TSP^{SM}—Leading a Development Team

TSP^{SM}—Leading a Development Team

Watts S. Humphrey

✛ Addison-Wesley

Upper Saddle River, NJ • Boston• Indianapolis • San Francisco
New York • Toronto • Montreal • London • Munich • Paris • Madrid
Capetown • Sydney • Tokyo • Singapore • Mexico City

CarnegieMellon
Software Engineering Institute

The SEI Series in Software Engineering

Many of the designations used by manufacturers and sellers to distinguish their products are claimed as trademarks. Where those designations appear in this book, and the publisher was aware of a trademark claim, the designations have been printed with initial capital letters or in all capitals.

CMM, CMMI, Capability Maturity Model, Capability Maturity Modeling, Carnegie Mellon, CERT, and CERT Coordination Center are registered in the U.S. Patent and Trademark Office by Carnegie Mellon University.

ATAM; Architecture Tradeoff Analysis Method; CMM Integration; COTS Usage-Risk Evaluation; CURE; EPIC; Evolutionary Process for Integrating COTS Based Systems; Framework for Software Product Line Practice; IDEAL; Interim Profile; OAR; OCTAVE; Operationally Critical Threat, Asset, and Vulnerability Evaluation; Options Analysis for Reengineering; Personal Software Process; PLTP; Product Line Technical Probe; PSP; SCAMPI; SCAMPI Lead Appraiser; SCAMPI Lead Assessor; SCE; SEI; SEPG; Team Software Process; and TSP are service marks of Carnegie Mellon University.

Special permission to reproduce "TSP process materials," © 2005 by Carnegie Mellon University, is granted by the Software Engineering Institute.

The author and publisher have taken care in the preparation of this book, but make no expressed or implied warranty of any kind and assume no responsibility for errors or omissions. No liability is assumed for incidental or consequential damages in connection with or arising out of the use of the information or programs contained herein.

The publisher offers excellent discounts on this book when ordered in quantity for bulk purchases or special sales, which may include electronic versions and/or custom covers and content particular to your business, training goals, marketing focus, and branding interests. For more information, please contact:

> U.S. Corporate and Government Sales
> (800) 382-3419
> corpsales@pearsontechgroup.com

For sales outside the U.S., please contact:

> International Sales
> international@pearsoned.com

Visit us on the Web: www.awprofessional.com

Library of Congress Cataloging-in-Publication Data
Humphrey, Watts S., 1927–
    TSP—leading a development team / Watts S. Humphrey.
        p. cm.
    Includes bibliographical references and index.
    ISBN 0-321-34962-8 (hardback : alk. paper)
  1. Capability maturity model (Computer software) 2. Software
engineering. 3. Teams in the workplace. I. Title.
    QA76.758.H863 2005
    005.1'068'5—dc22
                            2005014392

ISBN 0-321-34962-8
Text printed in the United States on recycled paper at Courier in Westford, Massachusetts.
First printing, September 2005

*I dedicate this book to all the teams
I have worked with over the years.*

*You have taught me that teams are the most powerful tool
mankind has yet devised for doing creative work.*

*Working with you has been the most
enjoyable experience of my life.*

CONTENTS

PREFACE

In the fifty-plus years since I started doing development work, I have worked on, led, managed, directed, assessed, or coached literally hundreds of creative development teams. While I have drawn many lessons and guidelines from this experience, the one clearest message is that leadership makes the greatest difference. Without exception, truly creative work is done by teams with very capable leaders. What is most interesting, however, is that these great leaders are generally ordinary developers like you and me, but when thrust into a leadership position, they do an outstanding job.

What is equally interesting is the converse. When development projects fail, it is almost always because of poor leadership. In this book, I describe the differences between an ineffective leader and one who does a superb job. The objective is to help you understand, anticipate, and correct the most common leadership failings before they cause you or your team problems. I wrote this book because I have seen many smart and dedicated developers make basic leadership mistakes. This is a shame, because it is totally unnecessary. Leadership is not a complex subject and anyone can be a great leader.

When I was first made team leader, I had just joined a development group at my first job and did not know any of the team members or have the vaguest idea what they were doing or why. I didn't even understand the organization or the technology. While things worked out well in the end, it was due more to the marvelous people on my team than to any special insight or skill on my part.

However, I have found that this is not unusual. Given half a chance, your people will be very helpful, even when you are the new boss and they know much more about the job than you do. While there will be occasional exceptions, people want to like and respect you and they want you to succeed. They will tolerate your dumb questions and silly mistakes as long as you are willing to admit your mistakes and laugh at your goofs. Be honest about what you know and don't know, and assume that management had a good reason to make you the team leader.

After I had worked for a few years, I was asked to lead a larger group in another department. I knew the people pretty well and also knew a great deal about the job. This time, however, my reception was not nearly as smooth. One of the more experienced members of the new group was older than I, and he and several team members thought that he should have been the team leader instead. While this situation took a bit longer to straighten out, the team finally came to terms with my new role and we established a good and productive working relationship.

The way teams perform depends to a great extent on how they relate to their leadership. However, I have found that the way your team relates to you will depend on a host of factors, many of which you can influence but some you cannot. In this book, I describe these factors and suggest ways to deal with them. These guidelines have helped me and I hope they will help you.

Who This Book Is For

This book is for people who are now leading or would like to lead a development team. It describes the team leader's job, the essential elements of leadership, and the many issues and problems you are likely to face. While I can't pretend to have all of the answers, I have had a lot of experience leading teams, and I have worked with a great many teams and team leaders. Since every team is different, and most teams grow and evolve over time, there is no magic formula for being an effective leader. However, there are some principles and guidelines.

Whether you are a new or an experienced team leader, this book discusses many of the issues you will likely face and has examples, guidelines, and suggestions on how to handle them. It summarizes my observations and experiences in a form that will help you to address almost any kind of team and team leadership situation.

The Kinds of Teams Addressed

While there are many kinds of teams, this book concerns leading development teams. A lot has been written about sports, military, and production teams, but little material is available on development teams and even less is written about leading such teams. Since many of the teams I have worked with have had leadership problems, I have concluded that this book is needed. My intent is to talk about leading any kind of development team, but most of my recent work has concerned teams that were developing software-intensive systems. Therefore, my examples and much of the process discussion concerns these types of teams.

In my work at the Software Engineering Institute (SEI) at Carnegie Mellon University, we have developed the Team Software Process (TSP). As the name implies, this process is designed to guide software development teams. The TSP has been used by many teams that included hardware, software, systems, requirements, test, and other professionals. It has also been used by some teams that have done little or no software development. So while the book mentions TSP in many places, you will find that the concepts and much of the guidance applies to any kind of development team. Few things that are worthwhile are free, however, and your people will need new skills to use the TSP. These skills are taught in Personal Software Process (PSP) training

How This Book Is Organized

The five parts of this book address the principal aspects of teams and team leadership. Part I discusses what management and the team expect from you. It then describes the conditions for team success and the kinds of teams needed to do development work. Following the discussion of *what* and *why* in Part I, Parts II through V and the appendices deal with *how:* how to do what it takes to be a great leader.

Part II starts with a brief overview of the Team Software Process and how it can help you to build the kind of team you need, even if your team doesn't do software development or even any kind of development. It then describes how to form teams and the TSP launch process. Part III discusses teamworking. It concerns following the plan, maintaining focus, and following the process to produce a quality product. Part IV discusses management reporting, project reviews, and your obligation to support and protect your team. Part V concludes the book with a description of how to develop the team and its members and how to best capitalize on your capabilities and your team's capabilities. The book's appendices then provide more detail on the TSP team roles and how to use them. They also discuss the communication and command networks in your organization and how to use them to accomplish your team's objectives.

Acknowledgments

This book is based on my experiences in working with development teams. What has consistently amazed me is how varied teams are and how much there is to learn about teamwork and team leadership. After many years of working with development teams, I still learn something from every one. That is why I dedicate this book to the many teams I have led, coached, or observed. I owe each one a debt of gratitude, both for their unfailing dedication to their work and for their tolerance and good humor in dealing with me. While I can't thank everyone personally, if you have led or been a member of a team that I have worked with, I am thanking you.

In writing books, I have had the support of a very special team at the SEI: the TSP development team. The members of this team have all contributed to my work in many ways. For their help and support, I thank Dan Burton, Anita Carleton, Noopur Davis, Caroline Graettinger, Jim McHale, Julia Mullaney, Jim Over, Marsha Pomeroy-Huff, Mark Sebern, Dan Wall, and Alan Willett. I also thank Bob Cannon, Carol Grojean, and Don McAndrews for their helpful comments and suggestions on this book.

PART I

Introduction

On May 21, 1968, the 3,500-ton nuclear attack submarine *Scorpion* reported its position as it returned from duty in the North Atlantic (Sontag 1999). That report was the last that was heard from the ship and its 99-man crew. On May 27th, when the *Scorpion* did not arrive at Norfolk when scheduled, they knew it was lost. All anyone knew about the *Scorpion* was the time and place of the last report and that it was going to Norfolk. The wreck could be anywhere in 500 square miles of deep ocean. Finding such a wreck on land would be tough enough, but 5 miles deep in the ocean, it was an incredible challenge.

John Craven got the job of finding the wreckage. John had been on the search for the *Thresher* five years earlier, and he had led the successful search for a hydrogen bomb lost in the Atlantic off Spain. He lined up oceanography and submarine design experts. He contacted submarine captains and torpedo specialists. He consulted with modeling experts, nuclear engineers, and anyone else who might know something useful. He talked to the U.S. Navy hydrographic office to see if any explosion had been detected in the *Scorpion's* vicinity at the time of its last report, and he checked on prior problems with equipment like that used on the *Scorpion*. He next had a model built of how a submarine would sink. However, to run the model, he had to know when the Scorpion sank; its depth, heading, and speed; and the rate of descent. To determine this, he had to deduce what caused the sub to sink.

1

With this preparation, John worked with his informal team of experts to get some answers. Among other things, they concluded that the problem started with a battery explosion that caused a so-called "hot" torpedo. With a hot torpedo, the skippers said, they would immediately pull a 180 degree turn to deactivate the torpedo warhead. So the sub would have been headed east and not west when it sank. They also judged the speed, cruising depth, and timing of the fire and explosion that sank the *Scorpion*. When they ran the model and sent a deep-diving submersible to the spot 5 miles down in the Atlantic, the wreckage was 220 yards away.

Teams often produce amazing results like this. Well-formed and properly skilled and motivated groups of people produce much better results than any individual possibly could (Surowiecki 2004). The challenge for team leaders is to produce the conditions and provide the leadership and motivation to make such results possible. This book shows you how to meet this challenge.

The four chapters in Part I provide the foundation for everything that follows. Starting with a description of your job as team leader, these chapters cover leadership, the nature of teams, and motivation. They describe *what* to do to form and maintain a creative and effective team. The rest of the book addresses *how* to do it.

Chapter 1, The Team Leader, describes your job as team leader, what management expects from you, and what the team expects. It also summarizes your principal duties.

Chapter 2, Leadership, describes leadership, what differentiates leaders from managers, and the responsibilities of leadership.

Chapter 3, Teams, discusses the kind of team needed for development work. It introduces the self-directed team, describes why such teams are creative, and reviews your role in forming, launching, and leading such a team.

Chapter 4, Team Motivation, addresses the need for and principles of building and maintaining self-directed teams. It also describes how communication, commitment, and feedback affect team motivation.

References

Sontag, Sherry, and Christopher Drew. *Blind Man's Bluff*. New York: Harper Paperbacks. 1999.

Surowiecki, James. *The Wisdom of Crowds*. New York: Doubleday. 2004.

1

The Team Leader

As team leader, you are responsible for a project and your job is to use your team to get the job done. While you are the leader for all of the people on the team, you may not be their manager. Leaders must often lead groups that do not report to them. For good leaders, this is rarely a problem: people like to be led; they don't like being managed. This chapter describes what management and the team expect of you, the things team leaders must do, the way team leaders must behave, and the team leader's primary job.

1.1 What Management Expects

As team leader, you are part of management. While this does not necessarily mean that you will have an office and an assistant or that you will control salaries or promotions, it does set you apart from the team members. The essential difference is that you are now expected to get work done by delegating to other people rather than doing it all yourself. Most new managers have trouble accepting the fact that their job is to lead the people who do the work, not to do the work themselves.

While most team leaders who have been developers see nothing wrong with actually doing much of the work themselves, this is rarely a good idea and it can even damage your ability to be an effective leader. Even if you are the most skilled designer on the team, your job is to lead the team, not to be the lead designer. While you may have to provide detailed guidance on the design work, the best leaders show their team members how to do their jobs but do not step in and do the work themselves.

On a small team, you may decide to take on some of the team's roles and tasks yourself. But that must never be your primary concern and it must not distract you from the principal job of leading, guiding, supporting, and protecting the team. As far as management is concerned, your job is to use all of the team's resources to do this job. Everything else is secondary.

Some other things management expects of you are as follows.

☐ You will get this job done on the schedule and with the resources you have been given.

☐ The products you produce will meet both the stated and the implied requirements.

☐ You will keep management posted on your team's progress.

☐ You will inform management of any problems or issues in time for them to take corrective action.

☐ You will work cooperatively with all of the other parts of the organization.

☐ You will abide by all of the organization's rules, regulations, and standards.

1.2   What the Team Expects

While management's expectations are not very surprising, what your team members expect is much less well defined and often contradictory. Initially, the team members will have a collection of individual expectations. While these expectations could vary widely, there are a few common ones that team members almost always have of their leaders.

First, like everyone else, creative people share a basic need for job security. They want to keep their jobs and are understandably concerned about management's views of their performance. However, professionals' views of what makes a job interesting and rewarding often differ somewhat from management's priorities.

Second, what often is surprising to management is that the top priority for most development professionals is not about the product or the schedule. It is to work on a cohesive and cooperative team. In fact, even when the result is a total business disaster, if the team provided a rewarding personal experience, the team members will view the project as a success (Linberg 1999).

Third, the team members like to be successful. While this expectation will vary considerably from member to member, most would like to finish the job on time and to produce a successful product.

Fourth, and this expectation often ranks ahead of finishing the job on time, many team members want to do technical work that is interesting and that satisfies their personal goals and aspirations. This expectation is often hard to satisfy since it can change quickly. While a developer might be very interested in tackling a new challenge, once he or she has successfully handled a similar task once or twice, such challenges are much less appealing. In fact, every engineering challenge is much like a mystery story. Once you know the ending, it is easy to lose interest.

1.3   Management Priorities Versus Team Interests

In many respects, management's priorities are very consistent with the team's basic interests. They want skilled and satisfied employees and they need a stable and reliable workforce. Where their interests differ, however, is on the importance of building a cohesive and rewarding team environment. While few managers would object to such an environment, they have not generally thought much about it or given it a very high priority.

Resolving these differing priorities is a key part of your job and it is what makes leading development work so interesting and rewarding. The reason is something that many team leaders do not appreciate until after they have led several projects: when teams are cohesive and cooperative, and when they find their work most rewarding and enjoyable, they also do the best work. And that is also when they are most likely to meet their committed schedules and to deliver quality products. Convincing management and the team of this fact will be one of your more interesting challenges. A principal objective of this book is to show you how to meet that challenge.

Leadership is demanding, particularly for development work, but it is also exciting to have the support and allegiance of a capable, energetic, and enthusiastic team. You will find that once you have built a truly cohesive and energetic team, you will enjoy the work every bit as much as they do. However, to build such a team you must maintain a clear and consistent focus on the team's goals, set an example for the kind of performance you want, maintain high standards, and be responsible for all of the team's work.

1.4   The Team's Goals

To use a sports analogy, athletic teams strive to win every game. This typically means scoring more points than the opposition. Every team member knows what the goal is and strives both to score points and to prevent the opposition from scoring. While many strategies contribute to successful games, the goal is always clear, and it is the focus for everything that the team does.

In development work, goals are equally important but they are rarely as clear. While the ultimate goal is usually understood by all, there is often considerable confusion about short-term goals. A significant part of your leadership job is to keep the team's goals clear and well defined and to ensure that every team member knows how his or her current tasks contribute to meeting that goal. In addition, you want all team members to work energetically to meet their goals. As each goal is met, you help the team to move on to the next immediate goals, continuing until you meet the final objective. So goals are important. They provide the focus, motivation, and energy that make teams successful.

While establishing goals may seem simple, one team I worked with took over three hours to agree on their goals. The problem was that this team had three developers, two testers, a requirements person, someone from the support group, and the team leader, and that their interests and objectives were widely divergent. The goals discussion helped them to understand each others' objectives and to agree on what was important.

1.5   Setting an Example

As leader, your actions are highly visible and your behavior is seen by your team as an example. Lee Iacocca once said, "The speed of the boss is the speed of the team." (Iacocca 1984). You cannot expect your team to be any more committed or to work any harder or more carefully than you do. To get a full day's work from your people, you must put in a full day's work yourself. If you are not concerned about a one-day schedule slip, you cannot expect your people to work hard to make it up. If you don't seem to care about quality, usability, planning, or any of the other key aspects of the job, you can't expect your people to be concerned about these things either. Your energy, enthusiasm, and discipline set an example; when you take shortcuts, forget about the process, or ignore quality, so will your team. So remember to lead by what you do as well as by what you say.

1.6   Standards

The goals define what you and your team are supposed to do, but you are also responsible for how well that job is done. This is a matter of standards. A **standard** is a required level of performance or attainment, a comparator for quality, or a measure of acceptability. In engineering, there are many ways to measure and assess the work, but you are the only one who can monitor the team's performance and ensure that it meets the relevant standards.

There is an old saying in engineering: "If it doesn't have to work, we can build it pretty quickly." The essence of engineering is quality. Poor quality work is expensive, produces unsuccessful products, and is unsatisfying. Poor quality work wastes your time and your team's time, and it wastes your organization's money. Most developers intuitively understand the importance of quality and many even know how to do quality work. However, they often are not sufficiently skilled, motivated, and disciplined and don't have the leadership required to consistently produce quality results.

One of the key standards for a development team leader is the ability to get quality work from his or her team. Motivate your people to do the job correctly and, if they don't do it properly the first time, get them to do it over until it is right. If you settle for sloppy, incomplete, or inaccurate work, a sloppy and lazy attitude will infect everything that the team does.

Even more important than the quality standard is the team's standard of cooperation and support. While this standard is rarely stated or explicit, it is the team members' cooperative and supportive behavior that makes the working environment rewarding, productive, and fun. As pointed out earlier, a top leadership priority must be providing a cohesive and cooperative working environment. Accomplishing this is almost entirely a matter of behavior: your behavior, your management's behavior, and every team member's behavior. So, setting and meeting behavioral standards for yourself, for your team members, and for your management must be your top priority.

1.7   The Leadership Attitude

The way you act, your feelings, and even your private opinions will influence your team. For example, if you doubt that your team can succeed in its mission, even if you say nothing about your concerns, this belief will subtly affect your behavior. Your team will probably detect your doubts. When your team members sense that you do not believe in them, they will almost certainly fail.

If you do not believe that the team can succeed, sit down with the entire team and discuss your concerns. Don't tell them that you believe they will fail, but do get the risks and issues on the table and see if others share your concerns. Then, work with the team to figure out what must be done to succeed. Next, work with the team to make the required changes.

Your role is to motivate the team to do its utmost. To accomplish this, you must have confidence in all the members, believe that they can overcome the obstacles ahead, and trust that they are capable of producing extraordinary results. The most successful teams have energetic, enthusiastic, confident, and hard-driving leaders. If you don't have the required energy and drive, figure out what to change so that you do. If you can't see how to do that, either your team has a hopeless job or it needs a new leader.

1.8 Taking Responsibility

Finally, you are the boss. Your job is to get this project done and to use the resources that you have been given to do it. However, as boss, you are responsible for everything that the team does. You will get credit for the developers' achievements and successes, but you will also be blamed for their mistakes and failures. In short, as far as management is concerned, you *are* the team. This means that you had better make sure that the job is done correctly.

If the team is going down a blind alley, is wasting time on unproductive tasks, or is doing poor quality work, you must sooner or later answer for the consequences. Therefore, you had better make sure that the work is done properly. Doing this in a way that builds and sustains team motivation is not easy and there is no simple prescription that will fit all situations. However, there are some principles that can help you to define your own prescriptions. This book describes these principles and tells you how to apply them.

1.9 The Team Leader's Job

As team leader, you have several related jobs, and they must all be high priority. That is, there is no one job that you can ignore; if you omit any one, you and your team will fail. The three top priority jobs are as follows.

1. Deliver a quality product on the planned schedule and for its planned costs. As pointed out in Chapter 9, if you don't do that, you will have failed.

2. The second job for you and your team is to do quality work. Chapter 11 explains why the quality of your team's work governs the quality of your product and why product quality will determine the actual development schedule. Therefore, if you don't do quality work, you won't meet your obligation to deliver on the committed schedule.

3. The third job concerns high-performance teamwork. This subject is also discussed in Chapters 7, 15, 16, and 17. Teamwork is important because it drives team performance, which in turn governs the quality of the team's work. In short, without a smoothly operating, cohesive, and motivated team, you will not get the quality work that is required to deliver a timely or high-quality product.

As team leader, you have these three principal jobs and you must give them all top priority. Throughout the book, whenever I say that something must be your top priority, I am referring to one of these three top priorities.

1.10 Summary

This chapter describes the team leader's role, what management expects, what the team expects, and the basic responsibilities of the team leader.

Management expects you to use this team to get your assigned job done. This means that you must do the following.

☐ Get the job done on the schedule and with the resources you have been given.

☐ Produce products that meet their stated and implied requirements.

☐ Keep management posted on your team's progress.

☐ Warn management of any problems or issues in time to take corrective action.

☐ Work cooperatively with the other parts of the organization.

☐ Abide by all of the organization's rules, regulations, and standards.

While the team also expects these same things from you, it has other high priorities.

☐ That you will give them challenging and interesting work

☐ That you will recognize their achievements

☐ That you will foster and encourage a cohesive, cooperative, and productive working environment

Lastly, as a team leader, you must maintain a clear and consistent focus on the team's short- and long-term goals, set an example for how you expect this team to work, establish and maintain standards for how the team behaves and for the quality of its work, show confidence and enthusiasm for the team and its work, and feel and act responsible for the team and everything that it does.

Doing all of this in a way that motivates the team and all of its members will be your most important leadership challenge. The rest of this book describes how to do these things in a way that is rewarding for you and for the team and that produces the results management wants.

References

Iacocca, Lee, and William Novak. *Iacocca: An Autobiography.* New York: Bantam Books. 1984, p. 95.

Linberg, Kurt R. Software Developer Perceptions about Software Project Failure: A Case Study. *The Journal of Systems and Software.* Vol. 49 (1999), pp. 177–192.

2

Leadership

Now that you are a team leader, one of the first questions you face is: "What is leadership, and what must I do to be an effective leader?" That is the topic of this chapter, and its answer provides the foundation for the rest of the book.

2.1 Leadership Problems

To see why leadership is important, consider what its absence would mean. Have you ever worked in an organization that had an ineffective leader? You most likely have, and so have I.

My first brush with incompetent leadership was in one of my first engineering jobs. I was leading a team that was developing a military computer/communications system. This was a pretty advanced system, at least for the technology of the day, and I thought it had considerable commercial potential. I had convinced my immediate manager to launch a project to commercialize this military product and had also convinced the next higher layers of managers. Now I was in a meeting with the laboratory director.

After explaining this new product, I asked for his approval and support for a development effort. The laboratory director only asked me one question: "How long would it take for this product to become profitable?" I told him that it would probably be between 5 and 10 years before this product returned its initial investment and made a profit. He then said, "But I retire in four years."

I thanked the director for his time, folded my papers, and walked out, and that very afternoon I started looking for another job. I knew that this kind of narrow, parochial management would never survive the rigors of the competitive marketplace that any commercial product would face. In fact, even though this was an old company that had been highly respected, it was soon acquired by a larger company and no longer exists.

2.2   Symptoms of Poor Leadership

What are the symptoms of poor leadership? As this story illustrates, the first and most obvious symptom is self-centered, parochial, or narrow-minded thinking by senior management. These managers are so concerned about their current issues, problems, and interests that they can't see beyond their own narrow personal horizons.

Another and very common symptom of poor leadership is what I call "bureaucratic momentum." This is the "don't-rock-the-boat" environment where next year's budgets are determined by adding a percentage to this year's budgets. Whatever is being done now is justified, and anything new or any proposed changes must fight for survival. While this approach is common in most large organizations, at least for much of their operations, it has the unfortunate consequence of building entrenched, bureaucratic, and inefficient groups.

One illustration of this phenomenon was in the British army. Shortly after World War II, staff writers were preparing a new manual for artillery crews, and they could not understand why there was a fifth person on each gun crew. The writers asked everyone in army headquarters. Finally, one senior officer suggested that they call the retired general who had written the original manual. The retired general knew immediately what the fifth person was supposed to do. "Why," he said, "he holds the horses."

The British army had not used horses for over 20 years, but the old manuals had never been updated and the gun crews continued to have a fifth person to hold the nonexistent horses. With a bureaucratic leadership style, no one tries to eliminate the obsolete jobs or to reexamine the organization's resource distribution in light of current priorities, technologies, and goals.

Another characteristic of poor leadership is management's inability to make effective decisions in a timely way. This problem usually results from a lack of vision. Management has no clearly defined concept for what the organization should be in the future, so there is no sound basis for setting priorities or allocating resources. One symptom of this problem is the common corporate obsession with growth: our goal is to grow at 15 percent a year, or we strive to grow as fast as the industry. However, size is not a vision. Do these companies offer anything unique, do they contribute to society, or do they develop powerful new products or services? Without a meaningful goal, there can be no leadership.

While there are many symptoms of poor leadership, my final example is the leadership style that is so obsessed with change that the organization is in perpetual turmoil. Managers in these organizations do not recognize that people work most effectively in a stable environment. Productivity is directly related to workplace stability and changes must be parceled out at a rate and in doses that do not saturate an organization's tolerance for disruption. By exceeding that capacity, executives can quickly destroy an otherwise capable organization.

2.3 The Fundamental Leadership Problem

As a team leader, you will not generally face the problems of organization-wide change. However, it is important to consider the common symptoms of poor leadership and to ensure that your leadership style does not create similar problems. Poor leadership has many symptoms, but it generally stems from a failure to see what is needed and to set a direction that takes advantage of the available resources and opportunities.

It is often difficult to be objective and to establish goals for what to do and how to do it, but the key is to realize that you do not need to do it all by yourself. The modern world is simply too complex and no one person is smart enough or has enough knowledge to figure out everything without assistance. While you likely must make many leadership decisions yourself, you should take advantage of the intelligence, ideas, and creative suggestions of your team.

There is ample evidence that the combined intelligence of a group produces better results than even the most skilled and talented individual (Humphrey 1997, 159). So use your team. It needs leadership; it wants leadership; and it will gladly help you to provide that leadership.

2.4 Leading Versus Managing

Management uses resources to accomplish results; leadership motivates people to achieve objectives. Managing is impersonal and can be demeaning. It presumes that those being managed don't have ideas and feelings and must be told what to do and how to do it. Management is appropriate for handling inanimate objects or routine jobs. However, people like to be motivated to accomplish more challenging tasks, and they do not like being herded and directed as if they were so many cattle.

Most of us enjoy technical work, and we sought development careers because we like to do creative and challenging things. We also like to see the results of our labors, particularly when our products work the way we intended. But when someone treats us as if we were stupid or unthinking, we lose our energy and creative spark. As team leader, you will probably have to manage at least some routine work, but development engineering calls for leadership and for energetic and motivated teams. That is the only way to consistently produce truly superior results.

2.5   Leaders Have Followers

One principal distinction between leaders and managers is that managers direct people to obey their orders while leaders lead them. This crucial distinction is best illustrated by an example. One software manager, Ben, told me how he learned what leadership was all about. He was a marine lieutenant in Vietnam and, for the first time, he was leading his platoon into combat. As they approached the front lines, the captain told him, "Take that hill." "That hill" was where the enemy was dug in with a machine gun. There was no time for a discussion, so Ben told his troops, "Follow me," and he started running up the hill. He told me that all he could think of as he ran was not whether he would get shot or what would happen if he got to the top. The question that kept running through his head was, "Are they following?" It turned out that they were and they took the hill, but Ben told me that he learned right then that the two key ingredients of leadership are getting out front and trusting your troops to follow.

So leadership is intensely personal. It is not something that you can order and it is not something that you can measure, evaluate, and test. It is a property like loyalty or trust. It cannot be bought or inherited. It must be earned, and earned through long and often painful experience. It can, however, be lost in an instant. All you need to do is to stop behaving like a leader. Then your followers will stop following. They may continue to obey you, but you will soon sense that you no longer have their loyalty and trust. You can only tell if you are a leader by what happens: you are leading and they are following their leader.

2.6   The Leader's Vision and Commitment

What sets leaders apart from everyone else is that they have followers, and what attracts followers is a challenging and rewarding goal. It is impossible to be an effective leader without being committed to a cause that animates you and motivates your followers. Your energy and drive then come from your personal commitment to accomplish this objective.

This can't be just any goal—it must be something that you feel strongly about and will strive to accomplish. You must be sufficiently committed to this goal so that you can exhort your troops to achieve it, in spite of all obstacles. While development projects can have this character, that is not always the case. But, as we shall see, it is usually possible to excite creative people about the challenges and rewards of producing something entirely new and original.

2.7 The Leadership Attitude

How do you feel about the job you have to do? Are you excited about it and dying to be part of creating this marvelous new product? If you view the job as just another chore, you have little chance of building the team's excitement to the feverish pitch required for great work. Excitement is contagious, but so are boredom and laziness. As a leader you not only set the team's pace, but you also establish the attitude. If you want this team to win, they must act like winners. And for them to act like winners, you must act like a winner and also treat them as winners. It all starts with you.

Think about your job and what you can do to make it an exciting project where people will want to work. If you wake up in the middle of the night with ideas on how to attack a major challenge, share your enthusiasm and excitement with the team. When your people have great ideas or accomplish a key task, cheer them on and help them celebrate. Involve the whole team and make this a rewarding and fun place to work.

2.8 Transformational and Transactional Leadership

Getting people excited about a goal, and convincing them to follow you to achieve it, is called **intrinsic motivation** or **transformational leadership** (Humphrey 1997, 6). This is in contrast to the more mundane working situations called **extrinsic motivation** or **transactional leadership**. Transactional leadership is where you essentially make a deal with your people: "If you will do this job, I will reward you with a salary, a pay increase, or some other compensation."

The distinction between these two kinds of leadership is in the motivation involved. With transformational leadership, your team is striving to achieve an objective. While the financial and other rewards are important, the real objective is the achievement, not just the reward. With transactional leadership, the true objective is the promised payment and the project is just a necessary step to obtaining it.

With transactional leadership comes all the problems of defining appropriate rewards, measuring achievements, and ensuring that people merit what they earn. This leads to the practical problems of measuring piece work, managing sales commissions, and so forth. In all of these cases, the workers' objectives and yours are diametrically opposed: they want to minimize the work required to get their payment, while you want to get the maximum work done for any given reward. Unfortunately, neither of you is totally focused on doing a creative and productive job (Austin 1996).

When people are not intrinsically motivated by their work, they generally find creative ways to do less work while earning more money. Since this attitude hardly makes for successful or creative projects, your objective must be transformational leadership.

2.9   Becoming a Leader

If you are in a leadership situation for the first time, you may wonder how you can meet all of these requirements. Many people view leaders as having a special charisma, vision, and energy that is quite out of the ordinary. But leaders aren't born, they are made; more often than not, they are made by their circumstances.

For example, one of the principal distinctions between superior troops and poorly led ones is in their leadership. In many armies, when a unit's officer is killed, that unit is disabled. But with superior military units, when the officer is killed, a sergeant steps forward to fill the leadership role. And if there is no sergeant, a corporal or private takes over. While these aren't born leaders, they know that the troops have to be led so they step in and do the job.

Harry Truman, for example, was a failed businessman who became an unremarkable congressman. Then Franklin Delano Roosevelt picked him to be his vice president. When FDR died, Truman became one of the most effective leaders of the free world. He had a job to do and he did it to the best of his ability. He created the Marshall Plan, launched the United Nations, and fought the Korean War. Then he had the guts to fire General Douglas MacArthur, a national icon, when the general wouldn't follow orders. In my mind, what set Truman apart was his basic humility and personal honesty. He never pretended to know something he didn't know, and he didn't hesitate to ask for advice. But when he had to make a decision, he did so, and he did it to the best of his ability without worrying about who agreed or how it would affect his reputation.

Like many seemingly ordinary people, when thrust into a challenging situation, Truman did a remarkable job. There is no reason that this approach can't work for you. If you are open and honest, get the best help you can find, and keep your eyes fixed on the goal, you too can be a great leader.

2.10   Acting Like a Leader

When you are a member of a team and are made the leader, it will usually take some time to realize that you are no longer just one of the boys (or girls). While you will almost certainly have the same nickname and eat the same lunch with the same crowd, you are no longer just any old team member—you are the leader.

While being a leader will not make you any smarter or give you any special insight or added knowledge, you now have a responsibility and you carry that responsibility into every situation. When the team is confused or doesn't know how to proceed, you can no longer hope that somebody else will step forward— you have to make sure the confusion is cleared up. While you do not have to solve every problem, you must make sure that the right steps are taken to find a solution. Once you become a leader, you are out front, in the lead, and in charge. And you are always in charge, even during coffee breaks, on vacation, or when you are asleep.

2.11   Leading from Below

A lot has been written about the job of leading large corporations. It seems that every retired CEO wants to write a memoir that includes his or her personal "10 rules of effective leadership." While these rules are usually interesting and often useful, they don't address the most common leadership issue that I see in large organizations. This issue concerns the department or team leaders that are way down in the organization's hierarchy, and how these "subordinate leaders" behave. Most of these leaders rarely meet a senior executive; as a result, they don't have executive role models to emulate.

The essential problem of subordinate leadership is working in an organization that appears to be incompetent. In large organizations, the senior managers are often forced to make decisions about subjects that their subordinate managers know a great deal more about than they do. One of the best examples of this problem is a situation that developed shortly after I took over as IBM's Director of Programming. Our two largest locations were in Poughkeepsie, New York, and

San Jose, California. Because the Poughkeepsie group had grown to nearly 1,000 developers and because it still needed many more people to handle its committed work, we had decided to move the data-management mission from Poughkeepsie to San Jose. The problem was that the interface between the Poughkeepsie operating system work and the San Jose data management products had not been defined.

We had told the two groups to agree on the interface definition and to come to me if they could not. Unfortunately, the interface definition had become a highly contentious issue with no clearly best answer and the two groups were unable to agree. One morning, the two laboratory managers with about thirty of their best technical people showed up in my office with two competing proposals. Although I knew less about this subject than anyone else in the room, I ended up designing the interface. I told the groups to either make my definition work or to agree on a better solution and to let me know what they agreed on. They never came back.

While in retrospect I can think of better ways to handle this issue, it is a good example of the kinds of decisions senior managers and executives have to make all of the time. Your job as a subordinate manager or team leader is either to make these decisions come out right or figure out how to change them so that they are right. Unfortunately, even when subordinate managers do this, they also often complain loudly to their teams about "those dummies upstairs." The messages this complaining attitude sends to the team are the following.

- ☐ I wasn't party to this decision and I can't be blamed if it doesn't come out right.
- ☐ I didn't agree with this decision and I am unable to get it changed.
- ☐ This place is badly run and does not have much of a future.
- ☐ When I get a better offer, I am out of here.

Even if this is how you feel, as a leader, you will damage yourself by saying it or even implying it. Do your job, motivate the team, and don't spend your time carping about what a terrible place this is to work, even if you feel that way. As a leader, you do have some limited power and you must decide where to apply it. While lots of the issues you see may be annoying, concentrate on those that really impact the job and don't complain about the others. Of course, when asked by your superiors, offer suggestions on how to fix the bureaucratic nonsense that you and your team deal with. Otherwise, concentrate on the important stuff and don't let these bureaucratic annoyances get you down.

2.12   Summary

This chapter discusses leadership, leadership problems, and what makes effective leaders. Poor leadership has many symptoms, but the fundamental problem is often the leader's inability to set a clear and compelling direction or to capitalize on the energy, skill, and creativity of his or her people. To be effective, leaders must have followers, and what attracts followers is the leader's vision, energy, and drive to achieve the goal.

Managing is quite different from leading. In management, the manager controls resources to produce results. With leadership, the leader motivates people to achieve goals. The two basic kinds of leadership are transformational and transactional. In transformational leadership, teams are intrinsically motivated to achieve a goal. In transactional leadership, the work is done in exchange for some extrinsic compensation or reward. For superior technical performance, the work must be the objective. That takes transformational leadership.

When team leaders are open and honest and ask for help from their teams, they will grow into their jobs. Regardless of the challenges they face, if they keep their eyes fixed on the goal, they can become effective team leaders.

References

Austin, Robert D. *Measuring and Managing Performance in Organizations*. New York: Dorset House Publishing. 1996.

Humphrey, Watts S. *Managing Technical People: Innovation, Teamwork, and the Software Process*. Reading, MA: Addison-Wesley. 1997.

3

Teams

As team leader, you must lead, guide, and support your team. You therefore must know what teams are, how they work, and what makes them work most effectively. You also must decide what kind of team you want. Regardless of its other characteristics, the one thing you will certainly want is a team that meets its goals and consistently does outstanding work. This chapter starts with some general background information on teams and teamwork. It then describes self-directed teams, why they are important, and why they are essential for complex and creative work. Finally, it covers your role in building such a team and how having the right kind of team will help you to make your project a success. The rest of this book describes how to form, launch, and lead self-directed teams. The following topics are covered in this chapter.

- ☐ What is a team?
- ☐ The power of teams.
- ☐ Why teams are needed.
- ☐ The nature of self-directed teams.
- ☐ Membership and belonging.
- ☐ Commitment to a common goal.
- ☐ Ownership of the process and plan.
- ☐ Skill and discipline.

□ A dedication to excellence.

□ The need for leadership.

3.1   What Is a Team?

A team is a group of people who share a common goal. They must all be committed to this goal and must all have a common framework to guide them as they work to achieve the goal. The definition that best describes a team is one I have adapted from Jean Dyer (Dyer 1984, 286).

□ A team consists of at least two people.

□ The members are working toward a common goal.

□ Each person has been assigned a specific role.

□ Completion of the mission requires some form of dependency among the group members.

Each of these elements is important. For example, it is obvious that a team must have more than one member. The need for common goals, however, is more subtle. When groups of people work together without a common goal, they have no need to interact or to support each other. Even if the goal is simple, common objectives energize teams. Without some goal, people see no need to strive and they have no common group focus. Under these conditions, there can be no team.

Another reason for a common goal is that all of the members must be playing the same game. While this seems obvious in athletics, it is not as clear for development work. Unless the members are all playing the same game, their goals will be different, they are likely to work at cross purposes, and there will be little need or opportunity for them to cooperate. Everyone knows that mixing baseball and basketball players is not likely to produce a good ball team. The need for common goals and processes is equally true for development teams.

It also may not be obvious why the team members must have roles. Roles provide a sense of ownership and belonging, and they guide the members on what to do. Roles ensure that someone is assigned to each of the team's tasks. Roles also ensure that critical issues receive immediate attention. Chapter 7 and Appendix A discuss team roles in more detail.

A further important aspect of teams is cooperation or interdependence. This is where each team member depends to some degree on the performance of the other members. With a common goal and strong interdependence among the members, teams develop the trust and cohesion required for teams to jell. Tom DeMarco and Timothy Lister define a jelled team as follows (DeMarco 1987, 123).

A jelled team is a group of people so strongly knit [together] that the whole is greater than the sum of the parts. The production of such a team is greater than that of the same people working in unjelled form. Just as important, the enjoyment that the people derive from their work is greater than what you'd expect given the nature of the work itself.

3.2 The Power of Teams

Teams are common, and most creative product development groups intuitively understand what teams are and why they are needed. However, teamwork is a skill, and high-performing teams are not that common. Being a member of a well-run team that is creating a complex product is one of the most rewarding experiences a developer can have. Whether in sports, advertising, the performing arts, or product development, creative people like to work on teams and they will seek to join such teams whenever they can.

Teams derive their power from the way the members cooperatively work to achieve their goals. While it is essential to have trained and capable individuals on the team, the team's true power comes from its composite performance. This does not mean that the skill and ability of the members is not important, but that teams are most effective when their members cooperatively use all of their talents and skills to do their work. As the *Scorpion* submarine example in the Introduction to this part showed, when all of the members are fully and effectively utilized, teams achieve better performance than any of the individual members could possibly achieve alone.

3.3 Why Teams Are Needed

Today, many creative development projects are simply too large for a single person to complete in a reasonable time. For many businesses, time-to-market is the critical competitive measure, and the speed with which an organization deploys capable teams to develop or enhance products is the single most important factor in determining its market success.

Teams offer a range of talents and capabilities. Some jobs are so complex and involve so many specialties that few people could handle them alone. One person simply cannot know enough or have a broad enough range of experiences. With a team, the members specialize in the tasks that best fit their capabilities and interests. Reasonably sized teams contain a mix of talents, and one of the leader's principal responsibilities is to make the best use of these talents.

Participation on a team also improves individual performance. The members have complementary skills, learn from each other, and provide mutual help and support. They participate in product inspections, brainstorm designs, and get advice and assistance. By working with experienced professionals, beginners can learn more quickly than they could by themselves. Creative product development teams usually contain a broad range of talents and abilities and they provide a rich and stimulating environment for building talent.

3.4   The Nature of Self-Directed Teams

While it seems desirable to have a motivated and energetic team, why is it important to you? The best way to describe the value of such a team is with an example.

My very first development team was building a complex cryptographic system for the U.S. Army Signal Corps. We had just started life-testing the first model when a hurricane hit. This was some time ago and weather forecasting was pretty crude, so the storm was a complete surprise. By Sunday morning, I got so worried that I went to our basement laboratory in an old building in downtown Boston to see how the equipment was doing. Even though no one had called them, the entire team was there.

We spent the next several hours turning off and disconnecting the equipment and getting everything up on benches, desks, and crates. Water had been seeping up through cracks in the floor, and by the time we were done it was ankle deep. It took a lot of work for all of us, but everything was saved and the project finished on time.

This is characteristic behavior of self-directed teams: the members sense what is needed without being told, pitch in to help, and do whatever is needed to get the job done. This is their job, they own it, and they intend to finish it. This is why self-directed teams will stick together right to the end of the job. Typically, employee turnover on self-directed teams is zero. The members may know that the team will be dispersed, the organization disbanded, or the contract transferred, but this is their project and they intend to see it through.

While a self-directed team would be useful for any kind of job, such teams are essential for complex and creative development work. This kind of work requires everyone's wholehearted participation. If team members are not committed to the job and in agreement with its goals, they will not strive to do a superior job. Quality work is not done by mistake. It is done by thinking, caring, and motivated people. Self-directed teams have some special properties that set them apart from all other teams. The following are the five properties of self-directed teams.

1. A sense of membership and belonging
2. Commitment to a common team goal
3. Ownership of the process and plan
4. The skill to make a plan and the discipline to follow it
5. A dedication to excellence

Such teams typically devise their own development strategies, develop their own plans, and are motivated to do superior work.

3.5 Membership and Belonging

The members of a self-directed team are part of a cohesive and distinct group, and there is no question about who is on the team and who is not. All of the members share a common bond of membership and they seem to have a special communication medium. They are so familiar with the job and with each other that they can almost speak in shorthand. The most impressive aspect of a self-directed team is the way that its members work together. Cooperation is the essence of teamwork and it is the key to building the required trust and spirit. Self-directed teams are close-knit and cohesive groups and, while the members may not all be close friends, they are all valued contributors.

Cohesion is the bond among members that knits them together. Cohesion requires contact and close association. The team members must share a common workspace, see each other often, and communicate freely and openly. You can't legislate cohesion; it is a consequence of the team's working context. Cohesion is a fundamental property of a self-directed team.

Team cohesion is strengthened by the support the members provide to each other. Human beings are social animals and few people like to work entirely by themselves, at least not for very long. Team membership provides a comfortable human environment and a source of mutual commitment, support, and motivation. All of the members of such teams make a special effort to meet their obligations to their teammates.

When a team does not have clear boundaries and its members seem to randomly drift on and off the team, no one can assume responsibility and the members cannot rely on each other. This is the principal problem with part-time team members. When developers are simultaneously assigned to several projects, they have split loyalties and their teammates cannot rely on them for support and assistance. They are rarely available when needed and no one really knows whether they are on the team or not.

While it is normal for developers to have some demands from prior projects, these must be the exception and every team member should have a principal project assignment. Teams with a substantial number of part-time members can rarely jell. The reason is that it is hard for someone to feel committed to a project when management is unwilling to make it their principal job.

3.6   Commitment to a Common Goal

Self-directed teams share a common commitment to a goal. While the goal has importance to the organization, its principal value to you is to provide the focus for the team. The team members' motivation results from the common commitment they have made. Once they have decided to accomplish this goal, they will do their utmost to bring it off.

To maintain this commitment, the team must receive feedback on its work. Whoever heard of a winning team that didn't know the score? To be motivated, teams must know when they are ahead and when they are behind. They also must see progress every day. Only then can teams continue pushing to achieve their goals. For high personal and team performance, feedback is the single most important ingredient.

> Goal tracking and feedback are critically important. Effective teams are aware of their performance and can see the progress they are making toward their goals. In a study of air defense crews, those with frequent and precise feedback on goal performance improved on almost every criterion. This compares with the stable, unimproving performance of crews that did not get feedback (Humphrey 2000, 21).

3.7   Owning the Process and Plan

Another property of self-directed teams is ownership. This is not just any job these teams are doing; it is *their* job. They feel responsible for it and have decided just how to do it. Such teams speak of their work with a special pride. To have this sense of ownership, all of the team members must participate in defining their own processes, producing their own plans, and tracking and reporting on their own work. The members must be solely responsible for doing this job and they must know that nobody else will do it. This responsibility provides a sense of personal importance and a feeling of self-respect.

Finally, when a team has a defined process and a detailed plan, the members will know what to do. While this seems obvious, it is fundamental. When a group is unsure about what to do and it doesn't know where to get guidance or help, it cannot jell. It is merely a group of confused people looking for direction. Under these conditions, the members will work to different priorities, not support each other, and often work counterproductively. Following a process and a plan will provide stability and build the team's motivation and energy. To be self-directed, teams need a common goal, they must have a defined and understood process, and they must also have a detailed plan.

3.8 Skill and Discipline

Self-directed teams are especially well suited for creative development work. They define the process and the plan for doing the work and they have the discipline to follow that process and plan. Discipline, in fact, is what separates the experts from the amateurs in any professional field. Their willingness to rehearse, to practice, and to continually improve is what makes them experts. Studies have shown that the principal distinction between world class performers and those who finish in the middle of the pack is their disciplined behavior (Gawande 2002).

3.9 A Dedication to Excellence

The final property of self-directed teams is their dedication to excellence. For teams to work cooperatively and to maintain their energy and motivation, all members must strive to do more than their share of the work. Everyone volunteers for the tough assignments, pitches in, and contributes to the best of his or her ability. The spirit and energy of such teams depend, however, on the quality of everyone's work. If a member does sloppy work, makes frequent mistakes, and causes excessive rework, it wastes everyone's time. If this happens often, everyone will know the source of the problem and will resent it. Poor work by any team member can quickly destroy the team's spirit. Then you will no longer have a self-directed team.

3.10 The Need for Leadership

While these five properties—membership, commitment, ownership, discipline, and a dedication to excellence—are essential, they are not enough. Self-directed teams, above all, must have effective leadership. The team leader must motivate, coach, drive, and urge the members to perform to the best of their abilities. In short, the quality of your team's work depends, more than anything else, on your leadership. If the team is properly trained and built and if you are an effective team leader, it will perform superbly, almost regardless of the challenges it faces. But if you do not provide effective leadership, your team will not excel and it may not even do a competent job.

While providing such leadership may seem like a daunting challenge, particularly if you have never been a team leader, leadership is not that difficult. At least it is not difficult if you know how to go about it. While all of the conditions described in this chapter are needed for self-directed teams, meeting these conditions is not as difficult as it may seem. Teams like to jell, and when they are given the proper leadership and support, they generally will. That, in fact, is the principal objective of this book: to show you how to provide the leadership your team wants and needs to do consistently superior work.

3.11 Summary

This chapter describes the properties, characteristics, and behavior of teams and it provides the background you need to understand and fulfill your responsibilities as the team's leader.

A team can do a faster and better job than any individual could do alone. Teams provide a rich and supportive environment for doing complex creative work. However, the effectiveness of a team depends on its ability to fully utilize the special talents and skills of all of its members. To be a team, a group must have at least two members, a common goal, member roles, and some form of dependency among these members.

This chapter describes the special characteristics of self-directed teams. The principal conditions for self-directed teams are that the members have a sense of membership and belonging, they are committed to a common goal, they own their own processes and plans, they have the skill and discipline to follow these plans, and they are dedicated to doing excellent work. Self-directed teams, above all else, must have leaders who motivate, coach, and drive the members to perform to the best of their abilities. The self-directed team is the most powerful tool humankind has devised for addressing challenging tasks. This book shows you how to provide the leadership your team wants and needs to produce consistently superior performance.

References

DeMarco, Tom, and Timothy Lister. *Peopleware, Productive Projects and Teams.* New York: Dorset House Publishing. 1987.

Dyer, Jean L. Team Research and Team Training: A State-of-the-Art Review. *Human Factors Review.* The Human Factors Society. 1984, pp. 286, 309.

Gawande, Atul. The Learning Curve. *The New Yorker.* January 26, 2002, pp. 52–61.

Humphrey, Watts S. *Introduction to the Team Software Process.* Boston, MA: Addison-Wesley. 2000.

4

Team Motivation

Motivation causes action. Without motivation, nothing much happens. While some things people do are instinctive, such as eating and self-protection, most of our actions are the result of conscious choice. These choices are governed by our motivations. So motivation is key to much of what we do, and it is fundamental to creative behavior, both for individuals and for teams. But what is motivation, and how can we motivate people to do what we want them to do?

Motivation is a complex subject and many theories have been propounded to explain it. Nonetheless, enough is known about motivation to guide us in motivating creative people, particularly when they work in development teams. This chapter briefly discusses what motivation is and the principles that govern building and sustaining motivation. The rest of this book concerns ways to apply these principles to motivate your team to accomplish what management wants you to do.

4.1   What Is Motivation?

Motivation is an urge that causes us to act. The most basic motivations are to satisfy our needs to survive, to eat, and to make a living. Maslow defined human needs as having five levels (Maslow 1954). As shown in Figure 4.1, these levels are as follows.

☐ First come physical needs, like hunger and thirst. These are basic requirements for survival; they must be satisfied before anything else.

☐ Next come safety and the need to live in an unthreatening environment with reasonable security and comfort.

☐ Once these basic needs are satisfied, humans have emotional needs, like belonging to a family, a group, or a tribe, and being loved and cared for.

☐ Once we have achieved group membership, Maslow defines the next need as esteem and recognition. At this stage, we want more than just belonging; we want to be respected and to be appreciated for what we are.

☐ Finally, Maslow's highest level is self-actualization. This is where people's desires are no longer focused purely on themselves. With self-actualization, we focus on what we have done and what the accomplishment means rather than what people think of us. The self-actualizing person is concerned with results and is motivated by achievements, not approbation. While recognition is always welcome, the self-actualizing person is rewarded by personal achievement.

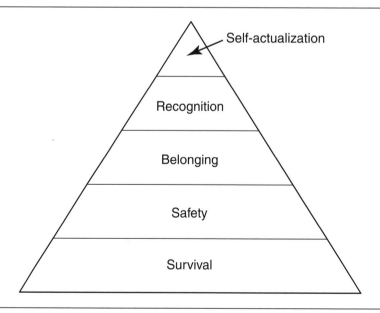

Figure 4.1 Maslow's Hierarchy of Needs

The self-actualizing level is required for development work, and this is the level development teams must reach to be consistently productive and successful. Maslow's hierarchy asserts that if a lower-level need is not satisfied, the higher-level needs will not provide much, if any, motivation. Therefore, for development teams to operate at the self-actualizing level, their lower-level needs must all be satisfied.

For example, when the developers on a team feel respected and recognized, they will no longer be concerned with their place in the group. They will then likely behave at the self-actualizing level. However, if one team member was excluded from an important team activity or otherwise felt rejected, he or she would probably be concerned about team recognition and acceptance. That team member would then not be a self-actualizing performer.

4.2 Goals and Motivation

Goals are an important aspect of motivation. The more important the goal, the harder we work to achieve it. An interesting corollary is that the harder we have worked to achieve a goal, the more highly we are likely to value it. For example, if you were to climb the stairs to the top of a tall tower, you would find the view more memorable than if you had taken the elevator.

Some years ago, Leon Festinger explained this phenomenon in psychological terms (Festinger 1957). He pointed out that the relationships among people's perceptions actually affect their behavior. For example, when we hold two related ideas that are in agreement, they are called **consonant** ideas and cause no problem. However, when we have two perceptions that are apparently in conflict, they are called **dissonant**. Dissonance makes people uncomfortable and causes them to try to bring their conflicting views into agreement.

An example of **cognitive dissonance** would be when management insisted that the team start system testing on a date that the team believed was unachievable. Cognitive dissonance would cause the developers to feel uncomfortable. Instead of striving to meet management's date, the team would likely argue that the date was not really that important. Therefore, unless you could convince the team members that the system test entry date was achievable, they would not likely work their hardest to achieve it.

Interestingly, the converse is also true: the more your team strives to achieve a difficult objective, the more highly the members will value that objective. Therefore, as long as the team members believe that the date is achievable and the harder they work to meet it, the more important it will become.

4.3 Feedback

The theory of cognitive dissonance also relates to feedback. For example, as long as the evidence indicates that we will likely reach a goal, we will exert ourselves to achieve it, even if this involves considerable effort. Feedback is important because it provides evidence of progress toward the goal (Parsons 1974). Assuming that the progress is close to that planned, feedback will reassure the team members that the goal is achievable and help to sustain motivation. Drucker points out three other reasons that feedback is important for individuals (Drucker 1999).

1. Feedback will identify your strengths and help you to concentrate your efforts where they will do the most good.

2. Feedback will quickly identify areas where you need to improve or to learn more. This will help you to get better.

3. Feedback analysis will also identify areas where intellectual arrogance or bias has caused disabling ignorance, which would be an obstacle to improvement.

4.4 Sustaining Motivation

While feedback impacts team behavior, it is not obvious how it relates to sustaining team motivation. Here we must consider something called **compensating feedback**. This is where the harder we push, the harder the job seems to get (Senge 1990, 58).

In the software field, there are many examples of compensating feedback. It happens when you respond to a demanding customer with one requirements change and then he or she demands another. You will soon feel that this customer will never be satisfied. This makes you much less likely to agree to the next change. System testing defects can have a similar effect: after every test fix, more tests are run and even more defects are found. Management can cause compensating feedback by removing team members from a successful team to help one that is in trouble. The "good" team members will then feel that the harder they work, the more work they will have to do.

To handle the problems of cogitative dissonance and compensating feedback, provide frequent feedback on team progress against its goals. However, since development commitments often span many months and or years, the goals may be far in the future and not very motivating. Eric Severeid, the war correspondent, used to tell a story about sustaining motivation over long periods (Severeid 1957, 140).

During World War II, I and several others had to parachute from a crippled army transport plane into the mountainous jungle on the Burma-India border. It was several weeks before an armed relief expedition could reach us, and then we began a painful, plodding march "out" to civilized India. We were faced by a 140-mile trek, over mountains, in August heat and monsoon rains. In the first hour of the march I rammed a boot nail deep into one foot. By evening I had bleeding blisters the size of a 50-cent piece on both feet. Could I hobble 140 miles? Could the others, some in worse shape than I, complete such a distance? We were convinced we could not. But we could hobble to that ridge, we could make the next friendly village for the night. And that, of course, was all we had to do.

Distant goals may seem exciting in theory but they are not very motivating in practice, particularly in the face of immediate problems. This means that distant goals are rarely useful motivators. The reason is that it is hard to generate timely feedback on goal attainment. You need short-term goals and ways to provide periodic feedback against them. This helps to sustain team motivation and to maintain team energy and enthusiasm. You also need a way to connect these many short-term intermediate commitments to the overall end commitment.

4.5 Motivation and the Job

An interesting aspect of motivating developers and other creative people concerns technical challenge. New and inexperienced developers are often reluctant to take on unfamiliar challenges. They lack the self-confidence and job security required to take the risk. More experienced developers, however, are often excited by new technical challenges and are eager to learn new methods and techniques. On the other hand, the same experienced developers will likely feel that repeated assignments of similar work are not interesting or motivating.

Some tasks are motivating because of working conditions. Developers will gladly join one team while a similar assignment on another team will offer little or no attraction. Motivation is a complex mix of talents, experiences, preferences, and attitudes, and what will motivate one developer at one time may not be motivating to the same developer at a different time or under different conditions.

4.6 Kinds of Motivation

For the workplace, the three principal motivators are fear, greed, and commitment. Fear can be an effective motivator, and a team leader who is also a manager can resort to it when needed. All you have to do is to say, or even just imply, that the team members could lose their jobs if they do not finish a task as directed.

While this is rarely a productive tactic, it is guaranteed to get a reaction. However, the reaction is often not what you would want. The reason is that fear engenders unthinking reactions rather than thoughtful creative actions. When management resorts to threats and fear, they force their people down the Maslow hierarchy. Now, instead of self-actualization and respect, they are concerned with membership and even personal safety. This can often induce protective or even irrational behavior.

A good example is the manager who launched a new quality initiative. He decided to measure the quality of each developer's work by the number of defects found in team inspections of his or her programs. He announced that each developer's job evaluation would be partly based on this quality measure. Thereafter, except for an occasional requirements mistake that could be blamed on somebody else, nobody reported any defects for any of their teammates. Since inspections were no longer useful for finding defects, they became an expensive waste of time. However, because the inspections were no longer finding defects, the quality of the team's products got worse instead of better. Fear is not a useful motivator, at least not for technical work.

Greed, or at least the normal desire for more money, is the most common workplace motivator. It is, after all, the basis for salary increases, sales commissions, and annual bonuses. People do tend to perform in ways that they hope will get them more money. However, these greed-related motivation systems have one big disadvantage: the reward must be coupled to the desired performance. This requires a measurement and evaluation system that permits management to calculate the appropriate reward for any given level of performance.

The problem with reward-based motivation systems is that few human activities are straightforward enough for simple evaluation measures (Austin 1996). Even piecework systems that base the pay on the number of products produced usually motivate counterproductive behavior. For example, in a typical manufacturing plant with a piecework pay system, people often produce exactly the standard quota every day; no more and no less. Anyone who produces more, in a desire for more money or promotion, could be castigated by the rest of the group. The workers know, or at least they suspect, that if anyone demonstrates an ability to produce more than the norm, quotas would soon be increased and they would have to produce more product to earn their current pay. The workers' fear of group displeasure overrides the motivation to get more money.

As noted in the Chapter 2 discussion of transactional leadership, a motivation system that uses financial or similar rewards switches the employee's objective from the accomplishment to the reward. This substitutes greed for self-actualization. Under these conditions, people will try to maximize their expected rewards while minimizing the effort required. While this may sound like what you want, it really isn't. For example, if you rewarded the developers for the vol-

Figure 4.2 Dilbert Cartoon on Software Quality[1]

ume of code they produced, you could expect to get at least some programs that had a lot more lines of code than would be needed by clean designs. Another example is illustrated by the Dilbert cartoon in Figure 4.2.

4.7 Commitment

Since greed and fear are not appropriate motivators for development work, this leaves us with the third motivator: commitment. A **commitment** is a promise to do something. What makes commitments motivating is the person's or team's desire to do what was promised. As we shall see, the level of motivation is almost entirely a function of how the commitment was made. The elements of commitment are negotiation, agreement, and performance.

Negotiation

Two parties are generally involved in a commitment negotiation. One party, the buyer, describes what is desired and tries to convince the other, the supplier, that the commitment is important and worthwhile but not that hard to meet. The supplier then responds with a proposal. If the proposal does not completely satisfy the buyer, the parties negotiate until they either agree or break off negotiations.

---

1. © Scott Adams/Distributed by United Feature Syndicate, Inc.

Agreement

The essential ingredient for an agreement is credibility. To reach agreement, the supplier must somehow convince the buyer that he or she can be trusted to perform as promised, and the buyer must assure the supplier that he or she can and will pay the agreed price. Since consistently demonstrated performance leads to credibility, credibility is related to performance. The buyer's ability to pay is usually easy to confirm, but if the buyer is not already confident of the supplier's ability, the parties must find some way to satisfy the buyer's need for a credible commitment. Typical ways to demonstrate this are with detailed plans, guarantees, or penalty clauses.

Performance

After the buyer and supplier come to agreement, the next step is doing the agreed work. This is where motivation comes in. The supplier, or in our case the development team, has made a promise to the buyer, or management, and is expected to do whatever is required to meet that commitment. For development work, this is critical. On development projects, for example, there are usually surprises, and there is an unwritten rule of engineering that all surprises cost time and effort. So, regardless of how carefully the commitment was made, a final Herculean effort is often needed to meet the committed date. But why do the developers make a crash effort to finish? The reason is that they are motivated by their commitment.

Team Commitments

People react in different ways to commitments. Some make extraordinary efforts to do absolutely everything they say they will do; others seem to forget commitments the minute they make them. After you have been let down a couple of times by someone, you learn not to trust that person's commitments. So the person making the commitment is key: is this someone you can trust?

What is most interesting about commitments, however, is that team commitments seem to have a much greater motivating power than individual commitments. Within broad limits, the bigger the team and the stronger its commitment and cohesion, the greater the motivating force. It seems that when all the members have participated in making a team commitment, and when the entire team depends—at least to some extent—on every member to meet that commitment, the entire team is highly motivated to do so.

4.8 Building Motivation

The four parts of motivating development teams are shown in Figure 4.3. The first requirement is that the commitment be voluntary. This suggests that managers ask for commitments rather than dictate them. Also, of course, these managers must not direct, force, or otherwise browbeat their people into agreeing to a commitment. In short, voluntary means voluntary.

Second, the commitment must be visible. This means that development teams must be somehow involved in negotiating their own commitments and that the negotiation process must be transparent and have documented results.

Third, the commitment must be credible. While there are many ways to make commitments credible, one of the most reliable ways is to support it with a detailed plan. By producing a plan, you and your team demonstrate that you have thought through what must be done and are convinced you can do it with the resources and on the schedule to which you have committed.

Fourth and last, the commitment must be owned by the people who will do the required work. The only way to reliably meet this condition is to have the people who will do the work develop the plan to meet the commitment. These people must also be involved in negotiating the commitment with management.

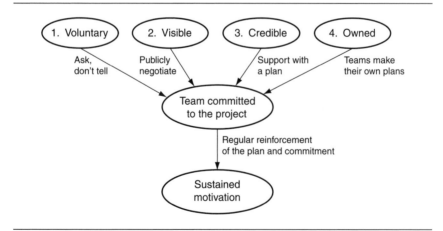

Figure 4.3 The Elements of Motivation

4.9   Sustaining Motivation

These four conditions provide the basis for *making* a team commitment, but they do not provide all of the conditions necessary to *sustain* this commitment throughout a long and challenging project. For that, you need some way to periodically reinforce the commitment throughout the job. This reinforcement must be frequent enough so the team members can see the immediate next steps required to meet the commitment.

To provide timely feedback, break the overall commitment into milestones that can serve as intermediate progress measures. Then identify and plan the steps to meet each milestone commitment. Next, manage the work according to the plan and track progress weekly or even daily. Finally, all of the team members must believe that the commitment is achievable. If at any time the team begins to doubt the feasibility of completing the job as planned, address that concern directly. If the team members start to feel discouraged and defeatist, their work will suffer. While there are many ways to address such problems, one of the most effective is to conduct a Team Software Process (TSP) team relaunch, as described in Part II of this book. The TSP was developed by the Software Engineering Institute (SEI) to address the teambuilding and teamworking issues that are common with development teams.

The combination of the elements described in this chapter forms a motivation system that will build motivated teams and sustain them throughout long and challenging projects. The next sections of this book describe ways to accomplish the objectives outlined in this and the previous chapters.

4.10   Summary

This chapter is about motivation: what it is, why it is important, and how to motivate development teams.

Motivation can be viewed as a hierarchy. Most basic is the need for food and drink. Then comes safety followed by the need to belong to a group or family. Next highest is the need for recognition, and finally comes self-actualizing behavior, the level required for creative and innovative work.

According to Maslow's needs hierarchy, people are only motivated to achieve the next level in the hierarchy when their needs at all the prior levels have been satisfied.

For development engineers, needs also vary with experience and working conditions. A job could be motivating at one time and under certain conditions but not at another time or under different conditions.

For professional work, the three most basic motivators are fear, greed, and commitment. Of these, commitment is the most useful and reliable for development work. When this commitment is made as part of a team commitment, it has the most motivational power.

A commitment is a promise to do something for someone at a specific time. To be motivating, the commitment must be voluntary, visible, credible, and owned by those who will do the committed work.

In summary, the requirements for a motivated team are as follows.

- ☐ The team must be committed to doing the job.
- ☐ To be motivating, this commitment must be important to the team.
- ☐ The commitment must also have been made
  - – voluntarily,
  - – visibly,
  - – and credibly (backed up by a plan).
- ☐ This commitment must be linked to the team and its members. This requires that the team make its own plan, and that all the members be involved in making the plan and negotiating it with management.

Once a commitment has been made, the team's motivation must be sustained during the job. This requires short-term milestone commitments that contribute to producing the desired result. These short-term commitments must be reinforced throughout the job.

If the team begins to feel that the project commitments are no longer feasible, you, as team leader, must take whatever steps are required to change that perception.

References

Austin, Robert D. *Measuring and Managing Performance in Organizations.* New York: Dorset House Publishing. 1996.

Drucker, Peter F. *Management Challenges for the 21st Century.* New York: Harper Collins Publications. 1999.

Festinger, Leon. *A Theory of Cognitive Dissonance.* Stanford, CA: Stanford University Press. 1957.

Maslow, Abraham. *Motivation and Personality.* New York: Harper & Row. 1954.

Parsons, H. M. What Happened at Hawthorne? *Science.* Vol. 183, March 8, 1974, pp. 922–932.

Senge, Peter M. *The Fifth Discipline: The Art and Practice of the Learning Organization*. New York: Doubleday. 1990.

Severeid, Eric. The Best Advice I Ever Had. *Reader's Digest*. Vol. 70, no. 420, (April 1957), p. 140.

PART II

Building Teams

November 20, 1962, was the day before Thanksgiving and I had just gotten home for dinner. This was only a couple of years after I had left my first development job to join IBM. At my prior job, I had enjoyed designing complex military computer-communications systems, but had concluded that the future of the computer business was with IBM. I was looking forward to a relaxed Thanksgiving weekend with my family when the phone rang. It was Learson's secretary. She told me to be in his office at 9:00 AM Friday.

Vin Learson was the IBM Senior Vice President for Marketing and Product Development, and I was a lowly project team leader in the marketing division. I spent the next 40-some hours wondering what Learson could possibly want with me. When I arrived at 9:00 AM on Friday, Frank Carey, the marketing division president, and George Kennard, the development division president, were already there. Apparently, nobody else was coming.

Learson got right to the point. The FAA had just issued an RFP (request for proposal) for the largest computer system procurement IBM had ever received. It was for hundreds of specialized computers to control the U.S. airspace. The proposal was due on January 1, only five weeks away. The marketing and development divisions disagreed on almost every aspect of this proposal. They had different system design ideas, wanted to handle the proposal differently, and could not agree on who should be the proposal manager. Under pressure from

Learson, they had compromised on me as the proposal manager: a development engineer who worked in the marketing division. I was to report to Learson and, for this proposal, Carey and Kennard were to work for me.

I spent Saturday in Washington with the marketing team and Sunday in Poughkeepsie with the development team. While both teams had great ideas, they were not communicating and we did not have time to settle the many disputes long distance. We moved everybody to Poughkeepsie, even though the only space we could find for 50 people was in the dance hall owned by the volunteer fire department in Red Oaks Mill. This was about ten miles from the IBM Poughkeepsie lab. It had one big open room with an old upright piano. We put tables and chairs around the sides and an old blackboard in the middle as a meeting point. By Tuesday afternoon both teams were there.

I held resolution sessions and invited everybody who wanted to contribute. It took one very long day to settle on the design and the proposal strategy. After that, when people had questions or issues, they would bang out a tune on the piano and announce the topic. Everybody who was involved would come to a stand-up meeting at the blackboard and we would hammer it out.

In my first status meeting with Learson, Carey, and Kennard, Learson didn't agree with our design strategy and started to tell me how to change it. I stopped him right then. "Look," I said, "if you want to design this system you can, but you will have to run the proposal too. If I am to do the job, I'd be glad to listen to your ideas but it's too late to change the design." Learson backed off and I finished the status review.

I later wondered how I had the nerve to take such a strong position on this issue. Learson was reported to be hard as nails. What could possibly have gotten into me? It was years before I figured it out, and the answer is an important part of what makes the Team Software Process (TSP) so effective.

We did submit the proposal to the FAA on time, and the team did such a remarkable job that IBM won the contract. That system and its extensions have controlled U.S. airspace for over 40 years.

Part II discusses how to build self-directed teams. Since we do this with the Team Software Process, this part starts with an overview of the TSP. The other two chapters address the issues of selecting, training, and building such teams. The topics in these three chapters are as follows.

Chapter 5, TSP Overview, briefly describes the purposes and objectives of the TSP and how it will help you to address the leadership responsibilities described in Chapters 1 and 2. The TSP is designed to guide you, your team, and your management in building and maintaining a self-directed team. The end of the chapter explains how the TSP launch helps you to negotiate with management (and how I got the nerve to handle the FAA design issue with Learson the way I did).

Chapter 6 covers team formation. Whether you start with a fully staffed team or must recruit some or even all of the members, you face special problems that must be addressed before your team can start working on the project. This chapter describes these staffing issues and some steps you can take to address them. It also discusses the skills and training required for self-directed teams and the steps required to provide this training.

Chapter 7 is on the TSP team launch. Once you have assembled and trained the team members, you must form them into a cooperative and productive team. The process for doing this is called a team launch, and the TSP process guides and supports the launch activities. This chapter describes the TSP launch process, how a launch helps you to build a self-directed team, and your responsibilities during the launch.

5

TSP Overview

Now that you know what self-directed teams are, we can discuss how to build and motivate these teams. This chapter summarizes the Team Software Process (TSP) and describes how it can help you to build, lead, and motivate a self-directed team. The remainder of the book then describes how you can use the TSP to help you and your team develop a quality product, on its committed schedule, and for its planned costs. This and subsequent chapters also describe your role in this teambuilding and teamworking process and suggest how to handle many of the issues you will likely face. The chapter starts with a summary of what the TSP does and then describes how the TSP process does it.

5.1 The Team Leader's Objectives

To meet your objectives as a team leader, you need to do three things: build a self-directed team, motivate this team to do your job, and then maintain this motivation throughout the job. The TSP is designed to help you do this. First, as described in Chapter 3, self-directed teams have the following five properties.

1. A sense of membership and belonging
2. Commitment to a common team goal
3. Ownership of the process and plan
4. The skill to make a plan and the discipline to follow it
5. A dedication to excellence

Second, once you have a self-directed team, you need to motivate all team members to do this job. The requirements for a motivated team are summarized in Chapter 4 as follows.

□ The team must be committed to doing the job.

□ To be motivating, this commitment must be important to the team.

□ The commitment must also have been made
   – voluntarily,
   – visibly,
   – and credibly (backed up by a plan).

□ This commitment must be linked to the team and its members. This requires that the team make its own plan, and that all the members be involved in making the plan and negotiating it with management.

Third, once you have a motivated and committed team, you must maintain this motivation throughout the project. Also as described in Chapter 4, you can do this in the following way.

1. Break the team's long-term goal into a sequence of smaller and shorter-term milestone commitments.
2. Plan the detailed steps to meet each of these milestone commitments.
3. Track and regularly review the team's progress against its plan.
4. Provide regular feedback on the team's performance against these shorter-term milestones.
5. If, for any reason, it appears that the commitment is unachievable, take whatever action is required to change that perception, even if it means modifying the team's plans or changing management's goals.

5.2   Meeting the Team Leader's Objectives

The TSP process was designed to build a self-directed team; it helps you to motivate that team and it provides the data, methods, and support you need to maintain that motivation. The TSP has three general parts. The first part is team formation, during which you recruit potential team members and provide them and their managers with any needed training or orientation. Second comes the team launch, in which management tells the team what they want done and the team builds its plan to do the necessary work. The third part is ongoing team operation, where the team follows its plan to do the job. The rest of this chapter provides more detail on these three topics.

5.3 Forming the Team

The principal activities in forming the team are shown in Figure 5.1. The first step is to get management's agreement to the needed resources. While the team will not have made its own plan yet, most projects start with at least a preliminary estimate of the expected or allowable costs. In fact, many projects start only after a procurement phase, where the organization has submitted a competitive proposal and has been awarded a contract. So management will almost certainly know roughly how many team members to plan for.

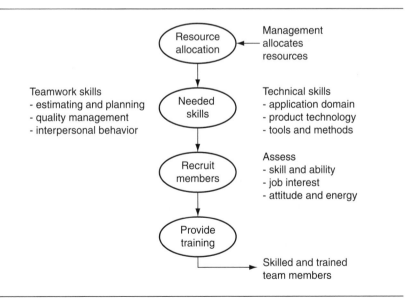

Figure 5.1 Team Formation

You don't want just anybody on this team. You need a particular mix of skills and abilities. Before starting the recruiting process, define these needs so you can build a suitable team. Often, however, team leaders are given projects with all or many of the team members already selected or at least identified. In this case, you are fortunate in not having to recruit new people, but you must also assess the needed skills and identify any shortcomings. Then you can either get additional team members or arrange for any needed training or support.

Needed Skills

As shown by the second element in Figure 5.1, the needed skills fall into two general categories: technical and teamwork. For technical skills, the three basic categories are as follows.

1. **Application domain.** Depending on team size, you will need one or more team members who thoroughly understand the application domain. That is, if you are developing a missile system, you need someone who knows about missiles and how they work. Similarly, for a financial system, you will need people who understand financial operations and know how key financial functions are performed. When teams lack domain skills, they are likely to produce unattractive or even unusable products. While training can be helpful in building such skills, it is no substitute for experience. A competent understanding of any but the most trivial application domain requires years of experience. While all of the other skills and abilities are important, satisfying this one is critical.

2. **Product technology.** Any large system will generally include several different types of products: control programs, file systems, communication facilities, and the like. There is a wealth of experience about each of these categories, and it is important that your team have some members with such experience. If you do not have several such skilled members, team progress will be painfully slow at least until your people get comfortable with the product technology. Since most development work involves modifying or interfacing with existing products, the lack of this skill can seriously lengthen the project schedule.

3. **Tools and methods.** While this area is also important, it is not as critical as the prior two. Most competent software professionals can pick up a working knowledge of any needed tool or method in a few days or weeks, particularly if they have access to local experts. If the needed experts are not available locally, you can often retain them until your people have come up to speed.

Teamwork

Also as shown in Figure 5.1, there are three important teamwork topics.

1. **Estimating and planning.** If none of the members on your team have these skills, you will not be able to build a self-directed team. However, since estimating and planning are not common software skills, all team members will probably have to be trained. After describing how the TSP process works, the final section of this chapter briefly summarizes the team-member training required for the TSP and how this need can be met by training the developers in the Personal Software Process (PSP) (Humphrey 2005).

2. **Quality management.** As discussed further in Chapter 11, quality management is an essential aspect of all TSP projects. The software team members must be competent in this skill and they must all believe that it is important to personally manage the quality of their work, even when they are under severe schedule pressure. Also, as discussed at the end of this chapter, software professionals generally need special training before they can measure and manage the quality of their work. Quality management is also covered by the PSP training.

3. **Interpersonal behavior.** To work effectively on a team, all of the members must be able to work cooperatively in a group, participate in resolving issues, and help the other team members when needed. This requires individuals who can listen to others, make logical judgments, and accept majority decisions. With proper guidance and support, most professionals can work effectively on teams. However, a few troubled individuals cannot. Since even one troubled member can destroy a team, you must avoid recruiting such people. When recruiting from within the organization, you can generally avoid this problem, but when recruiting from outside it is much more difficult. Since references are rarely reliable on this subject, get as broad a judgment as you can. Then observe the new members to see how well they work with the rest of the team. This subject is discussed in more detail in Chapter 16.

5.4   Launching the Team

Successful teambuilding programs typically expose a group to a challenging situation that requires the cooperative behavior of the entire group (Morgan 1993). As the group's members learn to surmount their common challenge, they generally form a close-knit and cohesive group. The TSP follows these principles in molding development groups into self-directed teams. However, instead of using an artificial situation like rock climbing or white-water rafting, it uses the team launch. The challenge in this case is to produce a detailed plan for a complex development job and then to negotiate the required schedule and resources with management. While a TSP coach guides this effort, your role as the team leader is to lead it. As shown in Figure 5.2, the TSP team launch process has nine meetings that are typically spread over four days. In meetings 1 and 9, you and the team meet with management. In all the other meetings, you and the team work with the coach with no audience or outside observers.

The Opening Management Meeting

The first step in the launch process is a management meeting where one or more senior managers meet with you and your team to describe the product they want developed and to convince you that this job is important enough to warrant your wholehearted effort. The managers also describe any important project constraints, desired schedules, staffing limits, or unique functional needs and ask you and the team to prepare a plan for doing the work. Finally, the managers invite questions.

This presentation should be made by the senior manager who decided to start this project, and it should be attended by you, the entire team, the coach, and other invited guests. It typically lasts an hour or two. Its objective is to satisfy one of the principal requirements for building a motivated and committed team: to

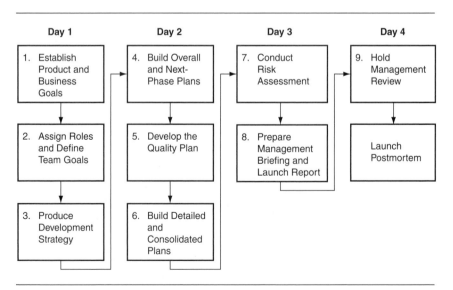

Figure 5.2 The TSP Launch Meetings

convince you and the entire team that this project is important and that it is worthy of the team's whole-hearted effort.

Your role in this meeting is to make sure that you and the team understand what management wants. If there are special priorities, unique needs, or unusual conditions, you and your team should ask about them. Throughout this meeting, your attitude should be that you will strive to make a plan that meets management's needs. Management knows what they want you to do but you do not yet know whether you can do it. After you and your team have made the plan, you will know enough to defend whatever plan you propose. In short, even if management's request looks totally unrealistic, you do not yet have a plan so it is too soon to debate it. Besides, any complaints about the schedule could imply to management that you will not really try to meet their needs.

Team Planning

Since management generally describes their desired schedule in the opening meeting, many teams question the need to make their own plan. However, as will be clear in Chapters 7 and 8, teams need detailed plans to motivate and guide them in doing the work. These plans also provide the checkpoints needed for project tracking and reporting and for timely feedback on team progress. Developing a plan is also the best way to protect you and the team from becoming committed to a job that you cannot do.

Following the opening management meeting, you and the team meet with the coach to develop a detailed plan for the work. This part of the launch takes several days, and no visitors or observers are allowed. In meetings 2 through 8, the coach guides you and the team through the following steps.

Meeting 2. Review and agree on the team goals and select the team member roles.

Meeting 3. Define the team's strategy and process for doing the job.

Meeting 4. Produce an overall plan for doing the job. If that plan does not meet management's needs, produce at least one alternate plan that meets management's schedule and one that does the job with the assigned resources.

Meeting 5. Produce the team's quality plan.

Meeting 6. Produce detailed near-term plans for each team member and then balance these plans.

Meeting 7. Assess project risks and devise mitigation plans for the few most significant ones.

Meeting 8. Prepare a presentation to describe the team's plan to management and to convince them that it is the proper plan for the job.

While you and your team must strive to meet management's goals, you will often find that you cannot. However, after trying and failing to devise such a plan, you will know why you could not do what management wanted and have the backup needed to negotiate a plan upon which you and management could agree.

Plan Negotiation

After you and the team have completed the plan, you will have produced the products shown in Figure 5.3. These products completely describe the job, how you plan to do it, how long it will take, and the major risks you anticipate. Now you again meet with senior management and anyone else who attended the opening meeting. In this meeting, you and the team present the launch results to management. Assuming that they accept the plan, you will then have a committed and motivated team that has a detailed plan for doing the job.

While there is no guarantee that this team will actually accomplish everything that it has committed, you will at least have a reasonable shot at doing so. You will also have a team where the members understand the job they are about to do and know their personal role in doing it. But what is most important: you will have a group that feels and acts like a cohesive team, has devised its own strategy, produced a detailed plan, and is motivated to do a superior job. In short, you will have a self-directed team.

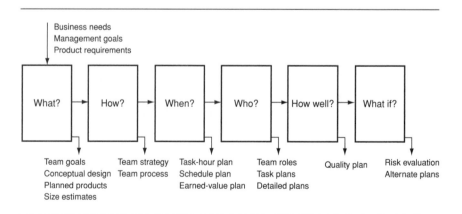

Figure 5.3 TSP Launch Products

5.5 Teamwork

Once management has agreed to the plan, you and your team can get right to work. While working on the project, the TSP provides the guidance and support shown in Figure 5.4. This figure shows the five principal teamwork activities as a sequential flow, but this is not the way it actually works. Because all of these activities are interconnected, a fully representative flow chart would be too complex to be useful. This section describes each part of this figure. Subsequent chapters provide further detail on these topics.

Data Gathering

While it may not be immediately clear why data gathering is important, getting the team members to consistently and accurately gather all of the required project

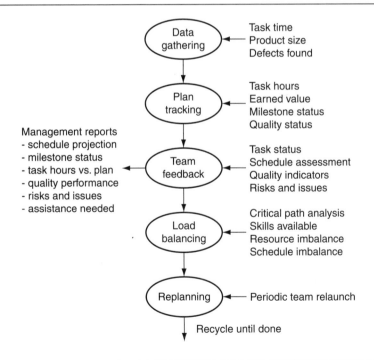

Figure 5.4 TSP Teamworking

and process data will be your most challenging initial leadership task. This topic is discussed more thoroughly in Chapter 10. However, the essential reason to gather project and process data is to provide the feedback needed to track progress, to report to management, and to manage the project. These feedback data also help you to maintain the team's motivation and energy.

Without these data, you will not precisely know project status, understand each member's status, or be able to devise solutions to the many problems you will face. In fact, you probably won't even recognize that you have problems until it is too late to do much about them. So, for the moment, accept the fact that data gathering is essential. The reasons will become clearer as you read subsequent chapters.

Plan Tracking

With a detailed plan and the data the team gathers on its work, you can see precisely where the project stands and understand plan deviations. The principal elements of plan tracking are as follows.

- ☐ **Task hours.** This is the time the team members spend working on planned tasks.
- ☐ **Earned value status.** This progress measure compares the actual to planned percentage of work that has been completed at any point in the project.
- ☐ **Milestone status.** With a detailed TSP plan, you will see precisely where you stand against each project milestone and what tasks remain to be completed before the milestone can be met. With the detailed TSP plans and data, you can generally tell to within a day where the team stands against its plan.
- ☐ **Quality status.** With the TSP, you can assess the quality of the team's work and take action while there is time to fix any potential problems.

Team Feedback and Communication

An essential element of maintaining team motivation is precise feedback on the work. This is provided in the TSP at the weekly team meetings. Here, all team members meet with you every week to review what they did in the prior week and what they plan to do next week. At the team meeting, each role manager also reports on his or her areas of responsibility. Problems with quality, schedule, support systems, or other areas are also raised and reviewed with the team.

The team meeting is also where team members arrange for needed support from their peers and when the team reviews its risk-tracking status. The weekly meeting is also where you review any management items that affect the team or that might be of interest to the members. This is also the time to ask the team for suggestions on items to review with management in your periodic management status reports.

Perhaps the most important reason to hold weekly team meetings is to provide a way for team members to communicate their problems and concerns to you, each other, and management. Most major project disasters are known by at least one team member well before they become serious, but that team member rarely has a way to communicate his or her concerns to management. By giving your team members a weekly forum for voicing their concerns, you can ensure that the team's key concerns are reported to management in time for them to take corrective action.

Dynamic Load Balancing

On any team, some members will work faster than others. This means that some will complete work ahead of schedule and others will fall behind. This is a normal consequence of the variations in estimating accuracy, the different productivity rates of team members, and the uneven difficulty of the work. A wide variety of distractions can also impact team-member performance as can many other factors. As a result, some team members will fall far enough behind their plans to threaten the team's performance. When team workload becomes unbalanced, it is essential to rebalance it. This will allow those members who are ahead to help those who are behind, either by assisting them with their tasks or by taking over some of their tasks.

Load balancing is important because it substantially shortens the time required to complete a project. Team productivity is maximized when all of the members are fully occupied, when they all work on tasks that match their capabilities, and when they consistently work on the most critical tasks.

While workload balancing seems like a normal and natural thing for motivated teams to do, it only works when teams are properly built, managed, and led. The reason is something we referred to in Chapter 4 called compensating feedback. Without a motivated and cohesive team, the developers will be focused only on their own work. Then, when some team member works harder and faster than the others, he or she would resent being given added tasks. These more productive developers would then feel that the harder they have to work, the more assignments they get, and the tougher their job becomes. To manage this problem, keep the focus on the team commitment and not on each individual team-member's progress.

The Relaunch and Replanning

In the TSP, teams periodically replan their work. This is necessary because it is difficult to make detailed plans that run for more than a few months. When people make longer range plans, they make so many assumptions that their plans are soon out of date. Also, even within a detailed plan's time horizon, development teams learn as they work, new requirements are added, or resources are changed. Unless the plans are regularly adjusted to reflect these changes, the plans will soon be useless for guiding the work and tracking progress. Finally, plans are necessarily inaccurate, particularly for first-time TSP teams. To correct these inaccuracies, you must periodically update the plan.

To address these problems, the TSP includes a relaunch step in which the team makes a new plan. The relaunch is generally scheduled as part of the project and conducted whenever the team feels it would be helpful. The relaunch helps the team by ensuring that it has a current and accurate plan to guide its work. The best way to determine when to relaunch is when the team members feel that their current plan is no longer useful in guiding their work.

5.6 Training

As noted earlier, the team members participate in all of the steps of the TSP launch. Then, in doing the job, they follow the process they defined in the launch, gather and analyze data, and track and manage the work. To do these things, they must have the proper skills. Unfortunately, few developers learn these skills in their academic training or on the job. The principal capabilities required by the TSP are provided by the Personal Software Process (PSP) course (Humphrey 2005). The PSP training teaches the following skills.

☐ **Defining and following processes.** Team members learn what an operational process is, how to follow such a process, and how to define processes for their personal and team use.

☐ **Gathering and using process data.** Team members learn the basic measures required for development work, how to gather data, and how to analyze and report these data.

☐ **Planning.** Team members use their personal data to estimate product size and development time. They also learn how to make task and schedule plans, judge plan accuracy, track earned value, and determine the likely time remaining to complete a job.

☐ **Measuring and managing quality.** Software professionals learn how to analyze quality data, how to use these data to assess the quality of their work, and how to manage the quality of the products they produce.

To learn the PSP and to be qualified to practice the TSP, developers must learn many facts concerning data, measures, and methods. Then they must develop various measurement and data analysis skills. Next, they must under-stand the principles of process design, quality management, and planning. Finally, they must gather and analyze sufficient data on their personal practices to become convinced that these methods will help them to do better work than they could do before. That is why PSP training takes time. It takes a substantial effort to gain conviction. However, until people have conviction, they will not voluntarily change their behavior.

When team members haven't had PSP training, they generally do not know how to make accurate and detailed plans or to responsibly negotiate these plans with management. Several software groups have tried to use the TSP without PSP training and no one has yet been successful. Trying to do so is a waste of time and risks seriously delaying your project. Also, as pointed out in Chapter 4, an essential element of motivation is that the team develops its own plan and that all team members participate in developing and negotiating this plan. If the members cannot do this, you cannot count on having a motivated team.

Equally important, without proper training your team will not be able to produce a detailed plan to guide its work. The team will then have no way to measure its progress or to understand its status. Without this feedback, it would be almost impossible to sustain its motivation and energy throughout the entire project.

Finally, without PSP training, your team members will not know how to measure and manage the quality of their work. As described in Chapter 11, quality management is a critical skill required by teams that develop sophisticated software-intensive products. Without properly trained members, these products have many defects and testing takes far longer than would otherwise be required. When teams are properly trained and when they use the skills they have learned, they inject many fewer defects, remove those defects earlier, and sharply cut their testing times. Then, the resulting products will be essentially defect free.

5.7 Team Ownership

In the introduction to Part II of this book, I described a situation where I had to confront an IBM Senior Vice President over a design issue. Since this VP was a very powerful man who was far above me in the IBM organizational hierarchy, I had long wondered where I got the guts to face him down. I learned the answer from the TSP. The design strategy we had adopted for the FAA proposal was not my design—it was the team's. After all we had gone through to produce it, I could not imagine going back to the team and telling them that Learson and I had decided to change it. Facing Learson was a lot easier. You will also find that when you involve the team in key decisions, you will not only have better decisions, but you will also have the evidence and conviction to defend them. The TSP will actually enable you to do things you could never do before!

5.8 Summary

This chapter describes how the TSP helps team leaders build and motivate their development teams. Starting with a summary of the requirements for self-directed teams, it describes the TSP process and how it helps to build and motivate such teams. The TSP has three principal parts: team formation, the team launch, and teamwork. During team formation, you are allocated some team resources, you assess skill needs, and you recruit the team members. If some needed skills are not adequately covered, you may also arrange for training or other support.

During the team launch, a qualified TSP coach guides you in forming a self-directed team that is committed to doing its assigned job. The teambuilding process starts with a management meeting where senior management describes their desired product and any project constraints. You and the team then prepare a plan to develop this product and review that plan with management. If you cannot completely meet management's requirements, you and the team members negotiate with management on a mutually agreeable plan for doing the work. The result is a self-directed team that has a detailed plan and is motivated to do the job.

To help you sustain the team's commitment during the project, the TSP provides for project measures, progress tracking, weekly team meetings, and regular management reporting. It also provides a relaunch process where you and the team periodically revisit your plan and recommit to the project.

References

Humphrey, Watts S. *PSP: A Self-Improvement Process for Software Engineers.* Boston, MA: Addison-Wesley. 2005.

Morgan, Ben B., Jr., Eduardo Salas, and Albert S. Glickman. An Analysis of Team Evolution and Maturation. *Journal of General Psychology.* July 1993, 120(3), pp. 277–291.

6

Team Formation

When you form a new team, you must select the members. They should have the right skills, want to do the job, and be able to work together. Otherwise, you cannot build a self-directed team. With a new team, you can select the members, but this takes time and you may not get all of the skills you need. This is particularly troublesome when, as is often the case, the skills you need are in short supply.

Another common situation is starting with a completely formed team. While you don't have to recruit the members, you must work with the people you have. If they do not have the right skills or cannot work together, you will have to make some changes. Since it is often difficult to change peoples' skills or behavior, you may have to replace some of the team members. If you can't get the proper mix of skilled and motivated people, you will almost certainly have a troubled project, regardless of the processes and methods used.

This chapter discusses the issues of team formation. Since every organization, project, team, and team member is different, no set of guidelines can cover every situation. The chapter, therefore, concentrates on the principles of team formation. It covers the following topics.

- ☐ The selection process
- ☐ Inheriting formed teams
- ☐ Selection criteria
- ☐ Training

□ Team players

□ Potential leaders

6.1   The Selection Process

While there is no foolproof way to identify suitable team members, the best method is to involve the entire team in the interviewing process. Have every available team member interview every candidate. Then ask all of those who did the interviews to participate in the hiring decision. Not only will you make more informed judgments about the candidates, but the team members will have a stake in helping the new members fit in and become productive.

For recruiting from within the organization, the team members will likely know more about the candidates than you could possibly find out, so listen carefully to their comments. While they will be relatively relaxed in commenting about people from outside the organization, they will be less direct when discussing fellow employees. The best approach is to treat any hesitancy or uneasiness as a sign of potential problems. In addition to asking your team members, talk to the candidate's prior managers and associates. Previous managers from within your organization will generally be helpful. However, current managers are sometimes less honest, particularly if this is a troublesome employee who they are trying to get rid of.

For outside candidates, check every reference for signs of problems. Unfortunately, this is not foolproof. The only way to get honest references is by talking with previous coworkers. However, unless you know the references personally, most of them will be so concerned about possible litigation that they will not say anything negative. I have learned that the only way to detect potential problems is by the absence of strong positives. In this highly litigious world, you will rarely hear negative comments from any outside reference, even from someone you know.

My worst experience with a misleading reference was for a candidate who was highly recommended by someone I knew personally. After we had hired him, we found that he was almost impossible to work with. He insulted his teammates, made disparaging comments about their work, and refused to work cooperatively with anyone on the team. We were all surprised, since this behavior was totally different from what we had observed in the team interviews or learned from the references. While it took a while for this employee to do something so bizarre that we could dismiss him, he had learned to hide his flaws so well that they could not be discovered until after he had joined the group. In another case, in hiring an employee for a job that required a security clearance, a close friend gave the candidate a very strong reference without mentioning that he was a convicted felon. Needless to say, this made it hard to get the needed security clearance.

Difficult people are often very smart and have usually learned that they do not work well with other people. To get hired, many of these difficult people will be able to conceal their problems. While most people are straightforward and honest during interviews, some are not. For the most difficult people, interviewing is a highly intuitive process where you try to discover clues about how these people will behave on the team.

6.2   Inheriting Formed Teams

A common way to become a team leader is to inherit an existing team. Here, your problems are quite different from those in building new teams. You now must learn about the members you have and determine if any might be difficult to work with or be assigned to the wrong jobs. If you were promoted to leadership from within a team, you will know the members and be able to decide quickly what changes to make. However, if you were promoted from outside the team, you are the unknown and the members will generally not say anything negative about any other member until they know they can trust you. When hiring new members for this team, follow the guidelines already discussed for new teams. For the existing members, however, take the time to build a trusting relationship with the members before expecting them to talk about their problems. A TSP launch or relaunch will help you to do this. The team launch is also a stressful experience and often exposes teamworking problems.

6.3   Selection Criteria

While you will sometimes find the ideal mix of team members, that is rarely the case. You must then pick people who do not precisely fit your criteria and somehow mold them into a skilled and capable group. In deciding how to do this, consider the members' skills, aptitudes, and interests.

Skill Needs

Start by determining the skills you need and decide which can be learned on the job, which must be taught in courses, and which must be hired from outside of the team. While you should do this planning before the team launch, the launch will help you to refine your assessment of the team's skill needs. You can do this by considering the kinds of work to be done, the skills required for that work, and how many people you need for each skill category.

One common set of skills is fluency with the programming languages, tools, and development environments the team will use. Generally, these skills are trainable. If team members do not have needed language or tool proficiency, they can either pick it up on the job or can get it through training. Most tools and languages are simple enough so that competent developers can acquire a working knowledge relatively quickly. Because they must use these tools to do their jobs, their skills will improve rapidly.

Other skills, like planning, project tracking, quality measurement, and quality management, are quite different. While the technical content is modest, few developers use these practices in their daily work. Because these competencies will not improve as the developers work, such skills are harder to establish and maintain. Further, without repeated use, planning, tracking, and quality management skills will not improve, and any skill that the members do have will likely deteriorate. As a result, such skills must be learned and practiced in more extensive and time-consuming training programs.

As noted in Chapter 5, application and product-related skills are critically important to most projects. While training programs can provide some rudimentary background in these areas, true competence generally requires considerable experience. If you do not have at least a few people with such experience, make it a high priority to get access to suitably qualified people as soon as possible.

Aptitudes

While skills are generally trainable, aptitudes are not. For example, if your project is using C++ to develop a 30,000 LOC program, you might plan for nine developers. You cannot merely stop there, however, since all C++ developers are not the same. Some may be good designers, some may know the application environment, and others might be superb coders. Just as in forming a baseball team, you don't want nine left fielders or pitchers. This does not mean that all developers are frozen into a skills category. However, it does mean that some skills can be learned and others require certain aptitudes. Just as a left fielder could almost certainly play center field, a C++ programmer could probably develop a database system or work on test development. However, just as you would not expect many left fielders to become good pitchers, do not expect many coders or debuggers to develop into first-class designers.

Talents and aptitudes cannot be taught and often they cannot even be developed. Some people have the proper mental and physical equipment to perform some tasks and others do not. As the saying goes, you can teach tigers to roar and eagles to soar, but you can't teach tigers to soar or eagles to roar. Once you know the needed skills and capabilities, you must next ensure that the selected candidates have the right talents and aptitudes.

With experienced people, you can generally determine their aptitudes by asking about the work they have done and the jobs that they have most enjoyed. Since most people like to do the tasks they do the best, their preferences generally indicate their aptitudes. Comments from prior managers and teammates can also be helpful. For new or inexperienced candidates, it is harder to determine talents and aptitudes. However, their interests will often provide useful clues.

Interests

For intellectual work like design and development, interest is fundamental. Even if team members have all of the requisite skills and abilities, if they are not interested in doing the work, you will have trouble building an energetic and motivated team. People generally have a pretty good sense of what they are good at doing and are usually interested in jobs that offer them an opportunity to use their talents.

While interests are generally a reliable guide to aptitudes and talents, that is not always the case. In one example, Sam wanted to be the team's design manager and insisted that he could do a good job. It turned out to be a disaster. Sam wanted to design electronic systems, not because he had any special design talent, but because that is what his father and older brother had done. Sam felt that he had to be a design engineer too. Occasionally, someone wants to do some job, not because of any special talent or ability, but because of some unrelated personal need.

That is the key to identifying talent. Try to understand why the candidates are interested in the jobs they want to do. Is it because they have really enjoyed doing similar work or because they are trying to prove something? If they are trying to prove something, interests are not a reliable indicator of talent. Sam said he was interested in design work, but he had struggled through engineering school and labored valiantly at several development jobs. He just didn't have engineering talent. He later turned out to be a very successful paint salesman.

6.4 Training

Since training is critically important, it is essential that all team members be properly trained. If they are not, the untrained members will not be fully effective, no matter how hard they try. It is through education and training that we learn how others have handled the problems that we face. After all, building on the achievements of others is what separates engineering and science from superstition and craft. While a great deal could be said about the learning process, a fairly simple four-level framework is adequate at this point (Bloom 1956).

1. Cognitive learning—facts
2. Cognitive learning—understanding
3. Building skills
4. Establishing conviction

Cognitive Learning—Facts

Fact-based training concerns objective information. For example, in learning about a tool or a support system, we learn what commands or keys perform which functions and which functions perform what operations. This is the simplest kind of learning; it is largely a question of memorization and learning how to access available information.

Cognitive Learning—Understanding

Understanding-based training requires building true mastery. For example, when studying programming, one might learn the various techniques and strategies for designing compilers or the principles of operating systems design. Other understanding-based courses might deal with the elements of planning or the principles and methods of quality management. In these cases, the objective is to provide basic knowledge together with the ability to build upon and use the accumulated experiences of others. In the case of quality, for example, true understanding requires being able to explain the following.

☐ What is quality?

☐ Why quality is important.

☐ The ways to measure quality.

☐ The principles of quality management.

☐ Quality management methods and their application.

In understanding-based training, the student's objective is not just to develop a rote capability, but to acquire the ability to build upon and even extend the limits of prior knowledge.

Building Skills

Skills-based training generally starts with factual material followed by enough practice to build the requisite skill. Touch typing is a good example. Here, starting with the basic facts about keyboards and word processors, the training consists almost entirely of practice. Learning a programming language has much the same character: practice is required to truly understand the principal language functions and to become reasonably proficient at using these language constructs to rapidly build working programs. Learning a programming language is also much like learning a spoken language: to be really proficient, you must be able to think in that language.

As with any disciplined activity, fact-based and skill-based training require concentration, consistent effort, and a reasonable level of interest. However, fact-based and skill-based training are generally temporary: once learned, the facts and skills will soon be forgotten if not reinforced by reasonably regular use. That is why this kind of training should be given shortly before the skills are needed on the job.

Establishing Conviction

Conviction-based training is the learning level required to actually change behavior. It typically requires both cognitive and skill training as prerequisites. For example, this is the kind of training medical schools provide. They start by teaching surgeons about anatomy and the principles of surgical procedures. Then medical students build the skills needed to perform operations. Once they have the proper foundation, training then focuses on convincing them that following all of the required hygienic practices and safeguards is essential. While conviction-based training generally requires extensive prior fact-based training, skills-based training, and understanding-based education, it generally also involves substantial supervised practice. Only then will the practitioner have enough experience to be completely convinced that the prescribed methods are the most effective way to do the job at hand. PSP training starts with cognitive and skills training and then focuses on building conviction. Its objective is to change developers' behavior.

6.5 Team Players

In addition to getting team members who have the proper training, skills, and aptitude, you also need people who can work cooperatively on the team. While most people can work cooperatively in groups, some cannot. If any members of your team cannot work cooperatively with the other members, that will almost certainly destroy the team as a cohesive working unit. One example was Betsy's behavior on a five-member software team. She had asked to be on the team, but her behavior was troublesome from the start. She was late to the opening launch meeting and refused to stay after the normal working time when the team needed to. What annoyed her peers the most was that when she took responsibility for preparing part of the management presentation at the end of the TSP launch, she did not stay to finish the job. The others had to stay late to finish her work.

At team meetings, Betsy would sit by herself with her arms folded and a frown on her face. She did not participate in team discussions and accomplished little of her assigned work. While the team tried to do the job without her, that was difficult and team morale was destroyed. The team leader knew that Betsy was a problem, but it took him two months to get her removed. Even though he could not get a replacement, the team was happy to work without her. So little work had been accomplished during the first two months that the team could not make up the lost time and was a month late delivering the product.

Betsy's situation was an extreme case. I later heard that she was in the middle of a messy divorce, which probably contributed to her difficult behavior. However, such behavior will destroy a team, and you must take prompt action to address such problems. The subject of difficult team members is covered more fully in Chapter 16. In forming your team, try to avoid such problems if you possibly can.

6.6   Potential Leaders

When you become a team leader, you join the management team. It is thus important to consider your personal objectives. While this subject is covered more fully in Chapter 18, to be promoted and to advance in the management ranks, you should think about potential replacements. If you do well as team leader, management will probably want to promote you, but they cannot do this without an available replacement. The best way to ensure that you can be promoted is to have one or more potential leaders on your team. Then do your best to develop these people as candidates for your job.

This also means that, whenever there is an opportunity, you must offer your best people for promotion. This is not because you want to get rid of them, but because you must value your team members above your project. If you do not promote your people when there is an opportunity, they will likely find out about the opportunity and try to get it in spite of you. Then the team members will no longer trust you to look out for their interests and feel that they have to look out for themselves. Be known as a leader who promotes his or her people. It will make your team a more attractive place to work. It will also make you an attractive person to work for, and you will have no trouble finding replacements when you promote someone.

The best way to identify potential leaders is to ask them about their experiences and how they have handled themselves in various situations. If they typically take charge under confusing conditions or if they express an interest in becoming a manager, they are potential leadership candidates.

6.7 Summary

This chapter describes the team formation process, and it provides guidance on many of the issues you will face as a team leader. In forming a team, start by establishing selection criteria and identifying needed skills. Common skill areas include application specialties, design talent, and testing expertise, for example. During recruiting, look for the required skills and ensure that the candidates are interested in the type of work to be done.

While all of the required skills may be available, that is rarely the case. Then you must overcome whatever shortcomings remain. Training is the most common way to do this. The four kinds of training are fact-based, skill-based, understanding-based, and conviction-based. Fact-based training can often be handled on the job or with brief courses. Skill-based training can normally be provided with brief courses and short supervised practice sessions. However, understanding-based and conviction-based training almost always require professional courses that are long enough and intense enough to build the needed understanding and conviction.

One of the most important but difficult selection tasks is determining whether the candidates will be compatible team members. The best approach is to involve your entire team in the recruiting process and then to listen carefully to their views. In forming the team, also include some potential leaders. As a new leader of an existing team, you must generally take time to learn about the members' skills and problems before you make changes. Once you have established a trusting relationship with the members, they will be more likely to discuss their teamworking problems and to suggest ways to improve the team's effectiveness.

Reference

Bloom, Benjamin S. (Ed.) *Taxonomy of Educational Objectives: The Classification of Educational Goals: Handbook 1, Cognitive Domain.* New York: Longmans, Green. 1956.

7

The TSP Team Launch

After forming the team and training all of the members, your next priority is building a smoothly functioning and highly motivated working group. That process starts with the TSP team launch. This chapter describes the purposes and principles of the launch and your role in it. The principal topics covered in this chapter are as follows.

- ☐ Launch objectives
- ☐ Teambuilding
- ☐ Launch overview
- ☐ Launch support
- ☐ Launch preparation
- ☐ Leading a TSP launch

7.1   Launch Objectives

As discussed in Chapter 5, the TSP helps you to meet the following three objectives.

1. Building a self-directed team
2. Motivating the team to do the assigned job
3. Maintaining team motivation throughout the job

The TSP launch process addresses the first two of these objectives and it lays the foundation for the third. As described in Chapter 5, the five basic characteristics of a self-directed team are as follows.

1. The members all have a strong sense of belonging to the team.
2. They are all committed to the team's common goals.
3. The team owns its own processes and plans.
4. Each team member has the skill to make a sound plan and the discipline to follow that plan.
5. You and all of the team members are dedicated to doing a superior job.

As also described in Chapter 5, there are four additional characteristics of highly motivated self-directed teams.

6. The team is committed to doing the job.
7. This commitment is important to the team.
8. The commitment was made voluntarily, is visible, and is credible. That is, the commitment is backed up with a plan.
9. The commitment is clearly linked to this team and to all of its members. This requires that all of the team members participated in making the plan and negotiating it with management.

These nine steps are addressed by the nine TSP launch meetings, with special emphasis on the topics shown in the highlighted meetings in Table 7.1. The following sections describe the TSP launch meetings, how each meeting helps establish these nine team characteristics, and your role in this process.

Even though effective teambuilding involves a substantial number of conditions, teambuilding is not hard to do. However, without proper guidance and leadership, few teams are able to meet all of these conditions. The reasons are that these conditions are not intuitively obvious and that few organizations approach teambuilding in an orderly way. However, unless teams are guided through a structured launch process, they will not know what to do and will not build a fully effective team. The TSP process addresses these problems and you, the team leader, are an important part of this teambuilding process.

Table 7.1 The TSP Launch Meetings and Team Characteristics

Team Characteristics	TSP Launch Meetings									
	1	2	3	4	5	6	7	8	9	PM
1. Sense of team membership.		■							■	
2. Commitment to a common goal.	■								■	
3. Ownership of processes and plans.			■			■			■	
4. Members have skills and discipline.									■	
5. Dedicated to superior work.					■				■	
6. Committed to doing the job.				■		■			■	
7. The commitment is important to the team.	■								■	
8. The commitment is voluntary, visible, and credible.			■						■	
9. The commitment is linked to the team.							■	■	■	

7.2 Teambuilding

The TSP team launch jump-starts a project. That is, the launch not only builds a cohesive and motivated team, it also provides every team member with a plan and set of tasks to guide his or her work. This enables the team to start working right after the launch. A great deal is known about the teambuilding process, and the TSP launch was largely based on this experience. Throughout history, people have banded together into working, fighting, and playing teams. When faced with a challenge, we naturally form into groups. People generally feel more comfortable when working on teams than when working alone. That is why teambuilding is relatively easy to do. Your people want to become a jelled team and, if you give them a chance, they will help you with the teambuilding process.

Since well-formed teams are more effective than other groups, teambuilding has become a commercial endeavor. While many groups sell teambuilding methods, few of these programs achieve lasting benefits. The principal reason is that they are divorced from the team's job and working environment. As a consequence, they are rarely able to change workplace behavior.

Teambuilding Exercises

The typical way teambuilding exercises work is by presenting a group with a threatening or risky challenge that they must address as a group. This takes advantage of our natural tendency to seek support when under stress. Then, as the members work together to address their common challenge, they generally become a cohesive group. Typical teambuilding exercises are river-rafting or mountain climbing. Some of these adventures are downright dangerous, and they are all stressful. They generally require considerable personal stamina and a willingness to put up with privation and stress.

The Problems with Teambuilding Exercises

Commercial teambuilding exercises often have a fundamental shortcoming: they have little or no relationship to the working environment. The people who lead the teambuilding are usually strangers to the participants and they are only present during the exercise. Thus, even though the team may bond and some members may become lifelong friends, they get no guidance on applying this experience to the working environment.

Even though these teambuilding exercises are often successful, the members return to the same conditions that had previously made teamwork difficult or ineffective. Thus, while the teambuilding experience may have been exciting and the participants may even see how rewarding teamwork can be, they generally do not have the tools, methods, or support systems needed to use these teambuilding and teamworking methods to do their jobs. When teambuilding is disconnected from the working environment, it may leave exciting memories but it will have little or no impact on the job.

The TSP Teambuilding Strategy

The TSP process guides you and your team through the steps required to build a team for the job you have been assigned. In the TSP launch, the stressful and risky challenge is to agree on a project plan and strategy, to produce an accurate and detailed plan, and to negotiate that plan with management. Since you have a real project, and since implementing this project will be your team's principal job for the next several months or years, the outcome is important to all of you. Further, since management invariably wants you to complete this job on an aggressive schedule, the challenge carries a high level of risk and stress. Since the TSP team launch meets all of the conditions for a successful teambuilding exercise, and since it addresses a real team problem in your working environment, it will almost certainly impact the way your team works after the launch is completed.

7.3   TSP Launch Overview

The TSP launch is typically a four-day process that guides teams through producing a project plan. While the ostensible purpose of the launch process is to produce the team plan, its principal objective is to produce a jelled team. Think of the launch process as a teambuilding activity. Most important, recognize that the launch will not be successful unless it produces a cohesive team that is ready to jell. Jelled teams are the most powerful tool humans have devised for doing challenging work. That is what you want to build; it is your top priority.

The TSP Launch Process

The TSP launch process is shown in Table 7.2 and Figure 7.1. The script steps in Table 7.2 describe the launch meetings. By walking through this process, teams generally produce realistic plans and they usually jell into cohesive and effective working units. To jell, however, *all* of the team members must be committed to the plan and they must *all* have been involved in producing that plan. Thus, in addition to leading the team through the TSP launch, you must ensure that all of the team members are actively involved and that they all agree with the plan they are producing. The principal topics of this chapter concern ways to involve all of the team members in the launch process.

It is not easy to involve everyone in producing a complete and realistic plan. There are five principal reasons for this.

1. **History.** In most development organizations, managers have always made the plans.
2. **Experience.** The managers and lead developers know much more about the job than most of the developers. Therefore, it would seem reasonable for the managers to produce the plans.

Table 7.2 The TSP Team Launch—Script LAU[a]

Purpose	To guide integrated teams in launching a software-intensive project.
Entry Criteria	• The launch preparation work has been completed (PREPL, PREPT). • For the launch, the management and marketing representatives are prepared and available for meetings 1 and 9. • All team members and the team leader are committed to attend launch meetings 1 through 9 and the launch postmortem. • An authorized launch coach is on hand to lead the launch process.

General	Timing					
		Day	1	2	3	4
		Meeting	1, 2, and 3	4, 5, and 6	7 and 8	9 and PM

Step	Activities	Description
1	Project and Management Objectives	Hold team launch meeting 1 (use script LAU1). • Review the launch process and introduce team members. • Discuss the project goals with management and marketing.
2	Team Goals and Roles	Hold team launch meeting 2 (use script LAU2). • Define and document the team's goals. • Allocate team roles among team members.
3	Project Strategy and Support	Hold team launch meeting 3 (use script LAU3). • Produce a system conceptual design, and, if needed, a fix list. • Determine the development strategy and products to be produced. • Define the development process to be used. • Produce the process and support plans.
4	Overall Plan	Hold team launch meeting 4 (use script LAU4). • Develop size estimates and the overall team plan.
5	Quality Plan	Hold team launch meeting 5 (use script LAU5). • Develop the quality plan.
6	Balanced Plan	Hold team launch meeting 6 (use script LAU6). • Allocate work to team members. • Produce detailed near-term plans for each team member. • Produce a balanced near-term plan for the team and each team member.
7	Project Risk Analysis	Hold team launch meeting 7 (use script LAU7). • Identify and evaluate project risks. • Define risk assessment checkpoints and responsibilities. • Propose mitigation actions for near-term, high-impact risks.

a. Copyright Carnegie Mellon University

Table 7.2 (continued)

Step	Activities	Description
8	Launch Report Preparation	Hold team launch meeting 8 (use script LAU8). • Prepare a launch report for management.
9	Management Review	Hold team launch meeting 9 (use script LAU9). • Review the launch activities and project plans with management. • Discuss project risks, responsibilities, and planned actions.
PM	Launch Postmortem	Hold team launch postmortem meeting. • Gather launch data and produce a launch report. • Put the launch report in the project notebook. • Assess the launch process and prepare PIPs.
Exit Criteria		• The launch is completed with documented team and team member plans. • Team roles, goals, processes, and responsibilities are defined. • Management agrees with the team plan or resolution actions have been identified and responsibilities assigned. • The launch data are in the project notebook (NOTEBOOK specification).

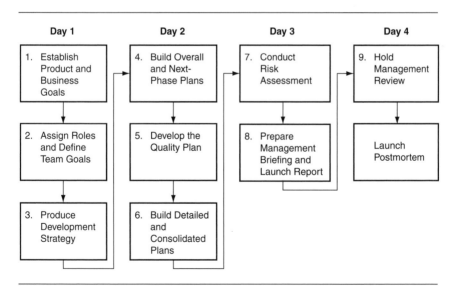

Figure 7.1 TSP Launch Meetings

3. **Pressure.** When everyone is in a hurry, nobody wants to make waves, so why not let the boss and the lead developer do the planning?

4. **Knowledge.** Often, most team members have limited knowledge of the product and would prefer to have experts give them the plan.

5. **Skills.** Unless they have been properly trained, few developers know how to make a plan or would even agree that a plan is needed.

If the objective of the launch were to quickly produce a detailed plan, a tool would be helpful. Remember, however, that the plan is not the objective. The principal launch objective is to have all of the team members cooperate in producing the plan, to have them all agree with the plan, and to have everyone commit to meeting it. Furthermore, after the launch, all team members must understand the plan and each of their roles and responsibilities for doing the job.

There are many tools that can generate plans. When properly used, they can even produce reasonably accurate plans. All you need to do is to plug in some factors that characterize the project, the product, and the team, and the tool will produce a complete and detailed plan. If you used such a tool to produce a plan that all of the team members would accept as an accurate representation of the work they had to do, you might get a good plan. However, you would not get a jelled and committed team and the launch process would have been a failure.

While sophisticated estimating tools can provide useful benchmarks, if they are used to produce the plan, the team members will not have thought through and agreed on what to build and how to build it or be committed to a plan for doing the work. Then you would lose a major benefit of the planning process. Estimating models can be useful, but they should only be used *after* the team has produced its own plan. The team could then compare its finished plan with the one produced by the tool and identify mistakes or oversights.

7.4   Launch Support

During the TSP launch, you have the guidance of a defined and detailed process and the support of a trained and qualified TSP coach. There are four reasons why coaching support is important.

First, you need a coach to guide you through the process. The TSP launch process is a guide to conducting the launch; it is not a tutorial on how to do it. The process is a little like the preflight checklist that pilots follow before starting a flight. While it does not tell the pilots anything they do not already know, it ensures that they do not forget anything and that they do the steps in the right order. In the TSP launch process, it is not always obvious how the steps should be performed. A trained and qualified coach can help you to understand how and why each step is done and guide you in doing it correctly.

If the launch were a simple process that always worked the same way, teams could quickly learn it and then conduct launches without a coach. However, every team and every launch is different. Because of these differences, teams often have trouble when they try to do a second launch just the way they did the first one. While the same process will work, the specific tasks can vary considerably depending on the team's experience and current situation. An experienced coach can help teams handle these variations.

The second reason for having a coach is to provide an independent party to resolve issues and to achieve team consensus. As team leader, you are an important part of the teambuilding process, but you cannot provide impartial guidance when your team needs to resolve issues. Even though you are perfectly capable of leading this team, and even though your people have no problems working with you, you are not just like any other team member. You are the leader and your words carry more weight than anyone else's.

The third reason that a coach is important is to facilitate the launch process. When you have the help and support of a coach, you can participate in the launch process without worrying about guiding and facilitating the launch meetings.

The fourth reason is that the team members will likely accept what you say, even if they do not completely agree. This can make it hard for the team to come to a fully agreed consensus. The presence of a coach can protect you and the team from the members' natural inclination to go along with what you say just because you are the leader. While this tendency could make meetings go more quickly and even accelerate an apparent consensus, its primary disadvantage is that the team may not achieve a true consensus. Then you will not have the benefit of everyone's views, the members will not be fully committed, and the team will not be as effective as it otherwise could be.

While the first three reasons are important, this fourth reason is crucial. The coach can help you to ensure that a true consensus is reached on the important team decisions. The coach can make sure that your views are properly considered by the team but that they do not unduly bias or dominate the views of the other members.

7.5 Launch Preparation

In preparing for the TSP launch, follow the steps described in the launch preparation checklist in Table 7.3. These checklist steps are discussed in Chapters 5 and 6 and they are required to satisfy teambuilding condition 4: that the members have the skill and discipline to make and to follow a plan. In addition, three other things are needed.

Table 7.3 TSP Launch Preparation Checklist—PREPL

Purpose	To guide launch preparation activities				
Weeks Prior to Launch	**Step**	**Description**			**Completed**
6–8	Pre-launch Package Sent	The launch coordinator has received and reviewed the pre-launch package.			
6	Project Identified	The TSP project has been identified.			
6	Person Responsible	A person has been named as responsible for launch preparation for the project.			
4	Team Ready	The team members and team leader are identified and have scheduled the launch period on their calendars so that they are available for the entire launch period.			
4	Project Profile Questions	The launch coordinator has returned the project profile to the launch coach.			
2	Launch Preparation Package	The launch coordinator has received, reviewed, and distributed the launch preparation package.			
2	Developer Training	All software developers on the team have completed PSP training.			
2	Management Training	• The team leader has completed TSP or PSP management training. • All involved managers and executives have completed TSP or PSP management training.			
2	Attendance	All launch participants know the attendance guidelines and are scheduled to attend. • The management, marketing, and other interested parties attend launch meetings 1 and 9. • The team leader and team members attend meetings 1 through 9, and the launch postmortem.			
2	Schedule	• All team members and the team leader are committed to attend launch meetings 1 through 9 and the launch postmortem, and management and marketing representatives are prepared and available for meetings 1 and 9.			

Schedule table:

Day	1	2	3	4
Timing	8:30–6:45	8:00–5:00	8:30–5:30	8:30–4:30
Meetings	1, 2, and 3	3(cont.), 4, 5, and 6	6 (cont.), 7 and 8	9 and PM

• The team may have to stay late (8:00 PM) on days 1, 2, or 3.

Table 7.3 (continued)

Weeks Prior to Launch	Step	Description	Completed
2	Facilities Needed for Meetings 1 and 9	• The room for launch meetings 1 and 9 is large enough to hold all the team members, management representatives, and observers. • An overhead projector and screen are available. • The room is available for the mornings of days 1 and 4.	
2	Facilities Needed for Meetings 2 through 8, Launch Postmortem, and Process Review	For days 1, 2, 3, and 4 (if needed) the following facilities are needed. • A conference room with desk-size working space for each team member, the team leader, and launch coaches • One or more personal computers with the Microsoft Office 2000 versions of Word, Excel, and Access database. • Two flip-chart easels and a whiteboard with pads and markers • A unit for projecting from a PC	
2	Process Review	All new TSP team members are scheduled to attend a TSP process review and workshop for the rest of day 4, after all other launch meetings.	
2	Team Preparation Package	The team leader and all of the team's developers have been given the team and team leader workshop preparation packages, respectively.	
2	Management Preparation Package	The senior manager has been given the senior management workshop preparation package.	
2	Marketing Preparation Package	The senior marketing manager has been given the marketing management workshop preparation package.	
2	Other Attendee Preparation Package	Any other attendees have been given the other attendee workshop preparation package.	
2	Catering	For days 1, 2, 3, and 4 (if needed), the following catering is planned. • Morning and mid morning break • Working lunch • Mid-afternoon break A working dinner (pizza?) may be needed for days 1, 2, or 3.	
2	Launch Notebooks	The launch notebooks have been distributed to all team members and the team leader.	

First, since you are presumably planning a new project, you will want as much information on that project as you can get. You will also want knowledge-able people to describe the job to the team in meeting 1. You must also personally understand what management wants your team to do.

Second, prior to the launch, you and your team members should have reviewed prior similar projects and brought any relevant data with you to the launch. Examples of such data include the sizes of prior products, development times and resources, test-defect data, and test-time histories. However, do not produce an early estimate for the job. While having such an estimate could greatly accelerate the launch process, the team members would not have been involved and they would view that preliminary plan as yours and not theirs.

The third launch preparation item concerns the product's conceptual design. On many jobs, particularly maintenance and enhancement work, the design is well known, so the conceptual-design step isn't necessary. However, if your team is developing a new product or making a major enhancement to an existing prod-uct, a substantial design effort is generally needed. In this case, one or two team members should think through the high-level design of this product and be pre-pared to present their ideas to the team during the launch. The conceptual design provides the basis for the team's size estimate and development strategy. It should be detailed enough to logically divide the work among the members but not so detailed that it would take more than an hour or two to describe.

An alternative approach would be to have the entire team produce the con-ceptual design during launch meeting 3. This is not usually a good idea, because there are many possible design approaches and the team could waste a great deal of time debating which one to pursue. Since the conceptual design is only needed to guide the team's size estimate and strategy discussion, it should merely be a safe or conservative design and not the design the team will ultimately use to build the product.

On most teams, there are usually one or two members who are the recog-nized design experts, and they will generally be best qualified to produce a useful and well thought out conceptual design. Also, by using a very few designers, you have a better chance of getting a logically constructed design instead of a com-mittee product that has the many little compromises usually required to get everyone's agreement. When selecting the members to think about the conceptual design in advance, try to pick the ones who are the most likely candidates for the design manager role. If you do, the rest of the team will likely accept their sug-gestions with little argument.

In addition to this preparatory conceptual-design and data-gathering work, you must also decide who will participate in the launch. Visitors, managers, and others are allowed in meetings 1 and 9 but not in any of the other launch meet-ings. Only you, the team members, and the coach participate in meetings 2 through 8 and the postmortem. By limiting participation to only those people who will be working essentially full time on this job, the launch can be an effective teambuilding activity. Experience shows that when visitors are present, many team members will not fully participate in the launch process. This often destroys the launch as a teambuilding activity.

There is also often a question of whom to consider as a team member. Some members may have commitments to prior jobs and have to spend time handling fixes or providing support for prior products. Requirements or systems development team members can often only spend part time on any one job. This can be acceptable as long as these members are properly trained and are committed to this team for a substantial portion of their time.

Projects also often involve many other groups that will want to be represented at the launch meetings. For example, support groups generally argue that if they do not participate in the launch, they will not be fully informed about the team's work. While it is essential that these groups' needs be addressed in the team's plan—and you may even want to coordinate with them during the launch—representatives of such groups must not be included in the launch meetings. The launch process is not the forum for negotiating with support groups. It is where you and your team decide how to do this job. When support groups object to being excluded, commit to keeping them fully informed but do not include them in launch meetings 2 through 8.

In some cases, groups such as requirements, test, hardware, or systems design have a large enough role in the job to warrant their inclusion in the launch. For example, if they have members assigned full time to the work, it may be more appropriate to use several different but coordinated teams. These are supported by the TSP with a TSP multi-team process. Before deciding to use a multi-team process, however, discuss the situation with the TSP coach to see if it would be appropriate. The material in this book describes the single team TSP process.

In considering whether to form a single or a multiple team, think of team membership in the following way: you would never form a ball team with football, baseball, and basketball players. Such teams are not effective because the members have different rules, goals, and skills. The same is true of teams with development, testing, and requirements members. They speak different languages, have different processes, and work toward different goals. Such teams rarely jell. Instead, they form into small cliques that work largely independently and often at cross-purposes. The TSP multi-team process is designed to handle this situation.

In the TSP multi-team process, separate but related teams are formed for each of the project's specialty groups. The single exception to having separate teams by discipline is for small integrated teams. For a small project with one or two hardware, software, requirements, and test specialists, for example, a single team with a common team launch could be effective. Since such teams are small with no dominant specialty, the members are less likely to split into factions. Such multiple-discipline teams can jell, particularly if the team leader is viewed as the leader for all of the members.

7.6   Leading a TSP Launch

The coach starts the launch process and provides an overview of every launch meeting, but you lead many of the launch steps. While it is important for all the team members to agree with whatever conclusions the group reaches, you must also agree. If the team has debated an issue and is settling on a position that you believe is wrong, do not be dominated by the team any more than you want the team to be dominated by you. Make the members convince you that they are right. If the issue appears unresolvable, get the coach to help you and the team identify the relevant facts and logically examine the issues and alternatives. Take the time to reach a full team consensus on every important issue. The resulting team cohesion and commitment will be well worth the time required.

Meeting 1: The Opening Management Meeting

Although the coach leads meeting 1, you are the host and are responsible for ensuring that the required people are there and properly prepared. You must also ensure that the team members know what to expect and that they enter this first meeting with the proper attitude. Even if management asks you to do the job in a fraction of the time you believe will be required, be positive. Understand what management wants and clarify any resource, schedule, or product constraints. At the end of meeting 1, every team member should know management's needs, understand the criteria for success, and be aware of the alternatives management will likely accept. In the rest of the launch, your team will do its utmost to make a plan that meets management's needs.

The time to discuss schedules is after you have made a team plan. In meeting 1, do not tell management that you believe their desired schedule is impossible or even difficult. If you do, no matter how hard you try, they will not likely believe that you will do your best to meet their needs. In meeting 9, it will then be much harder to convince them that you have a sound and realistic plan. In meeting 1, you and your team should demonstrate by your questions, your expressions, and your attitudes that you will do your utmost to meet management's needs.

Meeting 1 addresses points 2 (commitment to a common goal) and 7 (the commitment is important to the team) of the 9 conditions for a self-directed and motivated team (see Table 7.1 on page 73).

Meeting 2: Team Goals and Roles

Under the guidance of the TSP coach, you next lead the team through the goal identification and role selection steps in meeting 2. The first objective is to ensure that the team's goals address management's needs and are meaningful to all of the team members. One way to do this is to use some other team's results as a benchmark. While benchmarks are discussed more fully in Chapter 17, the idea is to establish goals that seem realistic and meaningful to the team. When you have data on other TSP projects, you can set goals to equal or better their performance in quality, productivity, test time, or any other key measure.

After agreeing on the goals, you next guide the team in selecting team-member roles. There are eight standard TSP roles (described in Appendix A) and, except for very small teams, the team leader should not take any of them. Your job as team leader is to motivate, guide, and oversee the work, not to do it. Role selection is a first step in establishing point 1 of the teambuilding conditions: the members all feel that they belong to the team. By taking responsibility for an important part of the team's work, each member gets a defined place on the team. This helps to build a feeling of membership and interdependence.

In this role-selection process, you must be comfortable with the team member assignments. If someone volunteers for a role that you think they cannot or should not do, discuss your concerns with the team. Do this only if you feel that this person's selection would be a serious mistake. Of course, you must be diplomatic in handling these discussions.

If, for example, you would prefer to have one team member be the design manager, try to address this problem before the launch. Ask that person to produce the conceptual design and to explain it to the team during the launch. If everyone knows about this assignment and if this team member does a good job, they will likely agree to him or her being the design manager. If you can, also make similar preparations for any of the other roles where you feel the selection would be especially critical.

One way to handle such problems is to think about which roles each team member would handle particularly well. Do not assign these roles, but if the team is about to make a selection that you think would be a serious mistake, tell the team that you would prefer this person's skill on the role you think they could best handle. Instead of making a negative statement about why Joe should not be design manager, for example, be positive about Joe and compliment him by saying how much you need his skill and ability in the support manager, test manager, or some other role. Make Joe feel wanted, not rejected. While experienced TSP team members generally know which roles to take, new members will not, and you may have to step in. However, in all cases, make sure that the team members agree with and accept their roles.

The first part of meeting 2 reinforces conditions 1 (sense of team membership), 2 (the commitment to a common goal), and 7 (the commitment is important to the team) for a motivated and self-directed team.

Meeting 3: Project Strategy and Support

In meeting 3, you lead the team in selecting its development strategy. This typically starts with a review of the conceptual design and a discussion of the various ways to build the product. The design manager is usually the right person to lead this discussion. You then lead the strategy discussion and the process manager leads the group in defining the development process. Finally, the support manager leads the team in defining its support needs. The coach guides all of you in doing this. While these steps are rarely a problem, strategy selection is particularly critical. Here the team decides how to approach the job. The prime objective is to address the major project exposures as early in the job as possible. This provides the time needed to address these exposures in an orderly way.

In developing the team strategy, consider first building a core or kernel system version and then enhancing this version in multiple builds or releases. This strategy provides an early development foundation and usually accelerates the entire project. It also gives you the most flexibility in adjusting the system's functional content in case you run into schedule problems. This also makes it easier to develop a wide variety of alternative plans by merely moving functions among the releases. Most importantly, a multiple-build strategy is effective for providing the kind of short-term concrete goals that best motivate and energize teams. The multiple-build strategy is almost always more successful than the more common strategy of building the entire system in one big step.

Meeting 3 addresses teambuilding steps 3 (ownership of the process and plan) and 8 (commitment is voluntary, visible, and credible).

Meeting 4: The Overall Team Plan

In meeting 4, the planning manager leads the team through overall planning. The coach guides this work and you participate along with everyone else. Since your views on size estimates and development rates may bias the team's decisions, and since you want the team estimate to be as accurate as possible, you should generally not state an opinion until after everyone else has done so.

In making the size and development time estimates, consider all of the available data and check that the results are consistent with prior experience. Also, have everyone participate in making the estimates. As long as the discussion is good-natured, disorderly meetings with everyone speaking up and occasionally interrupting generally produce better estimates than well-structured and orderly ones. Team members are more willing to participate in such freewheeling meetings where no one dominates the discussion. However, the coach and you should keep the discussion focused on the script topics. Take the time to produce a complete and thorough estimate and ensure that you have a record of why you picked the rate and size values that you did.

Once the team has made the overall plan and produced the resource and schedule estimates, you will probably find that the plan does not meet management's needs. That is when you need to consider alternative plans. Examples would be adding resources, lengthening the schedule, or deferring functions to later releases. Once you have examined the reasonable alternatives, decide which one to use for the base plan. If it is not clear which alternative would be best, consider seeking guidance from management before proceeding to meetings 5 and 6.

However, under no conditions should you base the team's commitment on resources that you do not have. If management promises to provide additional resources, tell them what the date would be if these resources were trained and available on the required date. However, emphasize that the team's commitment is only for the resources that you now have. When you get additional resources you will adjust the commitment, but you cannot do so until the people are trained, on board, and working.

Meeting 4 continues the teambuilding process by addressing points 3 (ownership of the process and plan), 6 (committed to doing the job), and 8 (commitment is voluntary, visible, and credible).

Meeting 5: Making the Quality Plan

Meeting 5 is led by the quality manager, and it can be a relatively mechanical process of estimating defect injection rates and defect removal yields. From your perspective, however, the point of meeting 5 is to establish team yield goals for each process step. For example, many inexperienced TSP teams establish a goal of 70 percent yield for all of the reviews and inspections. While this is laudable, it is a meaningless goal unless the team considers what yield each member has achieved in the past and what they will do to achieve the team's yield commitments for this project.

The TSP process provides four activities that help to produce quality products. First, all of the team members record every defect they find at every step in the process. This includes the defects found in compiling, testing, inspecting, and reviewing the product. These data provide the information needed for the other three quality activities. Second, the team members periodically use their defect data to update their personal review checklists. These checklists guide their personal design and code reviews. Third, the team members use their quality plan to track and manage the quality of their work. Fourth, the team holds reviews of every defect found after unit testing. For example, when the testing group finds a defect in integration or system test, this defect has escaped every quality step in the team's process and it could provide valuable information on how to improve that process. The entire team should discuss where that defect was injected, why it was missed in each subsequent review, inspection, and test, and how to prevent that type of defect from being injected again. You should also consider what other defects could have been missed in the same way and establish a plan to find and fix them.

Discuss all of these issues with the team in meeting 5 and agree on what steps the team will take to follow its quality plan and to produce a truly superior product. Also discuss how the quality manager can monitor and report on the team's performance and help you to meet your quality commitments. Suggestions on how to motivate quality work are discussed in Chapter 11.

Meeting 5 addresses teambuilding condition 5 (dedicated to superior work). While you presumably talked about quality goals in meeting 2, meeting 5 is where the team discusses these goals and decides how to meet them.

Meeting 6: Balancing the Team Plan

In meeting 6, the team members each start with the overall plan produced in meeting 4 and make detailed personal plans for the next several months. They do this in three steps. First, they agree on the duration for the work to be planned before the next team relaunch. Second, the team allocates its work among all of the members. Here, the team discusses the task assignments and decides which ones will be handled by which member. You typically lead this allocation process. Third, each team member makes a detailed plan that shows earned value progress every week. This generally requires that the tasks be estimated in chunks of 10 task hours or less. The earned-value measure is used to track progress against the plan. It is described in Chapter 8.

The principal concerns in task allocation are the required skills and knowledge for each task, available team member time, willingness to do the task, and willingness to work with the other team members who will be involved in each task. Do as thorough a job of task allocation as you can, because if the allocations are not reasonably balanced, the plan will have a longer schedule than it should. Then you will have to work with the team to reassign the work among the members, and the members will have to revise their detailed plans.

Meeting 6 continues the process of building the team's ownership and commitment to its plan. These are teambuilding conditions 3 (ownership of the process and plan), 6 (committed to doing the job), and 8 (the commitment is voluntary, visible, and credible).

Meeting 7: Project Risk Analysis

In meeting 7, you lead the team through identifying and analyzing the major project risks. The TSP process and the coach guide you in doing this. Again, ensure that all of the team members are involved and contribute their views. If one or more members are not participating, wait for an opportune time and ask for their views. They will often have useful contributions to make.

At the end of meeting 7, discuss and agree on mitigation plans for each of the principal risks and decide which team member will track each one. You also need mitigation plans for these key risks since management will likely ask for them.

Assigning risk tracking responsibility begins to establish teambuilding condition 9 (the commitment is linked to the team).

Meeting 8: Launch Report Preparation

The task of meeting 8 is to prepare the team's presentation for the final management meeting. While the team leader generally makes this presentation, consider asking one or more members to handle some of the topics for you. Before doing so, however, make sure that these members can give clear and succinct presentations and would like to participate in the management presentation.

The TSP scripts and standards provide suggestions on how to organize and give the final management presentation. While you must personally decide how to present the team's story, discuss your ideas with the members and get their suggestions. In producing the presentation, also get the team to help. Allocate parts of the preparation work to various members and schedule a review to rehearse the entire talk. Then check to make sure that the presentation covers all of the required material, that it describes how the team's plan addresses management's goals, and that everyone who will be involved feels comfortable about making the presentation. It is also a good idea to discuss with the team the kinds of questions management will likely ask and to ensure that you have the backup materials needed to provide factual and convincing answers.

Meetings 8 and 9 continue the process of satisfying teambuilding condition 9 (the commitment is linked to the team).

Meeting 9: Reviewing the Plan with Management

The TSP suggests several guidelines for conducting the management meeting. First, do not go through the entire talk and end with a surprise. If the plan has major problems or if you cannot fulfill some important management request, say so at the beginning of the meeting. Explain that you have prepared one or more alternative plans and that you and your team have developed the most practical and responsible plan for doing this job. However, you cannot completely meet all of management's requirements. Then describe the topics that you will cover and get started.

Second, provide a summary overview of the project that describes the product you plan to develop, how you plan to do the job, when you expect to complete the work, and why you selected this development strategy. Using just a few charts, describe the project in terms that any senior manager could understand, and list the major milestones, summarize the resource needs, and list the key risks. If, as occasionally happens, management agrees to the plan and has no questions, move immediately to step six below, the meeting conclusion. You have made the sale. Since management will usually have questions, however, you will probably be able to give the entire presentation.

Third, start the plan discussion by building your and your team's credibility. Describe the work you have done during the launch and explain the launch products. Also explain the data you have used to validate the plan and to guide the estimates. Then describe how you used any available data to check that the plan was both realistic and aggressive. Point out that you have produced a great deal of detail and that you have backup material on all of it. Volunteer to provide any additional information that they would like to see.

Fourth, move quickly. Assume that these managers are smart people and that they will quickly understand your points. Explain all of the key points clearly and avoid using special jargon or acronyms. Since senior managers do not like being lectured to, do not lecture or preach. The more senior the executives, the more likely they are to stop listening the moment you start to lecture. Next, and most important, do not repeat yourself. Make your points quickly and concisely and move on.

Fifth, stop when your audience is done. If the most senior manager agrees with your proposal, even at the beginning of the presentation, make sure that he or she is really in agreement, then stop. Continuing with a presentation after management has heard all that they need to know to make a decision will waste their time and risk having the decision reversed.

Sixth, at the meeting's conclusion, make sure that you understand what management wants you to do. If there are open issues or if you and your team have been asked to do more work, make sure that you understand precisely what they want you to do before you stop. It is generally a good idea to end the meeting with a brief review of all the outstanding action items, who is responsible for each, and when it will be completed.

Seventh, and finally, do not make commitments on the fly. If management asks how the plan would change with more resources or some requirements adjustments but you and the team have not already discussed this case, agree to examine it and get back to them. This is not just your plan; it is the team's plan, and you cannot change it without reviewing the changes and getting the team's agreement to these changes.

At the end of meeting 9, you will have completed the TSP launch process and will also have completed all 9 of the conditions required for a motivated and self-directed team. Now, all you have to do is to maintain the team's motivation and ensure that all of the team members follow their defined processes and plans. Of course, you must also work with the team to address all of the problems that will inevitably arise as you do the work.

The Launch Postmortem

The postmortem meeting is held after the end of meeting 9. It is a brief session where you, the team members, and the coach review the launch process and discuss how you could improve it for the next launch or relaunch. You should also ensure that all of the plan and launch data are properly recorded in the project notebook for later reference. The coach generally leads the postmortem.

7.7 Summary

This chapter describes the TSP launch process and your role as team leader in that process. It starts with a summary of launch objectives and then discusses teambuilding, how teambuilding is done, and how the TSP builds teams.

The bulk of the chapter describes the TSP launch meetings and your role in these meetings. The principal launch steps are as follows.

1. The opening management meeting (meeting 1)
2. Team goals and roles (meeting 2)
3. Project strategy and support (meeting 3)
4. The overall team plan (meeting 4)
5. Making the quality plan (meeting 5)
6. Balancing the team plan (meeting 6)
7. Project risk analysis (meeting 7)
8. Launch report preparation (meeting 8)
9. Reviewing the plan with management (meeting 9)
10. The launch postmortem (PM meeting)

PART III

Teamworking

A new TSP team had only been working for three weeks but it was already behind schedule. It was the first time Candy had led a TSP project, and she could see from the team's third weekly status report that they were falling further behind each week. In the Monday morning team meeting, she reviewed the data in the table on page 94 with the team. The first and most obvious problem was that the team members were not working enough task hours. While everyone was working a very full week, they weren't devoting enough of their working hours to project tasks.

Everyone agreed to put in more task hours, but Candy was not satisfied. "Just trying harder won't do it. I know you're all trying pretty hard right now. What are you going to do differently?"

This started an extended brainstorming session that produced lots of good ideas. The team finally decided on two actions. First, they would dedicate three mornings a week to project tasks with no meetings or other interruptions. Second, they would establish a policy to not interrupt anyone who had a "Do not interrupt" sign on their office door. The team's task hours improved immediately and, within a couple of weeks, they were caught up with the plan.

This is typical of TSP teams. They start the job with lots of energy and enthusiasm but then encounter all kinds of surprises and problems. The team can generally handle each issue, but each problem adds to the workload and progress

The TSP Weekly Status Report—Week 3

Weekly Data	Plan	Actual	Plan/Actual
Schedule hours for this week	112.0	83.9	1.33
Scheduled hours this cycle to date	336.0	226.3	1.48
Earned value for this week	6.5	3.8	1.71
Earned value for this cycle to date	19.5	10.7	1.82
To-date hours for tasks completed	184.4	218.6	.84
To-date average hours per week	112.0	72.6	1.54

slows. While these small delays are not normally visible, TSP teams can detect even a one-day schedule slip. Your job as team leader is to motivate your team to use this information to stay on schedule. The chapters in Part III describe how to do this.

Chapter 8 describes the importance of managing to the plan and some issues you will face in doing so. It describes handling the first crisis, maintaining and changing plans, dynamic planning, and workload balancing.

Chapter 9 discusses priorities and the need to maintain a consistent focus on the highest priority tasks. The principal topics in Chapter 9 are setting and changing priorities, overcoming obstacles, involving the customer, and setting short-term goals.

Chapter 10 concerns following the team's process while doing the job. It discusses the importance of following the process, building good team habits, and motivating sound team practices. It also discusses handling process problems, the benefits of quality work, and making such work visible and rewarding.

Chapter 11 deals with product quality. The principal topics here concern human failings, quality responsibilities, assessing quality, and gathering and using quality data.

As you use the information in these chapters to lead, guide, and motivate your team, remember that the TSP coach can be a big help (see Appendix B, section B3).

8

Managing to the Plan

Once you have launched the team, you are ready to get to work. In simplest terms, all you have to do now is to follow the plan. That, however, is not always easy. Few people have ever worked with detailed plans, and they will either not know how to follow a plan or will give up when the plan doesn't exactly fit the job. Plans are never precisely accurate and unexpected things always happen. With experience, developers learn to expect problems and to plan for them. However, until they have enough experience, they will need leadership and guidance.

This chapter discusses the problems of working to a plan. It describes the typical issues you will face and steps to take to address them. The following are the principal topics of the chapter.

- □ Following the plan
- □ The first crisis
- □ Dynamic planning
- □ Changing requirements
- □ Maintaining the plan
- □ Workload balancing
- □ Tracking progress
- □ Assessing status
- □ Getting help

8.1   Following the Plan

When TSP teams follow their plans, the team members perform the tasks in their plans. As they work, they record the times spent on each task, the sizes of the products produced, and the defects found. They must also coordinate with their peers on design sessions, team inspections, and other interdependent activities. To accommodate overall team needs, they must often do tasks in a different order than planned or they may have to suspend one task to complete one that a team-mate needs done.

Your job as team leader is to facilitate this process and to help all team members do their work properly, follow the team's defined process, and track and record their data. If this was all you had to do, your job would be fairly straight-forward. However, this will rarely be the case. The plan will be at least partly inaccurate, changes will arise, and there may be one or more crises. Your job is to keep the team working efficiently and effectively, regardless of any problems or distractions. You must ensure that the team follows its process even when under pressure. This, in fact, is when a process is most important: to prevent panic and to maintain an orderly rate of progress.

A key part of leadership is maintaining an orderly and productive team environment. If you find that either the process or the plan is not appropriate, help the team fix it so both the process and the plan help the team do its work.

8.2   The First Crisis

Marjory had been lead designer on her previous project and did such a fine job that she was made the leader of a new team. Her team had a major new system to develop at flank speed and all the members had agreed to an aggressive schedule. While Marjory had known these developers for several years, she had never worked with them on a project. She decided to take the design manager job her-self, at least until she knew which members were the best designers.

After a week, Marjory realized that they were in trouble. She had assumed that most of the team members were reasonably competent designers and that they could work with only modest guidance and direction. She found, however, that only two of them had previously done much design work and that most of them did not know how to produce even rudimentary designs.

To meet the schedule, Marjory decided to closely supervise all of the design work. Every day she met with one or two team members to review their work and to give them specific guidance. She then thoroughly reviewed every developer's designs before agreeing that they could be released for further work. After about a month, when Marjory's manager wanted to review project status, she realized that she had no idea where the team stood. They had not been following their plan so she had no way to measure their progress. She managed to bluff her way through the project review, but then she decided to take a couple of days to review status with the team and to produce a new plan that reflected what they were actually doing.

While Marjory managed to salvage her project, it took about three months of exhausting work. She also learned an important lesson that most army officers learn the hard way: "No battle plan survives first contact with the enemy." When a team first makes a plan, that plan is often unrealistic. When teams have not previously worked to detailed plans, they often encounter problems they had not anticipated. As they gain experience, they will make better plans, but even experienced teams occasionally run into surprises.

While Marjory's was an extreme case, your job as a team leader is to keep your team on a productive path and to rework the plan as soon as you have learned enough about the job to do so. Working with an unrealistic plan is always a mistake, but working without a plan is even worse.

8.3   Dynamic Planning

To address the problems of inaccurate and changing plans, TSP teams do what is called **dynamic planning**. This is when the team members adjust the plan to reflect what they have learned about the job. By doing this, teams can ensure that their plans are continually updated to reflect changes. Their plans will then be accurate and they will guide the team in doing the work. At the beginning of the job, when they are learning the most, team members may even have to make plan changes every week.

During the launch, when you and your team first made the plan, it helped you negotiate the schedule with management. Now that you are doing the job, the plan's principal value is in guiding and managing the work. To be a realistic and useful guide, however, the plan must accurately represent the situation you face, the resources you have, and the strategy you intend to follow. For projects with few unknowns and surprises, this is rarely a problem, but for more typical jobs, you will be learning as you do the work.

In software, our knowledge is dynamic. We constantly learn more about the users' needs, the system's design, and the effort required for each task. Software development is a learning process and, as we learn, we must adjust our plans to incorporate this new knowledge. The key to doing this is dynamic planning.

Many people mistakenly feel that plans are static and that once they make a plan, it cannot be changed. While you should certainly keep the old plans for reference and document and track all of your commitments, you must change your plans whenever the situation warrants. The best guideline is: *if you can't plan accurately, plan often.*

One potential problem with planning is the time it takes. However, with a defined process and historical data, teams can produce a completely updated plan in a few hours. The small plan changes that team members must make every day or two typically only take a few minutes. With dynamic planning, you will always have a plan that accurately represents the work that you have to do and the way that you plan to do it.

8.4   Changing Requirements

A common belief is that projects get into trouble because their requirements changed. This is an excuse. Requirements always change. Usually, the problem is with the way these changes are managed. When faced with lots of little requirements changes, it takes considerable effort to keep the plan up to date. However, if you don't, you will be working without a plan and can no longer track your work or estimate when the job will be done. While this often happens to projects, the problem is with how the project was managed—not with the requirements changes. Often, the requirements will change so often and in such small steps that you will have to constantly reassess your plan.

With a dynamic planning process, teams can assess the impact of each change and only agree to changes when management understands and agrees to the necessary schedule and resource adjustments. The team can then know the cost of each requirements change and can negotiate any needed schedule or resources requirements before committing to the change. While this sounds easy in theory, it is often exceedingly difficult in practice.

Dynamic planning will protect you from requirements creep. If you do not examine the impact of every change, you will be inundated with small changes. In effect, by accepting changes without adjusting the schedule or resources, you are telling the customer and management that changes are free. That both misleads them and invites more changes. If you do not control every change, your project will be overwhelmed with changes.

Act as if there is no such thing as a free change. This is, of course, an over reaction. There is a fine line between requirements changes and requirements clarifications. As the customer's understanding of the product matures, the only constraint on adding new functions and features is your ability to deliver. If you do not make that constraint known, you will mislead the business. The best way to do this is with dynamic planning. It is the only way to protect yourself from being nibbled to death by small changes.

8.5   Maintaining the Plan

The longer you work to a detailed plan, the more you will need to change it. This does not mean that you will actually change the plan, but that you will refine it. As the work progresses, the team members will better understand the work and be better able to make more detailed plans. While these small plan changes will usually be consistent with the original plan, this dynamic working plan will gradually diverge from the plan you made during the launch.

Suppose that, after a few weeks of work, one team member completes her planned tasks and is ready to start on some new ones. If the rest of the team is still following its prior plan, it might not make sense to conduct a team relaunch. Rather than have this one developer work without a plan, she could add some near-term tasks to her current plan and continue working. To allow for this possibility, it is generally a good idea to extend the team's planning well beyond the planned relaunch date. Rather than plan all of the future work in detail, however, the later tasks could be kept in larger chunks and only refined when needed. In fact, developers often find it desirable to defer detailed planning for their larger tasks until shortly before they start to work on them.

While it is often possible to keep extending the current plan, it is not a good idea to defer the team relaunch for too long. The relaunch is needed not just to update the plan, but to update the team's goals and to review the team's risks and role assignments. It is also a good time to assess the work that has been done and to agree on how to do better work during the next project cycle.

8.6   Workload Balancing

The principal reason for dynamic planning is to continuously rebalance the team's workload. Some members will finish tasks before the planned date and others will be late. This is normal. Individual times vary from job to job. Since some members have special skills and others will take on more work than they can do, the team must regularly rebalance its workload.

One example of an unbalanced workload is shown in Figure 8.1. Each of the nine members on this team estimated the times they needed to complete their

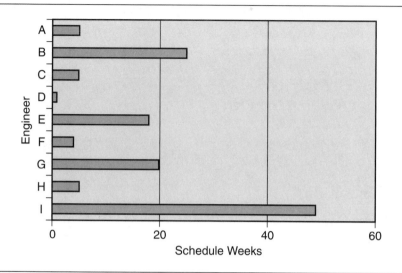

Figure 8.1 Unbalanced Team Workload

assigned near-term tasks. For this 16-week period, the lead designer (developer I in the figure) had 49 weeks of work to do in this next phase. Several other members had less than 10 weeks of assigned tasks.

Since the team members had each made detailed plans for the next phase, they could see the consequences of this workload imbalance. Without the TSP, team plans are rarely precise enough to show each member's weekly work. With typical high-level plans, workload imbalances are not apparent and some members will not be fully utilized. With such a team, the team leader will usually sense that there is a problem but not have the data needed to fix it. With a self-directed TSP team, the members have the data and the motivation to rebalance their own workloads.

Once the members of this team understood the workload imbalance problem, they reallocated their work and, in less than an hour, had produced the adjusted workload shown in Figure 8.2. In this rebalancing process, the members considered their individual skills, their product and application knowledge, and their preferences for working with other team members.

For any but the smallest teams, the workload is usually unbalanced. However, even when a team balances its workload, the workload will soon become unbalanced again. With self-directed teams, the members rebalance their workload as often as needed to keep every member productively occupied. While the team leader can assist in this process, only the team members have the knowledge to quickly and effectively rebalance their workload. As is clear from Figure 8.2,

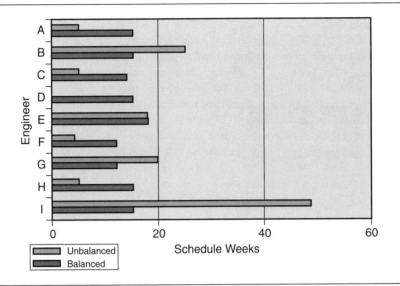

Figure 8.2 Balanced Team Workload

by taking less than an hour, these developers reduced the expected time for the next phase from 49 weeks to 17.

8.7   Tracking Progress

On development projects, team members constantly encounter new problems. That is the nature of development work: identifying and solving problems. Sometimes the team members can solve these problems by themselves and sometimes they will need help. With a detailed plan and the TSP's task and time measures, the team can determine precisely where it stands. This provides the information needed to decide whether the team can solve its problems by itself or whether you, the team leader, need to go to management for help. While you should not give up too soon, you must also know when to face reality and to ask for help. To do this, you must understand precisely where the project stands.

The two most useful measures of project schedule performance are **earned value (EV)** and **task hours**. EV measures the work completed to date. It is calculated by determining the percentage of total project hours planned for each task. For example, on a 1,000 task-hour plan, a task of 16 hours would have an EV of 1.6.

(For a more complete description of earned value, see Chapter 13, section 13.5.) The EV method allows the team to estimate when the project will likely finish. This estimate will be accurate as long as the original plan is reasonably accurate and the team members are following their plan. Suppose, for example, that your team had worked for 6 weeks and completed tasks that added up to 12 EV. Since the members are averaging 2 EV per week, and since the project will be done when all of the tasks are completed and since the team will reach 100 EV when all the tasks are done, this suggests that the project will take 50 weeks. Since they have already worked for 6 weeks, they have 44 weeks to go.

While a team's rate of earned value will fluctuate during the first few weeks, it will soon settle down. Once the team members are accustomed to following their process and plan, their EV rate will become a reliable indicator of schedule progress.

The second key performance measure is task hours. These are the hours the team members spend working on planned project tasks. Task hours do not include time for management and administrative meetings, training, e-mail, or any of the host of essential activities that team members must do. In fact, the weekly task hours for a team generally reach only about 15 hours a week after several months of work. They will then only increase gradually thereafter. The more task hours the developers spend each week, the more work they will get done, and the faster the project will be completed.

The best way to increase weekly task hours is to motivate the team members to increase their own weekly task time. If they do not strive to improve their own task hours, management pressure will not help and will probably hurt. Edicts to improve task hours are *always* counterproductive. While the reported task hours will almost certainly increase to the edicted level, the actual time worked usually declines, and often quite sharply. This is not because the team members are being rebellious, but because such edicts tell the team that task hours is management's problem and not the team's. The team will then not try as hard to meet management's goal as they would if the goal were their own.

8.8 Assessing Status

During TSP planning, teams estimate their weekly task hours and make earned-value plans. By comparing your team's progress with its plan, you can see where it is having problems and determine what to do about it. Suppose the team had been working for 6 weeks and achieved an EV of 12. At the rate of 2 EV per week, the total project will take $100/2 = 50$ weeks. Now suppose that the project was supposed to finish in a total of 42 weeks instead of the now expected 50. What could you do to finish on time? The EV measure can help you assess this situation.

For example, with only $42 - 6 = 36$ weeks to go and a total of $100 - 12 = 88$ EV of tasks remaining, the team would have to achieve an average of $88/36 = 2.44$ EV per week to finish on time. This is a substantial increase over the 2.0 weekly EV the team has earned to date. Does your team have any chance of producing 22 percent more work per week than it has produced so far? While such a sharp increase might seem unlikely, the way to find out is to look at the factors that determine the amount of weekly work the team members can do and the historical variation in these factors. They can either increase their productivity, do fewer tasks, or put in more task hours.

First, increasing productivity is always a good idea, but it is rarely possible, at least in the short term. Second, if you can identify any unnecessary tasks in the plan, you should drop them or defer them immediately. To see how many tasks you would have to drop to finish the job on schedule, you can make some simple calculations. For example, if you earned 2 EV per week for the remaining 36 weeks, that would be 72 more EV in addition to the 12 you have already earned. Therefore, to complete the project in 36 more weeks you must finish the job at an EV of only 84. This means that you must find 16 EV of unneeded work. Assuming that you made a reasonably competent plan in the first place, this seems highly unlikely. While you should identify any unnecessary or low priority work, you will probably not find very much. This topic is also discussed in the next chapter.

Third, assuming that you must do all of the planned work and that the team's productivity is unlikely to improve in the near term, your only alternative is to put in more task hours. This typically means either increasing the task hours that each team member spends every week or getting more people.

To understand what to do, first assess the task-hour rate the team has achieved versus what it planned to achieve. Since the key to improving task hours is the team members' motivation, conduct this review with the team members and have them participate in making the improvement plan.

While the situation might look pretty bad at first, don't give up too quickly. To assess the team's ability to increase its EV rate, look at the week-to-week variation in the team's performance. You will find that some weeks were much more productive than others. You can then work with the team to see how to improve average performance to near their best performance.

Similarly, you will also see wide variations in weekly task hours, both for the team and for the individual members. If some members are getting much higher task hours than others, find out how they do it and get their help in coaching the others. With a combination of persistence, ingenuity, and persuasion, you can usually improve team performance by substantial factors.

8.9   Getting Help

If, as occasionally happens, your project seems likely to miss its committed completion date, you must determine what to do. First, you could just continue working and finish late. Second, you could identify actions to increase weekly task hours and determine the effect of these actions on the schedule. Since management will almost certainly prefer this option over any other, make this more than just a casual review. Identify specific improvement steps and suggest where management could help. Also establish an improvement schedule with a weekly tracking plan to assess progress. Third, consider adding team members. Since these new members will have to be trained in the PSP, there will generally be a delay before they can be productive. Finally, identify any practical ways to deliver reduced product function on the committed date and include the remaining functions in later versions.

In any case, assemble your improvement plan as quickly as possible and meet with management. When you do, bring specific recommendations. Also, if possible, have the entire team participate. While it is always tempting to put off these discussions in hopes that the situation will improve, that is *never* a good idea. Take the time to understand the situation and make sure the team is doing its utmost. Then, as soon as you know that you need help and have a specific recommendation, get the story to management. The longer you wait, the harder it will be to solve the problem.

8.10   Summary

This chapter discusses the problems team leaders face in getting their teams to follow their plans. It also describes ways to address these problems. When teams first follow a detailed plan, they often encounter problems. While these problems can cause them to abandon their plans, this is almost always a mistake. As team leader, assess the situation, devise a solution, and then guide the team in revising the plan to address the new situation.

Dynamic planning helps teams keep their plans current. It is also an effective way to protect your team from requirements creep. While it is normal for requirements to change, there is no such thing as a free requirements change. The team should assess every change and understand its impact on the plan before agreeing to make the change.

With the TSP, teams can precisely track progress against their plans. The most useful measures are earned value (EV) and task hours. By assessing EV progress and task-hour performance, you can determine when the project will likely finish and what actions are required to meet the committed schedule. If, at the present rate of progress, your team will likely be late, work with the members to prepare and implement a recovery plan. As soon as you find that you need help, update the recovery plan and review it with management.

Since management will prefer that your team improve its task-hour performance over any other alternative, prepare a specific task-hour improvement plan and tracking schedule. If you find that you need help, report your problems to management as soon as you have an action plan prepared. Any delay will only make the problems harder to fix.

9

Maintaining Product Focus

As team leader, your top priority is building a quality product on time. Every-thing else is secondary. While you will face many pressures and distractions, your overriding objective is building this product. If you accomplish that and nothing else, you will be successful. However, if you don't accomplish that pri-mary goal, nothing else can make you and your team successful.

This chapter discusses the issues you will face in running a project. It covers the following topics.

- ☐ Defining success
- ☐ Setting and maintaining priorities
- ☐ Establishing short-term goals
- ☐ Overcoming obstacles
- ☐ Changing direction
- ☐ Involving the customer

9.1   Defining Success

In managing a project, consider what success would look like. In simplest terms, projects are successful if they deliver quality products on schedule and within planned costs. However, in different organizations, these three elements may have different priorities. Schedule is usually first, quality second, and cost third. In this case, if you do not deliver on schedule, the project will not be successful. Of course, if the product is on schedule but does not work, that too would be a failure. However, if the product worked but had some defects, the degree of success would be debatable. Many successful products have had defects and some have been highly defective. So quality judgments are often debatable. Everyone will agree that quality is important, but quality measures do not have the simplistic character of schedule measures. If the product is on schedule with some quality problems, it could be considered successful. However, if it had few if any quality problems but was significantly late, many development groups would consider it a failure. Schedule measures concern immediate gratification, but quality problems often persist. A product that was once considered successful could later turn into a failure if it was not a market success.

Finally comes cost. This again is a matter of judgment. If the product is on schedule with acceptable quality but is somewhat over the planned cost, it would probably be considered successful. This, however, depends on the business situation. For a fixed-price development contract, cost performance might be critical while for a cost-plus project or for a high-volume commercial product, development cost is not usually that important.

The strategy espoused in this book is to focus on quality as the best way to minimize schedule and cost. This strategy is based on the fact that, for software, higher quality products have shorter schedules and lower costs. However, many managers and most customers believe that improving quality necessarily extends the schedule and increases cost. If your managers or customers believe this, describe your quality improvement efforts as a way to shorten the schedule. Then explain how you plan to achieve that objective.

In managing your project, consider the business environment and the relative importance of cost, schedule, and quality to your management and customer. Then emphasize their priorities in explaining your strategy and plan.

9.2   Setting and Maintaining Priorities

Your job is to keep your team focused on its top priorities. While Frank had not run a project before, he did a creditable job of forming and launching the team. Shortly after the launch, however, one developer proposed that they use a seemingly attractive new design method. Since everyone on the team agreed, Frank went along. The team then dove into the challenge of learning this better design method. Before they knew it, they had spent two months studying this method but had produced little actual product design. Since none of the team members had used this design method before and only two of them had taken any design courses, the developers had spent most of the last two months understanding the new method and deciding how to use it.

At this point, Frank reviewed the project with his manager. When he explained why they were so far behind schedule, the manager blew up. He told Frank to focus on building the product, not on learning a new design method. Since none of the developers yet felt competent with the new design method, the team decided to defer their design education and to revert to their earlier well-known and familiar design techniques. While this problem was caught fairly early in the project, the team had lost two months and never did recover. Even though the developers ultimately delivered a quality product, it was late and the project was never considered successful.

What should Frank have done? New processes, methods, tools, and practices can often help teams meet their primary goal. On the other hand, learning a new and unfamiliar method takes time. Unless you have professional guidance, it is usually a mistake to try new and unfamiliar methods in the middle of a project. However, if you decide that the benefits are worth the risk, make an introduction plan that includes professional guidance and allows time to learn and to become proficient with the new methods.

Frank should have told his team that they had a project plan that they must follow. If someone suggested a better way to do the job, he would gladly consider it, but he should have refused to change the design approach until he saw evidence that the new method would help the team and not expose their schedule. He should also have insisted that the team make a plan for adopting this new approach, and then he should have reviewed that plan with his management before making the change.

Taking a blind leap into some promising but unknown new method without prior experience, professional guidance, an introduction plan, and management agreement is invariably a mistake. Your top priority is this job. Before agreeing to any change in direction, understand how it will impact the job. This applies to all changes, whether in design methods, new tools, requirements enhancements, or anything else that is not in your current approved plan.

9.3 Establishing Short-Term Goals

Schedules slip a day at a time (Brooks 1995). Few projects can detect a one-day schedule slip. To have any chance of meeting the project's schedule, you must meet all of its intermediate schedules. Because projects have many interrelated tasks, and because it is rarely clear how each of these tasks contributes to the overall project, developers rarely appreciate the importance of completing each day's scheduled tasks on that day. At least they won't understand it until the project is near completion.

Another leadership challenge is helping the team members set intermediate goals. While there is no general way to do this, one strategy is to break large projects into multiple releases and to establish planned dates for each release. Then hold periodic management review meetings on team performance against these goals. Before each review meeting, discuss intermediate goal status with the team and agree on recovery plans for any that are late. If the reviews are reasonably frequent and if the checkpoints are not too far apart, you can generally motivate the team to complete each intermediate goal before the next review.

People generally react to crises and little else. A slip of a few days on a one-year project will not generally cause much concern. However, a slip of a few days on a checkpoint that is due next week can be much more motivating. It will be even more motivating if there is a management review of the team's status next week, and if everyone who is late will have to produce and defend his or her recovery plan.

Even if there is no near-term build or release, you can create a sense of urgency. However, to be motivating, the urgent needs must be real, credible, and publicly committed. If, for example, your team establishes a date to release the initial design specification and you commit this date to management, you can track status against this commitment in each weekly team meeting. If you then schedule a management review, you can probably maintain the team's focus on this design specification commitment.

Suppose, however, that the design specification involved several months of work. What could you do? One approach would be to work with the team to establish checkpoints for each of the specification's chapters. Examples could be the first overall draft, the team inspection, and the final release. You could follow a similar strategy with almost any checkpoint.

While this strategy will expose you to missing an occasional checkpoint, weekly status tracking and periodic management reviews can help your team meet its intermediate dates. This will help you and the team maintain the urgency and motivation needed to complete the project on schedule.

9.4   Overcoming Obstacles

Development involves innovation. Our job is to do new things and to push new technological frontiers. While few projects are at the leading edge of technology, just about everything we do involves some unknowns and a few surprises. This means that we will often encounter obstacles and face new difficulties.

For example, the first version of any new product will likely have serious performance, memory, or usability problems. Security might be an issue or a planned COTS (commercial off-the-shelf) product might be too defective to use. While each new obstacle will be a surprise, the fact that you have problems should not be news. That is why you must base your plans on prior history and keep motivating the team to test every new technology or method as early in the project as possible.

When they hit new problems, developers can get discouraged. They may even want to throw in the towel and claim that the job cannot be done. Your role is to drive through every problem. Do not let the team give up. Insist that the members look for creative ways to overcome the problems. Keep the team thinking creatively and working hard. Most problems can be solved if you keep thinking about alternative approaches and don't give up. Many successful projects once teetered on the brink of failure but were brought off by a persistent and hard-driving team leader.

9.5 Changing Direction

While relentlessly driving for a goal is the mark of a seasoned leader, blind persistence can lead to disaster. Not all goals are achievable, regardless of how hard you push. In the hardware world, there are fundamental limits of nature. But with software, ultimate limits are not usually as clear or even definable. The limits of software-intensive systems concern resources, schedule, and product trade-offs. These are business issues and practicality judgments. What is the likelihood that your team can meet its performance or size specifications within acceptable business constraints?

There will be times when driving your team to meet an objective will be a waste of time and money. The challenge is to drive relentlessly toward a goal while simultaneously assessing the chances of success. It is helpful to get the advice of experienced professionals who have faced similar problems. Keep your management appraised of the problems and tell them what you are doing to overcome them. While it is hard to pursue two contradictory strategies at the same time, that is the mark of a leader: pushing relentlessly for success while preparing for the possibility of failure.

As your team strives to succeed, there may come a time when you must change course. The factors to consider are the costs of continuing with current efforts, the estimated time required, and the likelihood of success. Assemble that information and discuss the problem with your management. At some point, such decisions are no longer technical and should be made with the guidance of the managers who initiated the project.

9.6   Involving the Customer

The final and probably most important part of maintaining a consistent product focus concerns the customer. Know your customer and ensure that he or she is closely involved in the project. This is a great way to keep your team focused on the project's true needs. Every requirements statement is a snapshot of the customer's views. However, that snapshot will be different every time you review it with the customer. This is because the customer is learning along with you.

As we devise newer and better ways to help our customers, our products change the customer's environment and they change the problems the customers face. So, as we define new products and as our customers better understand these new products, the customer's view of the requirements will change. This is particularly important when we encounter some seemingly insurmountable design problem. These insurmountable problems can often be solved quite easily by reconsidering the requirements. Often, particularly when attacking a challenging project, your knowledge of the customer and your ability to involve that customer in critical decisions can spell the difference between success and failure.

9.7   Summary

This chapter discusses the team leader's principal job of developing a quality product on its committed schedule and for its planned costs. It explains why you must maintain a consistent focus on the project's objectives and not let other opportunities distract your team from its primary goals. There are several techniques for maintaining a team's energy and commitment even when the delivery date is far into the future. These include multiple release targets and frequent management reviews.

In the development business, we often push the limits of available technology. This can lead to surprises and even to seemingly insurmountable obstacles. Since developers can easily become discouraged, your job is to maintain the team's energy and to keep all of the members striving toward the principal objective. Occasionally, however, goals cannot be met, at least not for realistic costs. So, even while pushing to overcome all obstacles, simultaneously examine the costs and risks of failure and keep management informed.

Finally, and perhaps the most important, is knowing the customer and involving him or her in the major project decisions. This can help you overcome seemingly insurmountable obstacles and turn a likely project failure into a resounding success.

Reference

Brooks, Frederick P., Jr. *The Mythical Man-Month.* Reading, MA: Addison-Wesley. 1995.

10

Following the Process

In the TSP launch, your team defined the process it felt was best for this job and based its estimate and plan on that process. The team then committed a date to management. Assuming that the plan is reasonably accurate and that you and the team follow the process, you should be able to meet your commitments. However, if some or all of the team members do not follow this process, the plan will no longer represent what you are doing and there is no telling what will happen. If history is any guide, when teams do not follow their agreed processes and plans, they take far longer than planned and they deliver poor quality products.

This chapter describes why it is important for everyone to follow the process the team defined for the job. It also discusses some common issues you will likely face in motivating your team. The following topics are covered.

- ☐ Why it is important to follow the process
- ☐ The logic for the PSP
- ☐ The logic for the TSP
- ☐ Why it is hard to follow a process
- ☐ Starting to use the process
- ☐ Gathering and recording data
- ☐ Handling process problems

☐ Data-related problems

☐ Motivating teams to follow their defined process

☐ The benefits of following the process

10.1   Why It Is Important to Follow the Process

The accuracy with which a team follows its process is called its **process fidelity**. Process fidelity is important because the quality of a software system is determined by the quality of its worst parts, and the quality of these worst parts is determined by the processes used to develop them. Even if only one member uses undisciplined practices, that will impact the quality, cost, and schedule of the entire project.

The second reason process fidelity is important is that it is an essential part of improving team performance. The cost, schedule, and quality performance of software groups has historically been poor, and the challenges and complexity of our work have steadily increased. Almost without exception, senior managers are dissatisfied with the performance of their software groups and seek better performance. However, you can only improve the performance of a group by changing the behavior of its members. The only way to do this is to define the practices the group should follow and then guide, motivate, and coach the members to follow the practices they selected.

Unless organizations change the way their people work, organizational performance cannot consistently improve. Management has made a substantial investment, and they want your team to do a significantly better job than you have done before. However, to get these benefits, the team must follow the processes and practices it defined for the job.

10.2   The Logic for the PSP

The TSP is built on the foundation of the PSP, and all TSP team members must be trained in and use the PSP. The PSP is, therefore, a fundamental part of the TSP, and the PSP principles and logic apply equally well to the TSP. The five basic principles of the PSP are as follows (Humphrey 1995, pp. 14–15).

1. A defined and structured process can improve working efficiency.

2. Defined personal processes should conveniently fit the individual skills and preferences of each team member.

3. For professionals to be comfortable with a defined process, they should be involved in its definition.

4. As the professionals' skills and abilities evolve, their processes should also evolve.

5. Continuous process improvement is enhanced by rapid and explicit feedback.

The logic for the PSP process was derived from these principles. This logic is as follows (Humphrey 1995, 14).

□ Software professionals will better understand what they do if they define, measure, and track their work.

□ They will then have a defined process structure and measurable criteria for evaluating and learning from their own and others' experiences.

□ With this knowledge and experience, they can select those methods and practices that best suit their particular tasks and abilities.

□ By using a customized set of orderly, consistently practiced, and high-quality personal practices, they will be more effective members of their development teams and projects.

The principal reason that PSP training takes as long as it does is to provide developers the conviction that will motivate them to use the TSP process. Once they have followed many of these practices during PSP training, they will have data that show how these practices helped them. Your job is to convince them that those same benefits are important to the project and that each team member should continue to use these practices on the project. While the TSP launch will help to build this appreciation, it alone will not overcome the developers' natural resistance to following a challenging process.

10.3 The Logic for the TSP

The logic for the TSP builds upon the logic for the PSP. This logic is as follows.

□ Teams work best when the members cooperate with and support each other.

□ Team members can best cooperate and support each other when they all use an agreed-upon and well-defined process.

□ Teams will understand and consistently follow a process only when they have participated in defining that process.

□ Teams will produce quality products for predictable costs and schedules only if they are using a defined process that will consistently produce quality results.

☐ Teams will define such processes only if the members know how to do quality work.

☐ Teams will follow such processes only if they are motivated to do so by their peers, leaders, and managers.

The reason that software professionals must agree with and define their personal and team processes is that software is intellectual work and it involves extraordinary skill and ingenuity. To do creative intellectual work, people must be motivated and committed to their jobs, and they must not be constrained or annoyed by some process or method that they feel forced to use. If software people don't agree with a process, they will not use it and, in spite of your best efforts, there is a good chance that you will never know.

As team leader, one of your principal challenges is helping your team produce the kind of process you need to meet your objectives and then motivating the members to consistently and faithfully follow that process. Reluctant conformance will not produce the needed results. Your objective is quality work on schedule, and your team's process was designed to accomplish that. Whether your team members say they are following the process or not, if they don't really use the process the way it should be used, the project will likely be in trouble. You want real process fidelity, not grudging acceptance.

10.4   Why It Is Hard to Follow a Process

It is hard to follow a process for the same reason that it is hard to do any demanding task: few people are willing to devote the time and energy to master a truly complex and demanding process. This is why there are so few skilled surgeons and musicians and why professional athletes command such enormous salaries. The first and probably most important reason that people don't consistently follow their defined processes is because it isn't easy.

The second reason it is hard to follow a demanding process is that it isn't the team members' natural way to work. Until they have followed the TSP for several months, it will not feel natural—they must constantly remind themselves to record data and to review and assess the quality of their work.

A third reason that it is hard to follow a process like the TSP is that the hard work and extra effort come up front while most of the benefits don't show up until near the end of the project. This is why the PSP course uses many small programs to give the developer-students immediate feedback on their process-improvement results. With the TSP, the jobs are larger and the feedback loop is much longer. This is another reason to break large projects into multiple small builds and releases. Each build provides feedback on the benefits of following the process and helps to motivate the team to continue following it.

The fourth reason it is hard to follow a process is that, often, few other people are doing so. This is a function of team behavior and how widely TSP is used in the organization. Those who first use the TSP are breaking new ground and, if they are the only ones doing so, they will find it hard to be trailblazers.

The fifth and final reason that it is hard to follow the TSP process is that, as far as the team members can tell, management often doesn't seem to care if they do or not. Managers just seem to care about the schedule; process and product quality are not generally stated as important management concerns. This is where you can have a major impact. As leader of the team, your views and attitudes will be particularly important to the team.

10.5   Starting to Use the Process

Consistently following a process is a question of motivation, training, and support. This is true in sports, the performing arts, science, and medicine. It is also true in software engineering. The important issues to consider in following a defined process are the following.

☐ What kind of behavior do you seek?

☐ Who do you want to behave this way?

☐ What are the most effective ways to motivate this behavior?

The behavior required by the TSP is of three types: following the defined process; gathering and recording data; and using process data to track, manage, and improve the work. While you want all of the team members to follow all of these behaviors, the second category, gathering data, is the most difficult. The principal concerns of this chapter are following the defined process and gathering the required data. Then much of the rest of the book deals with how to use process data to assess and improve the team's processes and products. However, before you can use these data, you must first gather the data. That is why data gathering is so important.

Following the Defined Process

For the first behavior category, following the defined process, the key is your personal behavior. Consistently following a defined process is principally a question of habit, and this applies to you as well as to the other members of the team. In fact, if you don't make a practice of personally following the defined process and if you do not require that your team members also follow the process, they are unlikely to do so.

While you almost certainly will have followed a defined process when you conducted the TSP launch, the first time you must follow this process on your own will be in the team's weekly meeting. The detailed script and form for this meeting are shown in Tables 10.1 and 10.2. Since you will typically lead these weekly meetings, read over the WEEK script in Table 10.1 to familiarize yourself with its steps.

Since the WEEK script is simple and straightforward, most people can follow it with little difficulty. However, they often do not actually do so. Generally, the reason is that after following the script for one or two meetings, they know the process and feel they can follow it without guidance. Then they start to run the weekly meetings without consulting the script. While this may not be an immediate problem, it soon will be. Then, even experienced team leaders start to skip steps. Among the first steps they skip are the following.

☐ Forgetting to assign meeting roles

☐ Failing to prepare or review the agenda

☐ Not following the agenda during the meeting

☐ Not recording and reviewing the action items

☐ Not producing and distributing the meeting report

Table 10.1 TSP Weekly Team Meeting—Script WEEK

Purpose	• To plan and conduct the weekly team meetings. • These meetings are held to ensure that all team members understand current project status and know what to do next.

Entry Criteria	• All team members have provided the planning manager with
	  – updated task and schedule spreadsheets
	  – development, role, and risk status and plans
	• The planning manager has produced copies for the team of the team earned value spreadsheets with status and projections
	• Forms: MTG, WEEK
	• Specifications: NOTEBOOK, ROLE, STATUS

General	• The meetings are scheduled at a standard time every week. • All team members should regularly attend.

Step	Activities	Description
1	Meeting Roles	• The team leader typically leads the meeting (script MTG). • The timekeeper and recorder roles can be rotated among the team members or regularly handled by the same members.

Table 10.1 (continued)

Step	Activities	Description
2	Meeting Agenda	• Review the meeting purpose and agenda and select the roles. • Check for any changes in the purpose or agenda.
3	Manager's Report	The team leader opens the meeting with a brief summary of any new developments or issues.
4	Role Report	The team members review their assigned role responsibilities and the status against each (specification ROLE).
5	Goal Report	Each responsible engineer reports on status against team goals.
6	Risk Report	• The team members review status and changes in their assigned risks since the last report, and highlight any impending flag dates and required actions.
7	Project Status	• Each team member reviews his or her progress and status. – actual versus planned tasks completed in the prior week – actual versus planned earned value and hours spent • The planning manager summarizes the team progress and status. – actual versus planned team earned value and hours spent – current earned value projection to complete
8	Next Week Plans	• Each team member summarizes tasks planned for the next week and any special dependencies. • The team leader reviews expected issues or actions. • The team sets task, hour, and EV goals for the next week.
9	Meeting Wrap-up	The team leader checks that all needed items have been covered. • All engineers have reported their project status. • All risks and roles have been reported on. • Any newly identified risks have been evaluated and assigned. • Any other agenda topics are covered.
10	Meeting Conclusion	The team leader asks if there are any further comments. • confirms the meeting decisions and planned actions • agrees on topics for the management and customer meetings (specification STATUS) • asks for any suggested improvements in the meeting process
11	Meeting Report	The recorder and team leader produce the meeting report (form MTG). • planned versus actual hours and earned value • risks requiring management attention and why • any decisions, planned actions, or other key information
Exit Criteria		The completed WEEK and MTG forms are filed in the project notebook.

Table 10.2 TSP Meeting Report - Form MTG

Name		Date	
Chairperson		Location	
Meeting Date		Time From:	To:

Subject/Purpose

Attendees

Name	Role

Agenda

Times (min.)			Topics	Discussion Leader
Plan	Start	Stop		

Decisions, Actions, and Key Information

What	Who	When

If you don't consistently follow a meeting process, your weekly meetings will soon take longer and be less productive than they should be. While there are many more parts to following the process, your behavior in the weekly team meeting will set the standard for the team.

To help your team follow all of its processes, verify that the process manager has documented all of the required process scripts and that they are available to all of the team members. This includes the scripts for the overall development process and the inspection process. It also includes all of the more detailed requirements, design, implementation, and testing scripts. You can either use the standard TSP scripts or prepare your own, but they should all be available and everyone should use them.

Next, make a habit of meeting with each team member every few days to review what he or she is doing and to provide any needed help or guidance. By showing continuing interest in the work, you can help to sustain the team's morale and maintain its performance. During these private team member meetings, check that each one is following the defined process and recording all of the required data. If not, find out why. If the process is incomplete or inconvenient, get it fixed, but if the team member is just not bothering, urge him or her to try a bit harder. Keep doing this until the team members are consistently following the process.

10.6   Gathering and Recording Data

Gathering data is most difficult for new TSP team members. Except during their PSP course, developers have not gathered precise data on their work. Unfortunately, until they begin to use these data for planning, tracking, and managing their work, they will not appreciate their value. However, if you emphasize that the data are important and that you want everyone to gather their data, most of the team members will go along. Then, over time, data gathering will become routine. Ultimately, when the team members start to use the data, the data gathering problems will gradually decline. When the developers see how little time data gathering actually takes, and when they start to use these data to plan and manage their work, data gathering should not be a problem. However, without consistent management interest and attention, some of the team members will stop gathering data and you will again have a process fidelity problem.

While your early emphasis on data gathering is usually all that is required, some team members will be more difficult. In any large group, a few members will be adamantly opposed to doing anything new or different. This will be your first serious process problem, and the way you handle it will determine your team's effectiveness.

10.7   Handling Process Problems

There are four principles for handling process problems.

1. Timing

2. Listening

3. Being firm

4. Getting management support

The Importance of Timing

Process problems are like fires: once they start to spread, they are hard to contain. The longer you let such problems fester, the harder they will be to handle. With few exceptions, employees who refuse to do what their managers or team leaders ask are bluffing. They are testing to see what they can get away with. Their initial complaints are designed to test your nerve and conviction. If you are uncertain and tentative or act apologetic, their tentative initial complaints will get louder and more strident.

As soon as they sense weak leadership, these difficult members start to undermine the performance of the entire team. What is most interesting is that these complaints will generally have little or no substance. For example, when members complain that gathering data takes too long, ask them to describe how they are gathering the data and why it takes so long. You will find that they have never actually gathered much data. These complaints are generally not about any specific item; they are about you. These members don't want to change how they work.

If you let these problems fester, these difficult members will soon seek allies and try to convince other members that data gathering, planning, quality management, or just about anything you want them to do is a waste of time. They will complain that the planning, tracking, data gathering, standards, and/or controls are difficult, take a lot of time, and limit their creativity.

To put these issues into perspective, nobody said software work was easy. These are professionals, and their job is to do difficult work. If they are not up to it, perhaps they should look for a less challenging field. Regarding the time required, the team members are paid for their time. If management wants them to spend time gathering data, that is management's prerogative. Once management decides that they are willing to pay for that time, the members are obligated to do what they are paid to do. If they refuse, you have a personnel problem.

In any large group, there will always be members who object to whatever you want them to do, almost regardless of what that is. There will also be another small group that understands the value of the process and will follow it from the start. Most members of any group will fall somewhere in between. They will go along if you are firm, but they can easily be swayed by outspoken opposition, particularly if you do not take a firm position from the outset. Then, what was initially a few minor complaints will quickly become a serious problem. You must decide at the outset: are you going to lead this team or not?

Listen to and Understand All Complaints

In handling process problems, the key is to separate the substantive complaints from the smoke. When people have real problems, encourage them to speak up. Then you can resolve the problems. The most difficult people will have characteristics that separate them from everyone else: their problems will sound plausible but will have little substance. While you may have to probe a bit to learn the facts, deep down, these hardheads are complaining because they object to any kind of constraints, not because of any real problems.

On one team, Greg, one of the developers, complained that recording task time was inconvenient and took him so long that he could not get much work done. Tim, his team leader, asked him how long it took to record a task. Greg said he was wasting nearly half of his time recording time and tracking interruptions. So Tim asked Greg to show him how he was gathering time data and to review some of the data he had gathered.

It turned out that Greg had not used the time log and had no LOGT entries to show. In fact, he was not even sure how to use the time recording log. Tim showed him how to track time and told him to use the time log for a few days and then to come back with some data. The next day, Tim checked with Greg and found that he was still not using the time log properly. The problem now was that Greg's plan was incomplete and did not include the tasks he currently had to do. After Tim showed him how to fix his plan, Greg was able to record his time with little trouble.

When your people complain, first make sure you understand the complaint. If the problem has substance, get it fixed. However, if it is fluff, insist that team members do their work the way they are supposed to.

Being Firm

When someone is refusing to follow the processes or testing your leadership in some other way, they probably do not really understand what they are doing, but their actions will be clear if you know what to look for. The most obvious clue is that they will argue with almost anything new that they are told to do. Their attitude has little or nothing to do with the issues they raise. These people are usually addressing some personal need in the only way that they know. Your job is to set the behavior limits for your team and to be firm about them. If you wimp out, your team will sense it immediately. Then you will be the team leader in name only. The members will know that they can push you around, and some of them will regularly do so.

Get Management Support

As team leader, there are some issues you can handle by yourself and some where you must have management support. For any issue that could potentially become a personnel matter, you must have management support. Process problems are potentially personnel problems because, when a team member refuses to follow the team's defined process, that team member is refusing to do his or her job in the way that the team and management have agreed it should be done. It would be like a basketball player who insisted on running with the ball. If you let this behavior persist, it will destroy the team.

Obviously, your first objective is to get any difficult team members to follow the process. If you are firm and have your management's backing, you will usually be successful. However, a few people will be so adamant that you must remove them from the team. You may even have to remove them from the organization. For that, you must have management support. Usually, these difficult members have tested prior managers in just the same way and have pushed their behavior limits beyond what you and your team can tolerate. If this member refuses to cooperate, remove him or her from the team. Chapter 16 discusses how to do this.

To ensure that you have management support when you need it, review the required practices with your manager and explain why it is important that everyone use them. Do this even before you are aware of any process problems. If your manager fully supports your position, you can be firm with any difficult team member. When you discuss the need to follow the process in advance, you can usually get management support. However, if you wait until you have problems, the focus will be on the team member's complaints. Then you will find yourself defending the need to follow the process to a manager who doesn't understand the process or why it is important. To avoid this problem, get management support at the outset and make sure to keep that support. You can do this by periodically reviewing your process with your manager and showing data on its benefits.

10.8   Data-Related Problems

If, as is likely, the process problems concern the team member's unwillingness to gather data, it is important to distinguish between the need to gather the data and the actual values of the data. As far as you and your management are concerned, you want the members to accurately and completely gather the process data. If they do, you will not need to look at any individual data values. Your focus will be on composite team data and on examining product and component data to identify and address any likely quality problems. Although you will have to occasionally look at individual data to assure yourself that the members are properly gathering these data, that is your only concern. The members' particular data values are not an issue.

10.9   Motivating Teams to Follow Their Defined Processes

Motivating people to follow a process is no different than motivating any other kind of behavior. Maslow's five-level hierarchy of needs, in Chapter 4, provides a useful motivation framework (Maslow 1954).

1. Physical needs, like hunger and thirst

2. Safety and survival, like keeping a job

3. Membership, such as belonging to a team

4. Recognition, as for some outstanding achievement

5. Self-actualization, as for the personal satisfaction of doing a superior job

Levels 2 through 5 all represent potential ways to motivate team behavior. However, you should focus on levels 4 and 5. At level 5, the self-actualizing motivator is the satisfaction of doing a superior job. An example would be entering system test with a defect-free product or achieving a 100 percent process yield with some component. Self-actualizing behavior concerns being best, beating records, and achieving a desirable and laudable goal. Self-actualizing performance is the only way to consistently motivate superior work. The typical way to do this is for the team members to set challenging goals for themselves and for them to understand that the only way to achieve these goals is to follow the process.

At level 4, the motivation of recognition is always helpful, even for team members who are working at the self-actualizing level. Each lower Maslow level is a prerequisite for all of the higher levels. Therefore, recognition is important at both levels 4 and 5. You and your management should frequently recognize the team's achievements and compliment any team members who have done particularly impressive work. When prompt recognition is provided after every significant achievement, it can be a powerful motivator. For example, if the organization typically celebrates major milestones, this would be the time to recognize the team's performance and to point out any noteworthy team member achievements.

The third motivation level, membership, has two facets. On one side, by working cooperatively as part of a team and by supporting the team members, the group will develop a team spirit that is highly motivating. For example, when everyone on the team is following the process, new members will be motivated to follow these same practices. Conversely, if one or two members refuse to cooperate, it will ruin the team's spirit and dampen the members' enthusiasm.

The flip side of membership is the threat of expulsion. If a team member refuses to cooperate or feels that the team's practices are too onerous or difficult, suggest that he or she consider switching to another project. Sometimes such hints will motivate the difficult member to cooperate. When team members are truly difficult, however, it is often because they do not feel comfortable in the group. Then, membership is not a useful motivator.

If all of your efforts fail, there is always level 2, safety and survival. Here, if the member does not perform, you can threaten his or her job. Essentially, you can say, "Do this or you're fired." For this, you must have management support and you should first read Chapter 16.

10.10   The Benefits of Following the Process

While it is not easy to follow a process, doing so can substantially improve performance. For example, when teams use the TSP, they consistently do better work and they do it on shorter and more predictable schedules. An SEI study of 28 projects in 4 organizations found the results shown in Figures 10.1 through 10.5 (McAndrews 2000). In these figures, the shaded boxes show the performance of the middle 50 percent of the population, with the top and bottom population limits shown by the horizontal lines. The circles and asterisks represent "outlier points." As is clear from these figures, by following the TSP process, these teams substantially improved their performance. However, the best process in the world cannot help if your team does not consistently use it.

In a 2003 study of 20 TSP teams in 13 organizations, the results were similar (Davis 2003).

> These TSP teams delivered their products an average of 6% later than they had planned. The schedule error for these teams ranged from 20% earlier than planned to 27% later than planned. This compares favorably with industry data that show over half of all software projects were more than 100% late or were cancelled. These TSP teams also improved their productivity by an average of 78%.

> The teams met their schedules while producing products that had 10 to 100 times fewer defects than typical software products. They delivered software products with average quality levels of 5.2 sigma, or 60 defects per million parts (lines of code). In several instances, the products delivered were defect free.

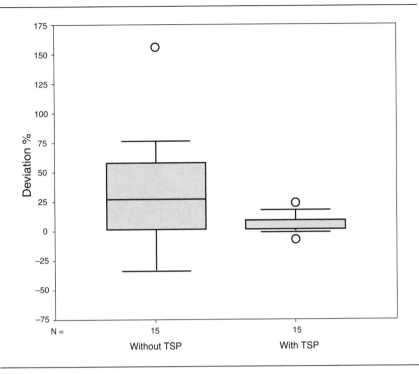

Figure 10.1 Schedule Error

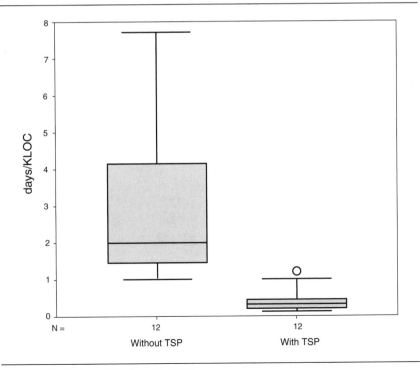

Figure 10.2 Reduced System Test Time

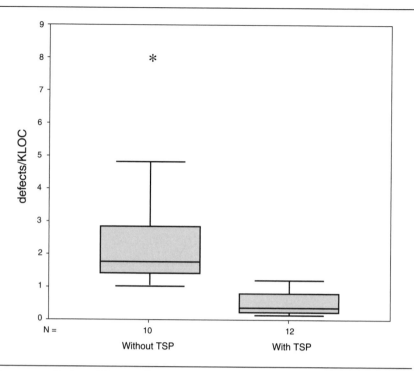

Figure 10.3 Reduced System Test Defects

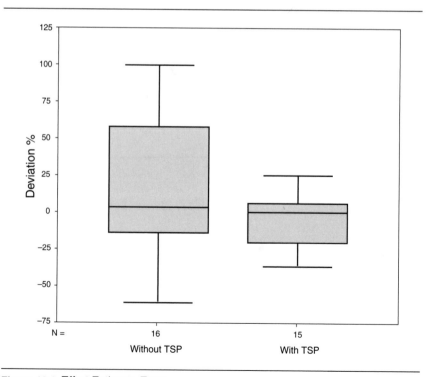

Figure 10.4 Effort Estimate Error

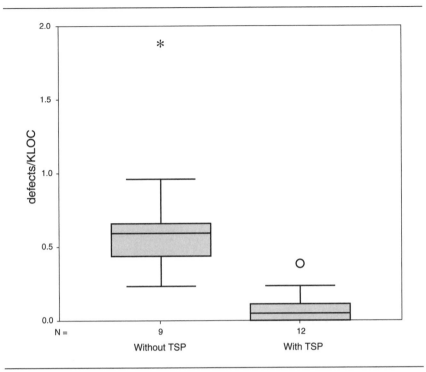

Figure 10.5 Improved Product Quality

10.11 Summary

The reason that teams should follow their processes is because that is the only way they can consistently and reliably improve their performance. Management has generally viewed the performance of software groups as unsatisfactory, and the only way to correct this situation is for teams to change their behavior. If properly used, the TSP process can help your team do this.

Since management wants its teams to do better work than before, you must somehow change your team's behavior. The principal behaviors required by the TSP are following the defined processes, gathering and recording process data, and using these data to manage the work.

Following the defined process is largely a question of your behavior. If you consistently follow the defined process and insist that the team members also do so, most team members will cooperate. However, many team members will initially view gathering and recording data as difficult. Most team members will gather the data if you urge them to but, in any large group, there will be some who object to gathering data or to following any other seemingly difficult practice.

The four principles for handling process problems are to act quickly but thoughtfully, to listen carefully to all complaints, to be firm about following the process, and to first get management support. Don't take any actions with a difficult team member without management support.

The Maslow five-level hierarchy is a useful framework for discussing motivation. At level 5, self-actualization, the motivation is the satisfaction of producing superior results. At level 4, the motivation is the recognition for doing a superior job. At level 3, the motivation is to be part of a cohesive team. Finally, at level 2, the team leader may actually have to threaten the difficult team member with dismissal. In all cases, however, it is important to either motivate the team members to follow the process or to remove them from the team.

Studies have shown that by following effective software methods, teams produce substantially better results. The results are typically better estimating accuracy, reduced development costs, shorter project schedules, and improved product quality. However, they will get these results only if they follow the process.

References

Davis, Noopur, and Julia Mullaney. Team Software Process (TSP) in Practice. *SEI Technical Report CMU/SEI-2003-TR-014*. September 2003.

Humphrey, Watts S. *A Discipline for Software Engineering*. Reading, MA: Addison-Wesley. 1995.

Maslow, Abraham. *Motivation and Personality*. New York: Harper & Row. 1954.

McAndrews. Donald R. The Team Software Process (TSP): An Overview and Preliminary Results of Using Disciplined Practices. *SEI Technical Report CMU/SEI 2000-TR-015*. November 2000.

11

Managing Quality

This chapter explains why and how to help your team do quality work. Quality management is important because poor-quality work is expensive, time consuming, and produces unsatisfactory products. Poor-quality products can damage your reputation, hurt your organization's business, and harm your customers. They could even kill people. The topics covered in this chapter are the following.

- ☐ What is quality?
- ☐ Why is quality important?
- ☐ Why manage quality?
- ☐ The principles of quality management.
- ☐ The quality journey.
- ☐ The TSP quality strategy.
- ☐ Gathering quality data.
- ☐ The developer's responsibility for quality.
- ☐ The team's responsibility for quality.
- ☐ Quality management methods.
- ☐ Quality reporting considerations.
- ☐ Quality reviews.

11.1   What Is Quality?

A quality product satisfies the customer. To satisfy customers, products must provide the functions and performance the users need, be delivered on time and for their expected costs, and must work reliably enough to do the customer's job.

Your organization will almost certainly focus on the first two of these criteria: that products have the required functions and performance and that these products be delivered on time and for their planned costs. These are the criteria that customers are initially most concerned about. However, if the product does not work reliably enough to do its intended job, the customer will be unhappy for as long as he or she tries to use it. Therefore, in the long run, the third criterion is most important to you. For a software product to work reliably and consistently, it must have very few defects. Regardless of anyone else's priorities, you must be concerned with defects. Here, a **defect** is a problem with any part of the product that, if not repaired, would cause improper design, implementation, test, use, maintenance, or enhancement of that product. While the other quality aspects are important and you must address them as a normal part of your job, in this book quality management means defect management.

11.2   Why Is Quality Important?

A few facts show why quality and quality management are important to you. First, with the current common "code it quickly and fix it later" programming ethic, testing takes as long as everything else a developer does. That is, testing takes about half of a typical project's development schedule. So, if you are like every other team leader I have known and are striving to meet an aggressive schedule, one of your top priorities must be reducing testing time.

Testing times are inherently unpredictable. Since there is no way to determine how many defects remain in a product, there is no way to know how much more testing is required. While there are various ways to use defect data to estimate test completion, none of them are very reliable. However, what is most important is that even the best tests find only a percentage of the defects in the product. Therefore, even after extensive testing, a test-based quality strategy produces defective products. While testing is essential and every system should be thoroughly tested, testing is an inefficient way to find and fix the volume of defects in most large software products.

Spacecraft Defects

To see why it is difficult to predict testing times, consider the data in Figure 11.1. This figure shows the cumulative defects found during system testing of the *Voyager* spacecraft (Nikora 1991). Since two of these spacecraft were sent on trouble-free missions to the outer solar system, it is likely that all or nearly all of their software defects were found and fixed during testing. However, it took 57 weeks, or well over a year, to remove most of the defects. Even then, one final defect was found in the 106th week of testing. All of this testing was required for a system of only 17,000 LOC. Since a small development team could develop such a system in about six months, the *Voyager* development schedule was dominated by testing time.

The *Voyager* system test data provide an example of why, even when testing is nearly completed, it is impossible to estimate the remaining testing time. Figure 11.2 shows the defects found per week. While one could say in retrospect that testing was completed at week 67, how about week 25? At week 25, no defects had been found for several weeks. However, if the developers had stopped testing at week 25, the product would have had 71 remaining defects and the mission would likely have failed.

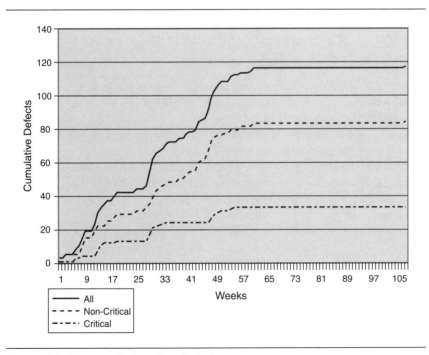

Figure 11.1 *Voyager* System Test Defects

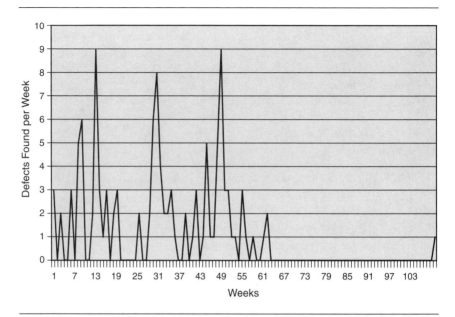

Figure 11.2 Weekly *Voyager* Test Defects

The *Magellan* Spacecraft

Consider the case of the *Magellan* spacecraft data shown in Figures 11.3 and 11.4. Here again, there were false completion indications at weeks 10, 46, and 102. Was testing over then? In fact, was testing over at week 125 when it was actually stopped? Since the *Magellan* mission had many software problems, even two and one-half years of testing was not enough. The *Magellan* system had only 22,000 LOC, and two and one-half years of testing did not find and fix all of the defects. There is no way to know from test data alone whether you have a quality product. That is why team members must gather quality data throughout the development process and why they must use these data to manage the quality of the products they produce. This is the only way to consistently produce quality products.

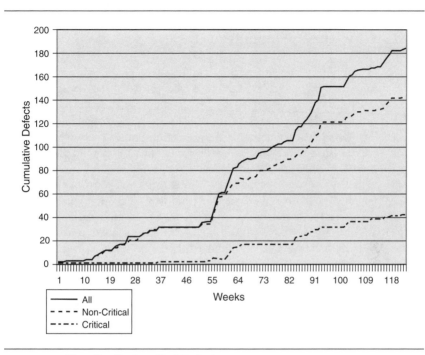

Figure 11.3 *Magellan* System Test Defects

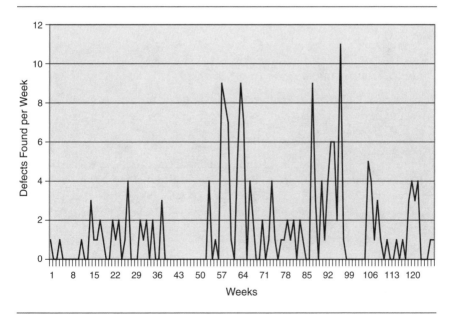

Figure 11.4 *Magellan* Weekly Test Defects

11.3   Why Manage Quality?

In this book, **quality management** refers to managing product defects. The reason to manage defects is not just to produce better products, but because defects are essentially random in nature and the costs of finding and fixing these defects increase exponentially the later in the development cycle you find and fix them. For development, defect management must be a top priority, because the defect content of the product will largely determine your ability to develop that product on a predicable schedule and for its planned costs.

Since most software developers inject substantial numbers of defects while writing programs, and since the later they find and fix these defects the more expensive it is to do so, poor quality management will result in excessive testing. Poor quality management also makes the work unpredictable. Since defect fix times are highly variable and the number of defects is generally poorly controlled, poor product quality will lead to wide variations in test time and an unpredictable product schedule.

Experience shows that software projects that do not manage defects have serious problems and that these problems are most severe in final testing. It is then so late that few groups will agree to do anything but test and fix. Also, as the *Voyager* and *Magellan* examples show, trying to fix defective products in test takes a very long time and is not usually successful. Thus, if you don't manage defects at the beginning of the project, those defects will manage *you* at the end of the project. In short, the reason to manage defects is to permit you to produce a quality product economically and predictably.

An Industrial Example

To appreciate the cost and schedule impact of defect management, consider two projects. One was an important new product being developed by a team of hardware and software developers. They were using the TSP process for the first time, and they did a competent job of following the process and managing defects. They delivered the 90,000 line-of-code product to engineering and field testing a few weeks ahead of schedule. After five weeks of testing, only two defects had been found and the customer accepted the product. Many hundreds of copies of this product have since been used by customers without any reported problems.

The other project was developed by a much smaller group of developers in the same company. They did not use the TSP or PSP and the only way they managed defects was with testing. Their 9,500 line-of-code product was delivered to field testing somewhat later than planned and, after 9 months of testing, over 50 defects had been found and fixed. The customer then reluctantly accepted the product. While the nine months of field and acceptance testing was done after the developers had completed their work, the unplanned time represented a major cost to both the customer and the company. The customer was unhappy with the product and he refused to pay for it until it had passed the acceptance tests.

The costs of poor quality may not be immediately apparent and the development team may never actually see all of these costs, but quality does pay. It generally pays even for the developers who do the work. This payoff is the satisfaction of producing a quality product, the rewards of doing a predictable job, and the recognition for doing professional work.

11.4 The Principles of Quality Management

The principles of software quality management are not new, and they come directly from general quality improvement principles. The basic principles of quality management have been used successfully in many other fields. These principles are as follows.

1. In any quality program, the principal objective is to satisfy the customer. First, for customers to consistently get quality products, they must recognize and demand quality. Second, even if the customer does not demand quality work, your obligation as a professional is to do quality work. Third, whenever possible, include the customer in your quality-improvement program.

2. Management must make quality *the* top priority, not *a* top priority. Unless quality is at the very top of management's priority list, you cannot maintain an effective quality program. Management must understand and support the principle that doing a quality job always pays, even if you cannot prove its value at the time.

3. The people doing the work must own the quality program. If the people who actually perform the work do not strive to build quality products, they almost certainly will not. To do quality work, all of the developers must feel that quality is important, and the entire team must participate in quality reviews. Since any defective part results in a defective system, every developer's work is important, and everyone must strive to produce defect-free products.

4. To improve quality, you must change the process. The quality of a product is determined by the quality of the process used to produce it. Just "trying harder" will not improve quality. If the process is wasteful or inefficient, product quality will ultimately suffer. It may not be obvious why, but improving a wasteful or inefficient process invariably results in faster, cheaper, and better products.

5. You must measure quality. Without measurements, quality is just talk. Since quality is a complex topic, no single measure will be adequate. You must use multiple quality measures and you must use them in scientifically sound ways.

6. Doing the job right always costs less in the long run. When quality improvement increases costs, that is a sure sign that you are doing something wrong. It costs less to do the job correctly than it does to fix the problems later, and it costs less to find and fix problems early than late. Since every defect represents an error, and errors are expensive to fix, no defect can be acceptable. Therefore, zero defects is the only rational and cost-effective quality goal.

As an example of principle 6, software managers often equate quality with testing. Then they argue that they can't afford to improve quality. These managers are failing to consider alternate and more effective ways to improve quality. While they can afford to improve quality, they can't afford to do more testing.

A great deal more could be said about each of these points, but most of the discussion would be to convince you that these principles are correct. There is, however, plenty of evidence to prove that they are correct (Davis 2003; McAndrews 2000). Since your team members will have already completed PSP training, they should agree with these points. However, most experienced developers have lived through at least one abortive quality-improvement program. Your challenge is to convince your team that *this time,* quality really is important. Once you do that, it should then be relatively easy to convince the members to follow these principles and to incorporate them into the project's development practices. If your management or any of the team members do not accept these principles, try to explain why they are correct. However, as the team leader, you must insist that all the members of your team follow these principles, whether or not they recognize their correctness.

11.5 The Quality Journey

People tend to think of quality as a final result or destination. It is not; it is a journey that never ends. As you measure and manage quality, you will learn more about it. Then each improvement step will provide the knowledge, experience, and data needed for the next step. Focus on continuous improvement and help your team to truly believe and follow the principles of quality management. Since each person's needs are different, you must recognize where each of your developers is on this journey and help every one to take the next step. The steps in the quality journey are as follows.

1. **Test and fix.** At first, the focus of almost all software groups is on getting products to work. The developers' objective is to get the product into test as quickly as possible, and then to test and fix (and test and fix and test and fix and...) until it works sufficiently well to ship to the users. At this stage, the only way that the members know to improve quality is to spend more time and money on testing. Your challenge is to move the team as quickly as possible to steps 2 through 8 of the quality journey.

2. **Inspect.** The next step is when the developers and managers start removing defects before test. This is usually done with various kinds of walkthroughs and inspections. The typical challenge in this step is to get the developers to do all of the required inspections and to do them properly.

3. **Partial measurement.** As inspection programs mature, some groups begin to measure and use inspection data both to improve the inspection process and to focus the inspections on the most defective product elements. The challenge is to get adequate data and to use these data to improve the products.

4. **Quality ownership.** As they participate in team inspections, developers may become more sensitive to the mistakes that they make and start reviewing their personal work in advance to eliminate as many of these problems as they can. Once developers reach this point, the quality of their products will quickly improve.

5. **Personal measurement.** To know how to improve the quality of their personal work, developers need objective data. The required data concern the defects they personally inject and remove, the sizes of their products, and the time they spend. The challenge is to get them to gather and use these data. As they examine the data on the defects that escaped to inspections, testing, and the final user, product quality will again increase sharply.

6. **Design.** Once developers have learned to manage their coding defects, they can focus on design defects. This requires precise and well-defined design practices and sound design verification methods. The challenge is to use sound design methods for all programs—large and small—and to use sound design verification methods in all design inspections and personal design reviews.

7. **Defect prevention.** While using sound design and measurement methods will reduce defect injection rates by about two times, effective defect-prevention programs follow a structured procedure to identify process problems and make the changes needed to eliminate even more defects. The challenge is to get the defect-prevention program initiated and then to sustain and broaden it to cover the full product life cycle.

8. **User-based measurement.** Ultimately, the quality program should be driven by user-based quality measures. The principal challenge here is to understand the quality characteristics that are most important to the users and to measure these characteristics in a way that is meaningful both to you and to the users.

An Alcoa executive once invited me to visit one of their plants that manufactured sheet aluminum. He said it produced the highest quality aluminum in the world. In talking to the engineers, I was surprised to find that their quality measurements weren't about making aluminum—they concerned making cans. For example, the thicker the aluminum, the more cans cost. However, the thinner the aluminum, the more likely it was that defects in the aluminum sheet would cause an expensive and time-consuming "punch-through" that would interrupt production. Alcoa was the market leader because their quality was so good, cans made with their aluminum were thinner.

The reason that the quality journey is never ending should be clear from this example. As long as technology advances and as long as it attracts newer and different kinds of users, we will face new quality needs. The principal message from this eightfold quality journey is that it must be traveled in steps. Until the developers have made reasonable progress with step 5, they will not have the data to support steps 6, 7, or 8. So, while you should take the long view, keep your team focused on the next step in this quality journey.

11.6 The TSP Quality Strategy

The TSP strategy for managing quality starts by training team members in the PSP. This training provides the skills and knowledge to progress through step 6 of the quality journey. Then the data and experience the developers gain in these first steps will prepare them for steps 7 and 8. However, even with PSP training, few software professionals can initially follow all of the rigorous practices required by steps 5, 6, and 7 of the quality journey. While fully following all of the PSP and TSP quality practices will be cost and schedule effective, it is counterproductive to push teams along the quality journey at too fast a rate. Ensure that the developers have mastered the skills for the current step and that they are ready and willing to move on to the next.

While rapid improvement is desirable, each step in the quality journey produces significant benefits. For example, in using team inspections at step 2, you will see immediate improvement in product quality, test time, and schedule predictability. As the team gets better at conducting inspections, these benefits will increase.

When teams do not use inspections, their shipped products typically have five or more defects per thousands of lines of code (KLOC). Just by starting to use design and code inspections, defect levels will improve by about two times. When teams gather inspection data and use these data at steps 3 and 4 of the quality journey, shipped defect levels will be cut to one per KLOC or less. This generally cuts test time in half and significantly reduces maintenance and customer support costs.

While many people might argue that one defect per KLOC is good enough, testing will still typically take about half of the development schedule and, for any widely used product, maintenance and support costs will exceed development costs. Further, even at only one defect per KLOC, large systems will have hundreds to thousands of shipped defects, each of which could cause customer problems and be expensive to fix.

By moving to steps 5 and 6 of the quality journey, test times will be reduced by another factor of five or more times and shipped defects will be further reduced by five to ten or more times. While the degree of improvement will depend on the discipline with which the team follows the TSP quality methods, there will be significant improvements with each step on this journey.

The essence of the TSP quality strategy is as follows.

1. Wherever you start on the quality journey, focus on doing the current step properly and on preparing for the next step.

2. Gather data on your work and assess the effort required and the benefits obtained from each step in the quality journey.

3. As long as the benefits are cost effective, continue with the quality journey.

4. If the next step does not appear to be cost or schedule effective, concentrate on improving performance at the current step and defer the next step until you are ready.

5. When developing or supporting systems that are either life or business critical, you may need to take quality steps that do not appear to have cost or schedule benefits.

As team leader, your strategy should be to celebrate each improvement step and to motivate your team to continue improving. To justify this effort, you will need quality data to demonstrate the benefits of the team's improvement efforts. You will also need these data to guide the next improvement steps.

11.7 Gathering Quality Data

Do not evaluate any developers based on the defect content of their programs. If you even imply that you blame a developer for the defects found in inspections or testing, you will destroy the team's commitment to quality. The developers know that everyone makes mistakes and that no one intentionally leaves defects in their programs. Therefore, if you judge any developer by his or her defects, you will no longer be able to trust any of the team's defect data. Defect data will have become threatening and no one will be willing to report any defect data on themselves or on any team member.

The data needed to guide your team on the quality journey are the time the members spend on various tasks, the sizes of the products they produce, and the defects they find. Assuming that the members have all been PSP trained, they will know how to gather these data. However, experience shows that developers will not consistently gather such data unless their team leader urges them to do so. Also, those who do gather these data will resent any team members who do not gather all the required data.

If the team members are not recording all of their process data, they are not being difficult or lazy. Gathering data takes effort, and developers would rather concentrate on development work. To them, coding and testing feels like progress while data gathering seems like a waste of time, particularly if no one uses the data they gather.

Encourage your team members to gather all of their time, size, and defect data but, for those who resist, be patient while continuing to press for improvement. If the team is not consistently gathering all of the required data, first concentrate on time data, size data, and inspection defect data. Then have the quality manager show you and the team how to use these data to improve the team inspections. Next, when inspections are reasonably effective, move to unit test defect data and again have the quality manager show you how to use these data to identify the modules to reinspect. Next, focus on the defects found in personal design and code reviews, and have the quality manager show the team how useful these data can be. Finally, focus on the defects found in compiling and on their potential uses. Until the team members see how to use their quality data to improve their personal work, some may object to gathering such data. If the quality manager is not sure how to use quality data in this way, get the team coach to help.

11.8   The Developer's Responsibility for Quality

A basic management principle is that people do what they are responsible for doing and not much else. For example, we know that when no one is responsible for doing a job, that job does not generally get done. Thus, to produce quality products, it is important to establish quality responsibility. Your team must understand that every member is responsible for the quality of the products he or she produces. It is not the responsibility of the testers or of quality assurance; it is theirs. If the developers do not strive to do quality work, they won't, and then someone will eventually have to fix their defective products. This fixing will cost time, delay the project, and cost more than it would have cost to do the job properly in the first place. You will also end up with a defective and heavily patched product.

The only way to economically and predictably produce quality products is for the developers to strive to produce such products. They must know what a quality product looks like, and they must know how to produce such products. Then they must do their work in just that way. When the developers take personal responsibility for quality, they will act and feel responsible for achieving the team's quality goals. Only then will you consistently produce truly high-quality products.

11.9 The Team's Responsibility for Quality

Hold the entire team responsible for the quality of the products provided to integration and system test. Although an individual developer will have produced any poor-quality program, the team inspected and approved that product, so it is up to the team to fix it. To meet this responsibility, a team must establish its own quality goals and make its own plans to meet these goals. It does this during the TSP launch. The team members should also agree on the quality methods to use to meet their goals. While the TSP suggests several such methods, teams should think creatively about their quality objectives and identify the methods they think will most likely meet their needs. Finally, teams must support their members as they follow the quality practices they have agreed to use.

These team responsibilities are much like those of winning teams in sports. In a hard-fought competition, all of the players must perform at their peak and several may even make spectacular plays. However, in the end it is the *team* that wins. Just as in sports, a software team is more than just the sum of its members. Each member must do superior work and each must also back up and support all of the other members. Team members are fallible human beings and they make mistakes, overlook defects, or have bad days. Here is where the team can be of most value. When one member makes a mistake or needs support, the others pitch in to ensure that the result is still a success. In sports these backup plays and grandstand catches can be spectacular; in software they are less visible but no less important.

There are many opportunities for software professionals to support each other. First, each team member has a role, and a big part of that role responsibility is watching all aspects of the work, anticipating problems, and seeing where some member needs help. Often, the developers may not even know that they have a problem. However, their teammates can tell and can step in to help.

An example of this support is team inspections. Here, several members review a developer's design or code. Their objective is to help that teammate produce a superior product. Similarly, the quality manager reviews each developer's data to identify troublesome modules. He or she can then work with that developer to determine how to address any quality problems.

Although you cannot measure individual developers on the defect content of their work, you can measure the team. The team must monitor the quality of everyone's work and not accept poor quality products into the system. If the team does not do this, hold the entire team responsible. The quality manager should make a quality judgment before any product is released, and if a product appeared defective, the quality manager should have alerted the team and gotten it fixed. Even though some developer produced the poor-quality product, the team let it into the system and it is the team's responsibility to get it fixed.

11.10   Quality Management Methods

Assuming that your team established challenging quality goals during the launch, its members must all use sound development methods to meet these goals. The principal quality management methods the TSP provides are the following.

☐ Plan reviews

☐ Design and coding standards

☐ Design and code reviews and inspections

☐ Defect reviews

☐ Quality analysis

The following sections discuss these methods.

Plan Reviews

To consistently produce quality products, developers must plan to do quality work. If they don't plan to follow a quality process, they probably won't. To help your team meet its quality goals, look at the developers' plans and discuss them with the quality manager. If any plans look questionable, talk to the developers to see how they produced their plans and to see if they are trying to do quality work. In this review, the topics to consider are the ratio of design to coding time, the ratio of design review to design time, and the ratio of code review to coding time. Also look at the planned inspection and review rates. If there are problems, ask the developers to adjust their plans. If you don't have time for all of these reviews, have the quality manager or the TSP coach do them and go over the results with you. You, the quality manager, or the coach must also monitor the developers' performance compared to their plans.

Design and Coding Standards

The limit on the quality of the programs the developers produce is determined by the quality of their design and implementation methods. To produce quality software, your team must know and consistently use sound methods. To improve your team's practices, have the design and implementation managers review the team's current design and implementation methods and propose a set of standards. Then have the team review these standards and agree with or modify them. If any team members are not reasonably fluent with the methods the team selects, arrange for any needed training and retain expert consulting assistance to help the team until everyone is consistently and properly using the selected design and implementation methods. Without proper training and support, developers often misuse new methods and thus generally take much longer to do their work than they should. Design work requires thinking, and until developers can think in the language of their design methods, they will not be fully productive and they will not consistently produce quality products.

Design and Code Reviews and Inspections

Good review methods are as important as sound design and implementation methods. People are fallible, and soundly performed design and code reviews can help them to find and fix most problems before the start of testing. Most PSP-trained developers review their designs just the way they review their code: by reading them with a checklist. However, it is almost impossible to find complex design problems just by reading a design. Most such problems can only be found by a careful design analysis. Developers will often argue that they could run a test much faster than performing a design analysis, but experience shows that it only takes an hour or two to completely analyze a complex design, while a single design defect can take several hours to several weeks to find and fix in final testing or during program use.

The quality, design, and implementation managers should discuss review and inspection methods with the team, and everyone should agree on the methods they will use. Urge the team to use proven methods, and then have the design, implementation, and quality managers check to see that the team members are actually using these methods in their work. Discuss any problems in the team meetings, and see what you can do to help the team use sound design-review and code-review methods. For a detailed discussion of design and code reviews, see Chapters 9 and 12 in *PSP: A Self-Improvement Process for Software Engineers* (Humphrey 2005).

Defect Reviews

Another useful quality management technique is to analyze test data. Here, the quality manager examines the team's data on the defects found in integration and system test and identifies those modules or components that are likely to have remaining defects. The logic for this analysis is that the number of defects found in a test provides a good indication of the number of defects likely to remain after that test. Thus, if a program module or component has many defects in integration or system test, it is likely to have many defects remaining after test.

Starting with unit testing, have the quality manager examine the quality data to identify any poor quality components. If the data for any component look particularly poor, have the team reinspect and fix that component. While this will take time, if there are many defects, it will take a great deal less time than finding and fixing those defects in integration or system testing. It will also produce a much higher quality product. The reinspections need not delay the project, since integration and system testing can continue while the components are reinspected. After reinspection, reintegrate the repaired components into the system and regression test them.

Quality Analysis

To maintain the team's focus on quality, have the quality manager, the TSP coach, and quality assurance work together to regularly analyze the team's quality data and review the findings in the team meetings. Have them work together to show the team's overall defect-removal profile and explain what the data mean. Then discuss the kinds of problems they see and their significance. Finally, discuss these problems with the team and agree on how to address them.

The coach or quality manager should also discuss the team's overall quality profile and PQI (the process quality index) and describe the kinds of problems it indicates (Humphrey 2005, 150). The TSP coach can help you and your team analyze and interpret these profiles. Be careful about showing the quality profiles for any individual developer's work. If the profile indicates poor quality work, this would be like presenting the responsible developer's personal data and could seem threatening. Ask the quality manager to discuss any troublesome profiles with the developers and agree on improvement actions. If the problems persist or the recovery actions are not adequate, make sure that these problems are brought to you for resolution.

11.11   Quality Reporting Considerations

Be careful how you handle quality data. If you press too hard to meet some quality goal, you will likely bias the defect data. Use data to motivate the developers to do better work, but not to embarrass or threaten them. Do not compare developers' data, and be sure to keep the quality discussions objective. Remember that everyone injects defects. Consistently emphasize process improvement, thorough data gathering, and careful reviews and inspections.

Some developers may object to recording some or all of their defect data. While gathering such data is not onerous or difficult, a few developers are likely to object to gathering these data until they see how useful they can be to them personally. While PSP training will have provided the basic skills and knowledge, it takes time and practice for developers to appreciate the value of defect data and for the data gathering process to become automatic.

If you maintain a consistent focus on process improvement and keep pressing the team members to gather and use their process data, their performance will gradually improve. In these periodic quality discussions, the team members should start to see this improvement. As you gather quality data, the TSP coach and you should be able to demonstrate the benefits of higher quality work and the need for the developers to gather and use quality data to do such work consistently.

11.12 Quality Reviews

One way to motivate your team members to follow sound quality practices is to hold periodic team quality reviews. The suggested quality review strategy has three parts. First, before the team starts each process phase, have the quality manager review the key quality goals for that phase. For the design phase, for example, the quality goals should include the ratio of design time to coding time, the consistent use of the team's design standards, and the use of effective review and design analysis practices. For the design-review and code-review phases, the goals should cover review rates, review times, and review yields. These same measures would also apply to the inspection phases. For the test phases, the quality review should cover desirable test practices, the importance of test defect data for assessing product quality, and the yield and efficiency of every previous phase.

Second, as the team starts each process phase, have the developers review and update their standards and checklists. Then have them use these standards and checklists in their work. Third, during testing, hold at least weekly reviews with the team to discuss every defect found in integration and system testing. Then determine what the team could do to prevent, find, and fix all similar defects before testing. If you hold these reviews regularly, product quality will steadily improve. Your team will also be more productive, reduce its test and development time sharply, and do more predictable work.

11.13 Summary

This chapter discusses quality management, how to improve product quality, and your role in motivating your team to do quality work. A quality product is one that satisfies the customer. To be fully satisfying, however, that product must have few if any defects. If it is not essentially defect free, the customers cannot consistently and reliably use its functions, regardless of the product's properties. While the functional and performance aspects of product quality are important, for the TSP, quality management means defect management.

Quality management is important to you because defect removal typically takes about half of the developers' time. By properly managing the quality of the work, TSP teams reduce the time they spend on defect removal by five to ten times. This improves the product schedule, cuts development costs, and produces better products.

There are six principles of quality management: focus on the customer, make quality the top priority, the developers own the quality program, quality improvement requires process improvement, quality management requires quality measurement, and it always costs less to do the job in the right way.

Quality management is an eight-step journey: test and fix, inspect, partial measurement, quality ownership, personal measurement, design, defect prevention, and user-based measurement. This journey never ends. Start by identifying where your team is on this journey and then motivate the members to take the next step. The TSP quality management strategy starts with PSP training and then follows this quality journey.

This chapter next discusses the developers' and team's responsibility for quality and briefly summarizes the TSP's principal quality management methods: plan reviews, design standards, design reviews and inspections, defect reviews, and quality analysis. In reviewing and reporting quality data, you must be careful not to embarrass or appear to threaten any team members. Finally, an effective way to motivate quality improvement is for you to have the quality manager, with help from the TSP coach and quality assurance, review the team's quality data in periodic team meetings. By showing the team members how to use their data to improve the quality of their work, these reviews will help your team to be more productive, to sharply reduce its test and development times, and to do more predictable work.

References

Davis, Noopur, and Julia Mullaney. Team Software Process (TSP) in Practice. *SEI Technical Report CMU/SEI-2003-TR-014.* September 2003.

Humphrey, Watts S. *PSP: A Self-Improvement Process for Software Engineers*, Boston: Addison-Wesley. 2005.

McAndrews, Donald R. The Team Software Process (TSP): An Overview and Preliminary Results of Using Disciplined Practices. *SEI Technical Report CMU/SEI-2000-TR-015, ESC-TR-2000-10.* November 2000.

Nikora, Allen P. Error Discovery Rate by Severity Category and Time to Repair Software Failures for Three JPL Flight Projects. Software Product Assurance Section, Jet Propulsion Laboratory, 4800 Oak Grove Drive, Pasadena, CA 91109-8099. November 5, 1991.

PART IV

Relating to Management

Sharif's team had finished development ahead of schedule, and the members had all done such a great job of managing quality that the testers had found no defects in system test. Instead of the planned six weeks of testing, they were done in a week and a half. In the final management review meeting, they saved the best for last. When Sharif finished describing their cost and schedule results, he proudly announced that the team had done such a superb job that the system had passed system testing with no defects being found.

The team expected some kind of enthusiastic reaction from management, but the general manager just sat there with a blank look on his face. He obviously had no idea how significant the team's accomplishment was. After a few moments, he said "Well, if that's the end of the story, I have to run to my next meeting. Thanks for the update, Sharif, and I'd like you to get started right away on that next project I told you about."

Talk about a letdown. All of the team's enthusiasm and excitement was gone in an instant. It was like puncturing a balloon. While it is said that good work is its own reward, winning teams need applause and cheers for a job well done. Maintaining your team's energy and enthusiasm is a key part of your job. You must ensure that your team's accomplishments are recognized and appreciated by senior management. In the traditional crisis-management environment, good work is invisible. Your job is to make your team's accomplishments visible and to ensure that they are recognized and applauded by senior management.

Part IV addresses the issues you will face in dealing with management. These include getting management support, reporting to management, handling management reviews, and protecting your team's resources. You must relate to your management in four ways: establishing a supportive relationship, providing information, working cooperatively, and providing the team with a sufficiently stable and protected environment so the members can do their work. These topics are covered in the three chapters of Part IV.

Chapter 12, Management Support, describes why management support is essential for building self-directed teams and some steps you can take to get that support.

Chapter 13, Reporting to Management, describes what management reviews and reports are, why they are needed, what to report, and how to conduct an effective project review. It also addresses the balance between being self-reliant and occasionally asking management for help.

Chapter 14, Protecting the Team, starts with a discussion of the manager's job, and then describes some of the most common management issues you will face and suggestions on how to handle them.

12

Management Support

To have a self-directed team, you must have management support. This chapter describes the kinds of support you need and some steps to take to get it. If you do not already have the support of your management, get it as soon as possible. The principal topics covered in this chapter are as follows.

- ☐ Management resistance
- ☐ Project control
- ☐ Inadequate resources
- ☐ PSP training
- ☐ Networking
- ☐ Defining team goals
- ☐ Team Planning

12.1 Management Resistance

The TSP will guide you and your team in building and working on a self-directed team. Since there is now plenty of evidence that these teams approximately double their productivity and produce much higher quality products, one might wonder how managers could object to using it (McAndrews 2000; Davis 2003). There are several reasons, most of which you can address if you have the facts and go about it in the right way. However, in some cases, the objecting managers may not explain why they do not support the TSP and some won't even tell you that they disagree. Typically, these managers will just delay doing anything. A more subtle delaying tactic is to keep asking you for more information.

When management really wants to do something, they can move quickly. When they take a long time to respond, it is hard to schedule meetings with them, or they keep asking for more information, the odds are that the manager either does not agree with what you want to do or is actively opposed.

If senior management disagrees with adopting the TSP, address that problem right away. Ways to do that are in another book: *Winning with Software* (Humphrey 2002). The material in this book assumes that you have senior management agreement but that you face resistance from one or more managers between you and senior management. You might wonder why, if senior management agrees, any intermediate manager would object. The reason is that TSP helps senior managers achieve their objectives and it helps you accomplish your objectives, but it can appear just to increase the workload for intermediate managers. The two most likely reasons for your manager's concerns are project control and inadequate resources.

12.2   Project Control

The most difficult form of management resistance concerns control. What makes this so difficult is that this type of resistance is almost always silent. Most managers have been promoted through the ranks and are now in positions of power. As working developers or team leaders, they had little control over resources, schedules, or priorities. Now they have the authority to make decisions and to give orders. They don't expect their people to argue or debate their directives, but to obediently try to do what they are told.

When organizations adopt the TSP, these managers must deal with self-directed teams. Now, instead of merely doing what they are told, self-directed teams make detailed plans and negotiate the schedules. Instead of meekly trying to do what they are told, they argue and debate. This is a shock for managers who like the feeling of being powerful and in control. Instead of having orders instantly obeyed, they must now negotiate. Just as parents often have trouble adjusting when their children become argumentative teenagers, some managers do not readily adjust to self-directed teams.

There is no simple way to detect this control problem. One common symptom is when a manager assigns added tasks but refuses to let you make a plan for the new work. While each such change might seem too minor to debate, after several of these changes, your team's plan will no longer represent what it is doing. Then, without a realistic plan, you and your team can no longer assess the impact of the changes or negotiate schedule and resource adjustments. That puts your manager back in control and destroys your self-directed team.

One effective response to this tactic is to quietly make plan adjustments for every change. Instead of holding a relaunch or making a major replanning effort, make small plan adjustments every week. This will keep your plan consistent with the work and it will allow you to negotiate every change. While your manager may not like this response, you are merely being responsive to the requested changes by planning how to implement them. You will also still have a self-directed team.

Assuming that senior management continues to support your using the TSP, this strategy is relatively safe. The only problem is when your manager gives you a large change that you cannot contain by adjusting your current plan. Now you must decide when to face the music. Since your team is committed to the original schedule but you have now been given a change that will cause you to miss the committed date, you have a problem no matter what you do. While it is always tempting to delay the day of reckoning, the problem will not get better. The typical result of waiting is that you end up telling management about the schedule problem when it is unavoidable. Then management will blame you for the problem and you will have failed as a team leader.

Since such management behavior seems highly illogical and since managers are generally smart people, you might wonder why they would behave this way. There are many possible reasons. The most common situation is when these managers are unwilling to argue with their own manager. For example, if a marketing VP or a powerful customer demands a change that involves more work, the intermediate manager might not be willing to argue the schedule and resource case in front of senior management. Your best strategy in this case would be to suggest that your team present the impact story to the executive. While you could also lose the argument with the executive, the odds are that you will not. This, of course, assumes that you can defend your plan. Such a strategy would resolve your commitment problem and maintain your self-directed team.

If your manager refuses to let you make your case to senior management, try to find out why. While there are lots of possible reasons, the three most likely are that, first, your manager does not believe you have a very good story and is trying to help you. Second, he or she could be in some kind of trouble and does not want to raise any contentious issues with senior management. Third, it could be that senior management is really impossible to deal with and that your boss is trying to protect you. While there are lots of possible reasons for these escalation issues, you should first take the time to understand why your manager is behaving this way. If he or she is really trying to help you, be careful to work with your manager and not at cross-purposes. If, however, you really conclude that your manager is being unreasonable, you only have three choices: you could go over your boss' head to senior management, you could do nothing and hope things will get better, or you could change jobs.

12.3   Inadequate Resources

If the problem does not involve management control, it probably concerns resources. While senior management may agree that the TSP benefits are attractive, they may not have given your manager the resources to introduce it. In effect, they have told your intermediate manager that, since the TSP will save time and money, he or she should contain the cost and schedule impact within the current plan. While some managers may have sufficient flexibility to do this, few can. Generally, the only way to handle this problem is to convince the middle managers either to request added resources from senior management or to defer some other commitments. While the TSP is an attractive investment, it does not pay off instantly. The investment must be made at the beginning of each project, but the cost and schedule benefits come at the end.

Tight resources can also show up as a training problem. Since most projects are on very tight schedules, managers are generally reluctant to stop development work for the two weeks of training needed for the TSP. While this schedule impact will be recovered in a few months, it will not be recovered instantly. Usually the best way to convince middle managers is to show them that by using the TSP, this project will save much more time than the training takes.

To make this case, explain that if your people are not properly trained, they cannot follow the TSP process and they cannot be a self-directed team. Without such training, the team members will not know how to plan and track their work, gather process and product data, or produce consistently high-quality products. The only proven way to teach these practices is to get the entire team PSP trained. The principal arguments you can use with your management concern test defects, estimating accuracy, and developer productivity.

12.4   PSP Training

The following sections provide some of the arguments and supporting data to use in explaining the importance and benefits of PSP training. Since many if not all of your team members will have been programming for several years, they will have personal practices that will not be easy to change, and as most software professionals object to being told how to do their work, they will not change their behavior unless they are convinced that the change will help them do their jobs. The PSP course is designed to do this. This training shows team members how and why to

☐ Define and use processes

☐ Gather time, size, and defect data

☐ Estimate, plan, and track their work

☐ Measure and manage the quality of their processes

☐ Measure and manage the quality of the products they produce

Several thousand software professionals have now been trained in the PSP and there is no question of its effectiveness (McAndrews 2000; Davis 2003; Humphrey 2005). The principal areas where PSP training changes a developer's performance are in product quality, estimating accuracy, and development productivity. To function as a self-directed team, developers must know how to gather and use data, how to define and follow a process, have experience estimating and planning their own work, and know how to measure and manage product quality.

Test Defects

During PSP training, developers start by using their traditional software practices to write one or two programs. Then, as they write more programs, they add measurement, planning, quality management, and design practices. By the end of the course, they are following all of the PSP practices and have the data on their own work to prove that their performance has improved. With few exceptions, these personal data convince them that the PSP practices actually help them.

Figure 12.1 shows data on 810 developers who completed full PSP training. The average defects found in unit testing declined by 3.6 times during the course. That is, for program 1, the developers found an average of 39.3 defects per 1,000 lines of code (KLOC), and by program 10 their test defects had declined to 10.8 defects per KLOC. The upper and lower lines on the figure show the upper and lower quartile ranges for these data. That is, at every point, 75 percent of the developers had test defect levels that fell between the upper and lower lines in the figure. The fact that these lines converge also indicates that the average quality of all the developers' work improved and that those with the worst quality on program 1 improved the most.

The PSP shows developers how to efficiently remove defects before compiling and testing. They will then find many fewer defects in integration and system testing and, as shown in Figure 12.2, system testing time will be reduced by five or more times. With such an improvement, a typical 10-month system testing cycle would normally be completed in under 2 months with the TSP. These test savings will more than make up for the 2 weeks of PSP training the team

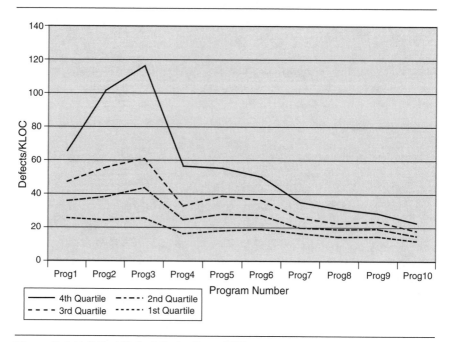

Figure 12.1 Unit Test Defect Reduction—PSP

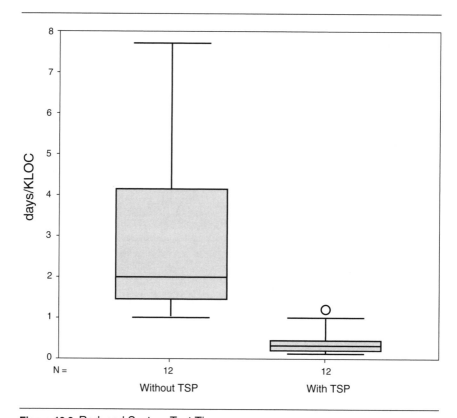

Figure 12.2 Reduced System Test Time

required. The data in Figure 12.2 are comparisons of TSP and non-TSP teams in four organizations. The data are for about a dozen teams that used the TSP and a similar number that did not (McAndrews 2000).

Estimating Accuracy

PSP training also shows developers how to use personal data to make statistically sound estimates of product size and development time. Improved team-member estimating accuracy enables teams to make accurate project estimates. This in turn helps you to better meet your commitments. Figures 12.3 and 12.4 show the improvements TSP teams typically experience. These results are from the same four organizations described earlier (McAndrews 2000).

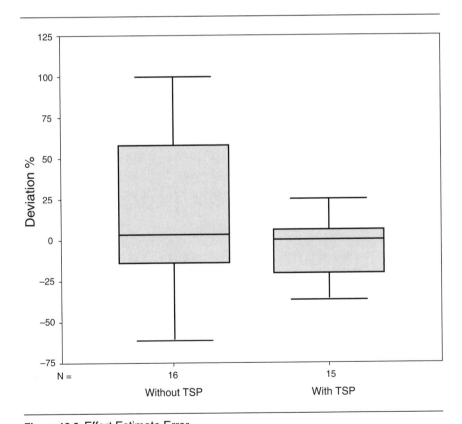

Figure 12.3 Effort Estimate Error

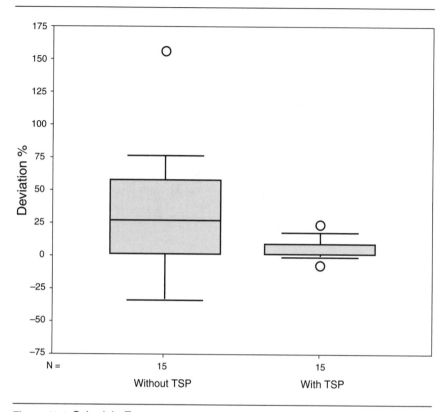

Figure 12.4 Schedule Error

Development Productivity

The story on development productivity is not as clear as it is for estimating accuracy and test defects. The reason is that the PSP requires developers to do things that they have not done before. Therefore, those developers who are highly adept with their current methods will probably not have significant productivity improvements and their productivity might even decline. The question for you and your managers to consider then is: are the planning, tracking, predictability, and quality management benefits sufficient to warrant the modest additional time required for your best developers to write code? Since coding is a relatively small part of most projects, and because team productivity typically improves by 50 percent to 100 percent with the TSP, the overall benefits should be clear.

To portray the impact of PSP training on developer productivity, data on the same 810 developers were divided into 4 groups according to the productivity with program 1. As you can see in Figure 12.5, the bottom quartile (4th) improved productivity by 73 percent, the middle two quartiles had modest productivity changes of plus and minus 12 percent, and for the top quartile (1st), productivity declined by 38 percent. The average productivity change for the group was –12.4 percent. This is why the most experienced and adept developers tend to take longer to be convinced of the PSP's benefits than those with less experience. In fact, just about everyone agrees after they have completed a TSP team project. By then the improvements are too obvious to debate.

Even though the fastest coders may take a bit more time to code and unit test their programs than they did before, team productivity will improve substantially. This improvement comes from the significant reduction in test time realized with the TSP. As shown in Figure 12.6, team productivity is significantly improved when testing times are reduced. For example, the bottom line shows that team productivity improves when test times are cut in half. Where the team typically had 50 percent of their development schedules in test, the productivity improvement was 50 percent. With the more typical four times reduction in test time (the middle line), the productivity improvement is 68 percent, which is the average for the TSP teams reported to date (Davis 2003).

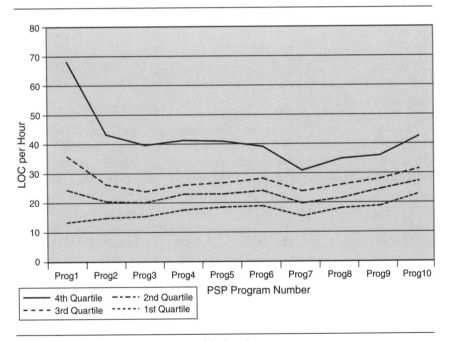

Figure 12.5 Productivity Results of PSP Training

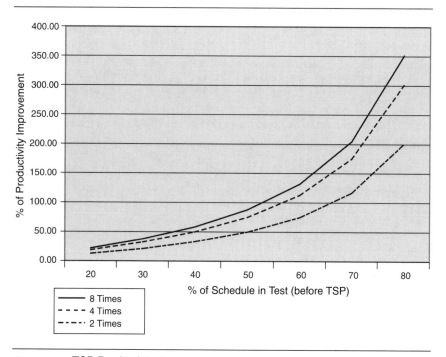

Figure 12.6 TSP Productivity Improvement

Training Time

In describing the impact of PSP training, explain to management that unless all team members are PSP trained, the TSP will not work. Brad's situation is a good example of what happens when team members are not properly trained. Brad's company had decided to start a trial TSP project. The effort started well with Brad and his people all being properly trained and coached. A few months after the initial project launch, Brad planned to add five additional team members.

Management had decided not to hire any new developers, so Brad arranged to borrow these new members from two other departments. However, since none of these developers had been PSP trained, Brad planned to delay the relaunch until they were. Brad's manager disagreed because he felt that the delay would jeopardize the project schedule. He told Brad to show the new members how to use the PSP but not take the time to get them trained.

During the TSP relaunch, the new members did not understand what was being done or why, so they did not participate. Without management support, Brad was unable to get these new members to follow the process so he let them use their traditional methods. Unfortunately, the result was that the team could not agree on a process or a plan. They even disagreed about how to manage quality. When the project finally reached the testing phase, many of the components had serious quality problems and testing took several months longer than planned. As a result, the project was late and was not a success.

Adequate training is essential for all team members. Any members who are not trained will not fully contribute to the project and will likely delay the schedule. They could even destroy the team as a cohesive unit. By saving two weeks of training time for one third of this team, Brad's manager cost the project several months of testing time. While it may be difficult to convince your manager to spend the time and money to fully train all of your people, it is critically important to do so. If you do not, you will waste the time and money you have already invested and you could even jeopardize your project.

12.5 Networking

Before you take any actions to circumvent your boss, make absolutely sure that you do not misunderstand the situation. With few exceptions, your managers will try to help you. Sometimes they will know things that you do not or they may see options and alternative courses of action that you have overlooked. Since a great many managers are poor communicators, it is easy to misunderstand them and to misinterpret their actions. However, if your boss really is being unreasonable, do something. But in taking action, keep your statements objective and focus on resolving project and not personal problems.

In small organizations, it is relatively easy to get to know everyone and to have friends in many parts of the organization. Here, when your manager is keeping you from talking to a more senior manager, it is usually easy to discuss the problem with some friends and have them pass the word up through their management that there is a problem in your department that senior management should know about. Any reasonably wide-awake manager, when hearing of such a situation, will ask some trusted aide to find out what is going on. This will usually resolve the problem without you having to confront your manager or making a career-risking move by going over his or her head.

In a large organization, particularly one that does not have established communication channels like open-door policies, it is often difficult to surface issues (Humphrey 1997). However, such organizations usually have various staff departments that assist management in identifying and resolving technical and business issues and keeping them informed about the organization's operations. These technical staffs can provide you the vehicle for indirectly communicating your issues to senior management. This suggests that you make it a practice to get to know members of these staffs so that you can call on them for help if you need to. Stick to the technical staffs, however, for any complaint to a personnel staff will be treated as a personnel and not a project issue. The key rule to remember is that in any disagreement with your boss, do not get personal or you will lose. Networking is discussed further in Appendix B.

12.6   Defining Team Goals

As discussed in Chapter 4, in addition to building a self-directed team, you must also motivate the team members to do the job your team has been assigned. The most important step in doing this is convincing the members that the job is important. While you might think you could just tell the team what management wants, that does not work. You must get management to personally explain to the team why they want this job done and why it is important. By having management explain their goals, they will reinforce the importance of the project and help you to motivate the team.

Furthermore, to do a superior job, the team members must understand precisely what management wants. While the managers will almost certainly know what they want your team to do, there is a good chance that they will not have made their desires completely clear. In TSP launch meeting 1, when management explains what they want and why, ask questions yourself and try to get your people to bring up their issues and questions. At the end of meeting 1, every team member should understand exactly how management's goals relate to what he or she is expected to do.

Barbara's team is one example of how management communication can motivate a team to do a job that did not originally seem very exciting. The VP personally attended the team launch and explained why the project was important. He explained that the initial project effort was to convert an old display system to a new technology. Since the new product's external functions would be identical to the existing product, the project had not seemed very exciting or creative to the developers. The VP explained, however, that the new technology was less expensive and would provide substantially higher performance than anything currently on the market. If Barbara's team produced a quality product, it would be the foundation for the company's future display product family. The VP summarized by saying that the team's objective was to furnish a solid foundation for the next 10 years of the company's business.

While the team had not initially been excited about the job, the VP's words made all the difference. Throughout the launch, the developers kept referring to the need to produce a high-quality foundation for the company's future product line.

12.7   Team Planning

Management must support the TSP strategy to have teams produce their own plans. If management does not agree to have them do this, the TSP will not work and you will not have a self-directed team. As discussed in Chapter 7, it is through the planning process that you build and motivate your project's self-directed team.

Managers often suspect that their development teams will not try to produce plans that would meet their desired schedules. Most projects start with a required completion date that is either set by customer contract or established by some business need. It would then be natural for management to worry that if the team made its own plan, the plan would have a later date than they wanted. Since TSP teams rarely produce plans that precisely meet what management requests, this is not an unreasonable concern. However, with few exceptions, when teams work to management's predefined dates, they rarely finish on time. Conversely, when self-directed teams work to their own plans, they generally meet the schedules they themselves established.

To put management's concerns into perspective, consider what management really wants. Management would like the product now. The only reason they pick a future date is that they know that product development takes time. However, since nobody knows how long the job will actually take, management pushes for the most aggressive date they think you could possibly meet. However, what they really need is a plan for the best possible date. Then, if the planned date is later than the desired date, they will have the facts needed to understand and address the scheduling problem. This is really a question of trust: can management trust this team to do its utmost to make a plan that meets their needs?

If management trusts the team to do its best, the odds are that they will agree to the team making its own plan. They intuitively know that the team that will do the work is the best one to make the plan for the job. They know this because the team is the only group that can make a plan that reflects what these team members can actually do. So, assuming that all of the members know how to make plans and that they all follow an orderly process to do so, you will have the best possible plan for the job. You should then be able to convince management that this plan is the most aggressive one they can reasonably expect.

Your job as team leader is to support your team during this planning process and to ensure that you and the team members do your utmost to meet management's needs. Then you must convince management that your plan is the best way to do this job. The TSP launch process will help you to do this.

12.8   Summary

This chapter describes the critical importance of management support in building and leading development teams. While senior management is often highly supportive, the intermediate managers are sometimes reluctant to adopt the TSP. This resistance is often because of a loss of project control or from inadequate resources.

The first place where team leaders are likely to face management resistance is in getting their people PSP trained. To overcome this resistance, show these managers the benefits of PSP training and explain how this training will actually save substantially more time and money than it costs.

The chapter also discusses the team's goals and the need for all team members to understand what management wants them to do and why. The best way to achieve this is to have the managers who decided to start this project explain to the team members what they want done and why.

This chapter also explains why management support is important for team planning. To obtain accurate and useful plans that will guide and motivate the team, the members must make their own plans. When properly coached and led, most PSP-trained teams can do this. However, management must be willing to let the team develop its own plan. If they are not willing to do this, the TSP will not be successful.

References

Davis, Noopur, and Julia Mullaney. Team Software Process (TSP) in Practice. *SEI Technical Report CMU/SEI-2003-TR-014*. September 2003.

Humphrey, Watts S. *Managing Technical People: Innovation, Teamwork, and the Software Process*. Reading, MA: Addison-Wesley. 1997.

———. *Winning with Software: An Executive Strategy*. Boston: Addison-Wesley. 2002.

———. *PSP: A Self-Improvement Process for Software Engineers*. Boston: Addison-Wesley. 2005.

McAndrews, Donald R. The Team Software Process (TSP): An Overview and Preliminary Results of Using Disciplined Practices. *SEI Technical Report CMU/SEI-2000-TR-015, ESC-TR-2000-105*. 2000.

13

Reporting to Management

As team leader, one of your most important duties is to regularly report to management. A management report really is a way of saying: "This job is under control and we don't need your help right now." Since this is the implicit message of every management review and report, you must make yourself completely clear whenever you do need help. From your perspective, management reviews and reports are important for three reasons.

1. You want to show management that you and your team are doing a good job and that you will deliver a quality product on schedule and at the planned cost.

2. To demonstrate that you are doing a superior job of leading this team and that all of the team members are following sound and disciplined practices.

3. Reviews can help to motivate the team and to keep the members working energetically and productively to meet the project's goals.

While your objectives and your management's objectives are somewhat different, they are not in conflict. That is, when the review is most successful from management's perspective, it will be most successful for you.

This chapter describes how to handle management reviews and reports and how they help you to do your job. It also discusses what to report and gives some reporting guidelines and an example. The chapter concludes with a discussion of self-reliance and the principles to consider when you and your team face serious problems. Here, your principal concern will be balancing your ability to solve your own problems with your obligations to protect management from unpleasant surprises. While you should certainly attempt to be self-reliant, management can be very helpful, so be sure to ask for help when you really need it.

13.1   The Logic for Reporting

While management could call for a review, you could initiate the review, or you could just write a report, there are several reasons that management reports are helpful. First, they will help you to see what you have accomplished. While this may not seem important right now, you will soon find it helpful. These reports provide a permanent record of what you have accomplished, and you will occasionally consult them to refresh your memory, to make future plans, or to answer questions about your work.

Second, it is helpful to periodically review your status and assess progress. It is easy to become enmeshed in daily details and lose sight of the big picture. While preparing a periodic report, you should assess project status and verify that you are still on the right track.

Third, while your managers are probably busy, they need to know your project's status. They must know what you have accomplished, how your actual performance compares with the plan, and what you will accomplish in the next period. They will also want to know about any problems that will affect them or the business. However, they don't have time to read lengthy documents or sit through extended presentations, so make your reports brief and factual.

Your management will almost certainly find your reports useful. When you make regular reports to your manager, he or she can answer questions from more senior management. If you are behind schedule, your manager will know why and can explain what you are doing to recover and when you expect to be back on schedule. However, your manager will not be able to say this unless you have briefly and factually explained the situation in a review or report.

Finally, periodic reports advertise your accomplishments. In most organizations, the management system is dominated by crises. Projects get into trouble, customers complain, and emergencies must be handled immediately. Crises are normal and almost everything managers do is driven by them. However, this means that the recognition and promotion systems are almost always geared to crisis management. The managers who rescue programs from the jaws of disaster are the heroes who get recognized and promoted.

While this behavior is natural, it has the unfortunate consequence of penalizing good performance. The teams and team leaders who quietly produce quality products on schedule can easily be overlooked and passed over for the plum jobs.

As you competently and effectively run your project, your successes can easily make you invisible. Periodic reviews and reports are an effective way to advertise your team's accomplishments.

13.2   What to Report

The key to making useful and effective management reports is to design them for the audience. Think about what is most important to your managers and then only provide that information, but do it clearly, completely, and concisely. While there will be many other items you would like to include, keep these "extraneous" items to an absolute minimum and keep them crisp, factual, and objective. If your team has accomplished something important, state the facts and even state what the accomplishment means for the project or the business. Be factual, but don't appear to brag.

Finally, in making reports, avoid describing problems without solutions or planned actions. Describe all of your serious problems, but also point out what you are doing about them. While it would be desirable to have an action plan for every issue, there will occasionally be problems that you don't know how to handle. The strategy in these cases is as follows.

1. Describe the action plan for addressing the problems.

2. If you do not have an action plan, describe what you are doing to develop one.

3. If you don't know how to prepare an action plan for this problem, describe what you are doing to find out. You might talk to experts or study previous projects to see what they did.

4. If you don't have the vaguest idea how to proceed, describe what you are doing to define the problem and its potential impact. Then say that when you have the full story, you will meet with management for guidance on how to proceed.

13.3   Report Contents

In making a report, start by addressing your management's principal concerns. Managers generally review projects for the following reasons.

□ They must know if you are on schedule or if there are problems that could jeopardize the job.

□ Management wants to know whether you are producing a quality product that will work properly and meet the customer's requirements.

□ Management needs to know how well you are running this project. They selected you to lead this project and they want to know whether you are doing a good job.

If you have made prior reports, first describe what you have accomplished since the last report. Keep this brief, but include the key items. This is where you can make some subtle comments about how well the team is performing and what this means to the business.

Second, summarize where your project stands against its commitments and plan. If you are on or ahead of schedule, be brief, but if you are not on schedule, expect to spend the entire meeting addressing such questions as

□ How late are you?

□ Why are you are late?

□ What actions are you taking to get back on schedule?

□ How do you plan to address the problems caused by the schedule delay?

If your project is behind schedule and you open the meeting with crisp and clear answers to these questions, there is a good chance the review can continue. If not, expect to have a difficult meeting.

Third, discuss your key problems and what you are doing about them. You must also provide management with timely and precise information about any impending disasters. Under no conditions should you allow your manager to be surprised by something that you knew about ahead of time.

In this report, briefly answer any questions but be prepared to provide as much detail as management would like. In describing the project's status, demonstrate comprehensive and precise knowledge about the work, where it stands, and when it will likely be completed. Your objective is to make management completely confident that you know what you are doing and that you have all of the issues under control.

In evaluating your performance, management will first ask about schedule status. Once they are satisfied about the schedule, they will consider how well you and the team are doing the job. If your managers have had extensive experience with TSP projects, they may use a checklist like that shown in Table 13.1. While the checklist is largely self-explanatory, if you have questions, ask any experienced TSP team member or coach. For a more complete description of this checklist and its contents, see my book *Winning with Software* (Humphrey 2002).

Table 13.1 The Quarterly Review Checklist

Purpose	• To guide executives and senior managers in conducting project reviews • To motivate the developers to do superior work
Entry Criteria	• All of the developers have been PSP-trained and the teams were launched under the guidance of a trained TSP coach. • The team has worked for at least a month since the TSP launch. • The executive or senior manager is familiar with the TSP process and has been given a copy of this checklist.
General	• The team leader leads the review, presents status, and answers questions. • If practical, invite the team members to attend the review. • Repeat the initial questions (1-8) until the results are satisfactory. • As soon as the developers are tracking time and earned value, move to questions 9–14. • Once some developers are tracking and using defect data, start asking about benchmarked improvement (question 15).

Step	Activities	Review Questions
1	Planning	• Do the developers have detailed plans, and are they following these plans? • Do these plans follow the defined team process? • Are the plans sufficiently detailed to guide the work?
2	Task Time	• Are the team's weekly task hours near or above the plan? • If not, are actions planned to improve the weekly task-hour rate?
3	Earned Value	• Is the team tracking earned value (EV)? • If EV is below the plan, has the team planned actions to recover?
4	Completion Projections	• Do the team's schedule projections indicate problems? • Has the team planned actions to address these problems?
5	Load Balancing	Is the team rebalancing its workload whenever necessary?
6	Time Recording	Are the developers using the time recording log to record their time?
7	Task Recording	Are the developers recording when they complete each project task?
8	Size Recording	Are the developers properly recording their size data?
9	Defect Recording	• Are the developers properly recording their defect data? • Are they using the defect recording log?
10	Reviews	• Is the team conducting all of the required reviews and inspections? • Are the developers using and updating their personal review checklists?
11	Review Rates	Is the team meeting its review rate plan?
12	Ratios	Is the team meeting its phase and defect ratio plans?
13	Yield	Is the team meeting its phase and process yield plan?
14	Defect Density	Is the team meeting its defect density plan?
15	Benchmarks	How does the team's performance compare with the benchmark teams?
16	Management Actions	At the conclusion of the review • Summarize the actions to be taken. • Verify that the team leader will write a brief review report. • If management actions are needed, check that responsibility is assigned. • Summarize the improvements you will look for in the next review. • Compliment the team and the team leader for the work they have done.

Exit Criteria	• The appropriate review stage topics have been covered. • Action items have been defined, reviewed, and assigned. • The meeting report responsibility has been assigned.

13.4   When to Report

Reporting frequency is a matter of management style. Some organizations have regular status review and reporting systems where immediate managers review project status weekly, intermediate managers hold monthly project reviews, and more senior managers hold quarterly reviews. In organizations with no regular reporting system, each manager and team leader must decide what to do. Typically, in these organizations, reporting is viewed as a major annoyance and few managers make reports. If you are in such an organization, consider instituting brief reports of your own. However, if your organization already has a reporting system, don't add a new one. Follow the established procedure, but take advantage of the TSP data to make your reports clear, succinct, and factual.

One TSP team worked for a management group that required weekly project status reports. This particular team had also been submitting its regular weekly status reports to the customer. The customer's manager found these reports so useful that he started asking a competitor for similar reports. Since the competitor was not following a detailed plan or process, he was unable to make satisfactory reports. The customer soon got so annoyed that he cancelled the competitor's contract and extended the first team's scope and funding to cover the work the competitor had been doing.

In organizations with no reporting systems, the managers typically only hear the bad news. They are then faced with a dilemma. On the one hand, they don't want to hear from their projects because they always get bad news. On the other hand, to do their jobs, they must understand where their projects stand.

This suggests the following approach. Start by producing periodic management reports, even every week if your manager would like. If you report monthly or less frequently and your manager occasionally asks questions about the project, treat this as a symptom that you are not reporting frequently enough.

13.5   A Report Example

In making a management report, start with a brief summary that describes the project, its principal commitments, and a brief overview of any major issues or problems. Put all the surprises in this first chart or report paragraph. Next, review schedule and quality status. The TSP provides the data you need to make brief reports that provide a great deal of information. A partial example of a team's standard TSP weekly report is shown in Figure 13.1. If this were your project, you should include the schedule points described in the following sections.

TSP Week Summary - Form WEEK					
Name				Date	
Team					
Status for Week	7			Cycle	
Week Date	1/7/05				Plan/
		Weekly Data	Plan	Actual	Actual
		Project hours for this week	170.0	162.0	1.05
		Project hours this cycle to date	972.0	886.0	1.10
		Earned value for this week	5.5	4.6	1.20
		Earned value this cycle to date	16.9	15.6	1.08
		To-date hours for tasks completed	814.0	729.2	1.12

Assembly	Phase	Tasks Completed	Plan Hours	Actual Hours	Earned Value
		MILESTONES			
Requirements	Req	Requirements inspection complete			
High-level design	HLD	HLD complete			
High-level design	HLDI	HLD inspections complete			
Detailed design	DLD	Detailed design complete			
Detailed design	DLDI	Detailed design inspections done			
Code	Code	Coding complete			
Code	UT	Unit testing complete			
		TASKS COMPLETED IN WEEK 7			
High-level design	HLD	Design standards reviewed	16.8	23.7	0.292
High-level design	HLD	Interface definitions specified	11.8	21.6	0.205

Figure 13.1 TSP Weekly Summary Report

Schedule Status

From Figure 13.1, you can calculate precisely where the project stands. The TSP uses a measure called **earned value** (EV) to determine project status (Humphrey 2005). (See the sidebar on page 177 for a brief summary of the EV measure.) Although not shown in the figure, this project was planned to take 5,750 task hours and 33 weeks. By using the EV measure, you can determine the percentage of the work done to date compared to the plan. As shown in the *Plan* column at 7 weeks, the team should have spent 972.0 hours and completed 16.9 percent of the job. According to the *Actual* column of the report, the team has taken 886.0 hours to complete 15.6 percent of the work compared to the planned 16.9 percent, so you are about 8 percent behind schedule.

EV Schedule Calculations

When using EV, there are several ways to estimate when you will finish the project. The simplest way is to assume that the team will complete EV in the future at the average rate of EV progress to date. Since the project has been running for 7 weeks and the team has completed 15.6 EV, that is 2.23 EV a week. With 84.4 EV to go (100.0 − 15.6), the team would take 37.8 weeks to finish.

Considering that you have completed 7 weeks, this would be a total of 44.8 weeks. That is 11.8 weeks later than the committed schedule of 33 weeks. Since you could expect management to be upset about such a big schedule slippage, it would be prudent to first show the project completion estimate calculated in the next three paragraphs.

Expected Completion Date

In estimating when the team will complete the project, note the bottom line under *Weekly Data* in the team's weekly report in Figure 13.1. This shows the to-date hours for the completed tasks. The team planned to spend 814 hours on the work done to date and it only spent 729.2 hours. Using this fact, you can show that the team is slightly ahead of schedule.

Using method 4 from the sidebar on the next page, the team has completed 15.6 EV in 779.2 hours, or 49.9 hours per EV point. At this rate, the total job will take 4,990 hours (49.9*100 EV). This leaves only 4,104 (4,990.0 − 886) hours to go. At the current rate of 162.5 weekly task hours, the remaining work would take 4,104/162.5 = 25.3 more weeks. Considering the 7 weeks spent to date, this would be 32.3 weeks or 0.7 weeks ahead of the original 33 week commitment.

Since there are several ways to estimate job completion and it is easy to make mistakes, it is always a good idea to make the estimates with each method. Then review the situation with your team and with the TSP coach to make sure everyone agrees and that you have not made any mistakes. This will also get them involved in preparing for the management review and in developing any needed recovery plans.

Quality Status

Until your managers have become familiar with the TSP quality measures, focus the quality review on comparisons of the team's performance to its quality plan. Some measures to discuss would be review rates and defect densities for the phases completed to date. Again, the team and your TSP coach can be helpful in preparing such reports and suggesting the actions needed to get back on plan.

Once your team is performing effectively against its plan, management may also want to see comparisons with other TSP teams. You can then show any available comparative data on productivity and quality performance as well as data on estimate accuracy and task hours achieved per developer week. Compare these data with other TSP teams in your organization or elsewhere as well as with other teams that are not using the TSP. Chapter 17 discusses benchmarking in more detail.

The Earned Value (EV) Measure

Purpose: The earned-value measure permits developers and their teams to measure project progress even when they complete tasks in a different order than planned.

Definitions:

- □ Planned value (PV) measures each project task's percentage of the overall project plan. Therefore, a planned 15-hour task in a 1,000-hour job would have a PV of 1.5.
- □ A project's earned value (EV) is the total of the PV of all the tasks that have been completed to date.

Ground rules:

- □ A task's PV is only earned when that task is completed. There is no partial credit.
- □ Regardless of the actual time the task took, the PV is used to calculate the EV. This is true even if the task took much longer than planned.

Project status:

- □ To determine project status, compare the total cumulative EV to date with the cumulative PV to date.
- □ If the total cumulative EV is less than the total cumulative PV to date, the project is behind schedule.
- □ If the total cumulative EV is greater than the total cumulative PV to date, the project is ahead of schedule.

Four methods to estimate project completion:

1. Assume that the project will continue to earn value at the same weekly rate that it has so far. Subtract the EV from 100 and divide by the average EV per week to get the weeks to go.
2. Assume that the project will continue to earn value at the rate it did in the most recent week. Subtract the EV from 100 and divide by the latest EV per week to get the weeks to go.
3. Using the actual hours for tasks completed to date, calculate the hours per EV. Next, estimate the total hours for the project (EV per hour times 100). Then subtract the actual project hours this cycle to date from the estimated total hours and divide by the team's average hours per week to determine the weeks to go.
4. Using the actual hours for tasks completed to date, calculate the hours per EV. Next, estimate the total hours for the project (EV per hour times 100). Then subtract the actual project hours this cycle to date from the estimated total hours and divide by the team's latest hours per week to determine the weeks to go.

Cautions:

- □ The EV method only works for projects with reasonably accurate plans.
- □ The EV method assumes that the rate of estimate error is reasonably consistent across the project.
- □ The EV method assumes that the project resources will remain constant.

13.6   Asking for Help

Fundamentally, the engineering management job is about identifying and solving problems. To do your job, you must identify the team's problems as early as you can and get them addressed in an orderly and effective way. Do not shy away from problems. They are your job, and if you had no problems, management would not know what you were doing. However, in reporting problems, make sure your management knows that you are addressing them.

One mistake new team leaders often make is to think that, as managers, they now need to know how to handle every problem. Since you will be exposed to many more problems than your team members, you will often know how to handle them. However, when you first lead a team, you will see many issues for the first time. Often, common sense and an understanding of human nature will be an adequate guide. However, sometimes, particularly for issues that involve difficult people, you can easily get into trouble. So, when you face a problem that is new to you and you have questions about how to proceed, ask for guidance.

In deciding whom to ask for guidance, consider who would likely be most helpful and whom you are most willing to talk with openly and frankly. Assuming that you are on good terms with your immediate manager, he or she will almost always be the first person you should talk to. However, be careful not to run to your manager any more often than you need to.

Finally, don't ask for advice if you don't intend to take it, particularly from your manager. There are few things more annoying than being asked for advice and then having it ignored.

13.7   Summary

This chapter is about management reporting. It describes management reviews and reports and explains how they can help you do your job. The chapter also explains why these reviews and reports are needed, what to report, what not to report, and when to report.

In any review of your project, management will probably ask first about the project's schedule status. If the team is behind schedule, start the review by explaining why the project is late, the actions you have planned to get on schedule, and your current estimate for when the project will be completed. If management is satisfied with your answers, you can probably spend the rest of the review on the topics you want to cover.

   This chapter also includes guidelines on the content of effective management reviews and reports and provides suggestions on how and when to ask for management's help.

References

Humphrey, Watts S. *Winning with Software: An Executive Strategy.* Boston: Addison-Wesley. 2002.

———. *PSP: A Self-Improvement Process for Software Engineers.* Boston: Addison-Wesley. 2005.

14

Protecting the Team

As team leader, you are part of the management team but you are also part of the development team. You are responsible to management for the team's performance and you are responsible to the development team for explaining what management does. This chapter discusses this dichotomy, some of the issues you will likely face, and suggestions on how to handle them. Every organization and every team is different, and you must consider these differences in deciding how to handle each situation. However, based on experience with many TSP teams, there are some issues that you will almost certainly face and that you should be prepared to handle. While there is no magic formula for handling any of these issues, this chapter describes some approaches that other team leaders have found helpful.

14.1 The Manager's Job

Before discussing the problems you will likely face, first consider the typical manager's job and the issues commonly faced. While first-level managers, like team leaders, usually have relatively clear responsibilities, as they move into more senior management positions, however, they generally have multiple roles that often conflict. For example, your immediate manager will likely be responsible

for several project teams as well as some other administrative and support functions. Examples of such functions might be

☐ Continuing support for older products

☐ Supporting business operations

☐ Technical assistance to other departments

☐ Managing a line of products

Your manager will also be responsible for appraisals, salaries, hiring, and
firing. Any time any of the people in one of his or her groups has a personnel
problem, the manager must be involved, and often full-time until that problem is
resolved. Finally, your manager almost certainly has scarce resources and a great
deal more work to do than the available staff can easily handle.

Remember that your manager, and every more senior manager, is under
enormous pressure and will not be sympathetic about your problems. Your problems are also minor compared to many of the problems your manager faces.
While these problems are important to you and to your team, your manager
undoubtedly has higher priority crises. Third, and most important, even though
your manager may not seem very sympathetic to your problems, he or she knows
that if these problems get out of hand, they will become crises that must be handled, and probably immediately. So your arguments to your manager should be
based on preventing your project from becoming a crisis that will demand his or
her immediate attention.

The following sections discuss each of the problems you will likely face and
some of the considerations to keep in mind as you address them. Some of the
most common of these problems are the following.

☐ Handling requests

☐ Frequent changes

☐ Staffing

☐ Training

☐ Workspace

☐ Data confidentiality

☐ Balancing priorities

14.2 Handling Requests

Managers quickly learn that when they have something important to do, their first
reaction should be to find somebody to do it for them. Successful managers know

that their job is to manage the work of others, not to do that work themselves. As a consequence, your manager will often have tasks that he or she would like you or your team to do. Many of these added tasks will relate directly to your project but many of them will not.

The suggested strategy for handling such requests is to assess every one and to determine its impact on your principal job. If handling a request would jeopardize your team's ability to do its job, tell your manager about that impact before you agree to do the requested work. This is particularly important when the requests are for very small items. You will find that the cumulative effect of these many small requests is a bigger problem than the occasional major assignment.

Generally, with a self-directed team, you can help your manager handle occasional requests without impacting your team's work. The tasks to worry about are the ones that take the team members away from their principal project tasks. If you and your team estimate the work required for every one of these added items, you will have the data to support you when you must either refuse a request or ask for more resources or a longer schedule to handle it.

Without such data, your manager will likely think you are being unreasonable. After all, how could a request for an hour or two of work possibly impact the project? With data, you can demonstrate the frequency of these requests and the disruptive impact they are having on the team. Since such requests will be a key reason that your team cannot meet its task-hour plan, you will need your manager's support to reduce the frequency and duration of these small interruptions.

Another important step would be management's agreement to funnel any requests for help through you, even if it is only for an hour or two of work. Your people are under the same pressures that you are, and they will get many requests that you normally never hear about. However, in protecting your team, do not cut off all contact with the rest of the organization. Your people will also occasionally need help and, if you antagonize these other groups, your team members will be less able to get help when they need it. By all means, be as responsive as you can, but limit the frequency and duration of these small interruptions.

14.3   Frequent Changes

The most common problem most team leaders face, particularly at the beginning of a project, is the constant stream of changes. Many of these changes will come from the team members themselves as they learn more about the job. Others will come from outside the team, and many will have strong management support. Since most of the changes will improve the function, performance, or usability of the product, you and your team will be highly motivated to agree to them. Also, since many of these requests will be minor and could reasonably be considered within the agreed scope of the job, you must be reasonable about handling them. However, since none of these requests will come with blanket permission to slip the schedule, remember that all added work delays the delivery date. The only question is how long that delay will be and when your management and customer should know about it.

While the rule for dealing with changes is precisely the same as for handling new commitments, there is one critical difference: these requests often come from the customer. Most such changes can be used as a basis for negotiating added funding or for changing the schedule. Do not, ever, under any circumstances, pass up an opportunity to reset your project commitments based on customer or marketing requests for changes. If the change is small, agree to add it to your existing list of outstanding changes and to consider it along with all of the other changes when you next update the plan. In the interim, keep a record, including who made the request, when it was made, and any justification provided. To be completely safe, document this change record and send copies to your manager, the program manager, and the customer. For all major changes, adjust the plan immediately. If you don't, you will be working without a plan and, just like driving without a map, you will soon be lost.

14.4   Staffing

Staffing problems are typically of two kinds:

- ☐ Part-time team members
- ☐ Delays in getting promised staff

Part-Time Team Members

A common problem for many teams is part-time members. Sometimes, these members will be part-time until their current project is done, but often they will be part-time for the duration of the job. Occasionally, these part-time arrangements are unavoidable, as for occasional expert assistance. Sometimes the team members will have special skills or knowledge that are needed to support other projects.

When organizations make a practice of simultaneously assigning team members to several projects, these developers will be much less efficient than the full-time members. It is never easy for developers to switch from one job context to another, particularly for creative work like software development. It takes time to refresh your memory about a complex design or the details of a functional change. Such job switches waste time and are highly error prone. Unless your people have scarce skills that the other projects require, get full-time people assigned to your project whenever you can.

Staffing Delays

Another common team problem is obtaining promised people on the dates when they are needed. It always takes longer than planned to get new people. When you make the team plan, emphasize that the basic plan is for the staff you currently have on board. Tell management that the date committed in your current plan is based on having the promised new people trained and at work by the promised date. If this staffing plan is not met, the project will be delayed. Until these people are on hand and trained, reemphasize this staffing issue in every management meeting and status report. As long as the needed staff are not yet available, make sure that management knows the impact of late staffing on the project's schedule.

14.5 Training

Sometimes your team members will not be fully productive. This problem has three typical causes: the people may not have the proper skills, they might lack required knowledge, or they could be unmotivated or unwilling to do a proper job. For this third case, consult Chapter 16. In the other cases, assess the problem and determine whether it can be addressed with training and support or of it cannot be remedied in time to help your project.

Training will solve many skill problems, but it is often a difficult issue for management: managers can readily see training costs, but the benefits are rarely as clear. PSP training, for example, takes about two weeks. However, with this training, the quality of a developer's work is substantially improved and testing time is sharply reduced. For any but the smallest products, testing time will be reduced by much more than the two weeks of PSP training. When team members are not properly trained, they take longer to do their jobs and they produce poorer quality products. Proper training in the project's tools and methods will also generally shorten the overall project schedule by more than enough time to compensate for the training time.

If additional training is required, determine what is needed and how to get it. Then estimate the likely costs and benefits. One way to do this is to estimate the impact of poorly trained people on testing time. Available PSP data can help you to make these calculations. Figure 14.1 shows the average defects per KLOC

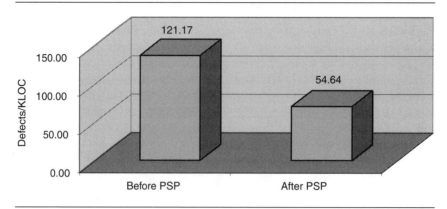

Figure 14.1 Average Defects Injected (827 Developers)

injected by 827 developers at the beginning of PSP training compared to the number injected when they finished. These same developers reduced their injected defects by over two times and, as shown in Figure 14.2, they cut unit test defects by nearly four times. This suggests that with PSP training your product will have one-fourth as many defects in system test as it would have if it were produced by untrained team members. Actual TSP data from several dozen teams show that the improvements in project performance are actually better than these PSP data would suggest (Davis 2003; McAndrews 2000).

Figure 14.3 shows that the average time for developers to produce quality products is only slightly longer than before PSP training. These same developers

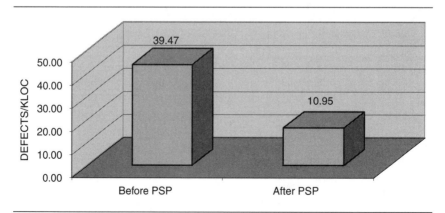

Figure 14.2 Average Unit Test Defects (827 Developers)

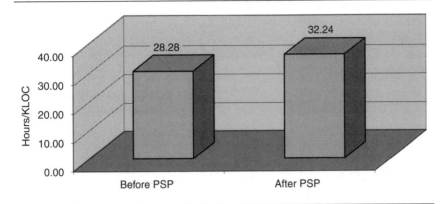

Figure 14.3 Average Development Time (827 Developers)

took 28 hours to produce 1,000 LOC before PSP training and 32 hours afterwards. This shows that the four times improvement in product quality does not significantly reduce the developers' productivity. TSP team data show that team productivity improvements average about 68 percent (Davis 2003). For example, by reducing testing times from 40 percent of the schedule to around 10 percent, using the TSP will increase team productivity by about 50 percent (Humphrey 2002, Appendix F).

With these data, you can explain to management that the project schedule is based on using PSP-trained team members. If you cannot train the team members, you must revise the schedule to include additional testing time. If you cannot train everyone, don't assign the untrained members any of the product's detailed design or implementation tasks. Use them on testing, test development, product documentation, or almost anything else. If you do have untrained people produce parts of the product, the added defects they inject will significantly increase testing time and delay the project. You will also get a poorer quality product.

14.6 Workspace

Space is tight in most organizations, and the practice of using cubicles or open workspaces is common. While there are many reasons for these arrangements, the fundamental driver is cost. Space is expensive, and the more people who can be packed into that space, the more money management can save. However, the quality of the physical facilities can substantially affect team-member performance, particularly for creative intellectual work like system development. Whenever possible, arrange for a reasonably quiet and stable working environment. To be most productive, the team's workspace should have the following characteristics.

- ☐ The space should be contiguous; that is, all of the team members should share a common workspace and be able to communicate frequently and easily.

- ☐ The team members should each have an available private workspace. When team members are producing complex designs, they need to think. This is difficult in shared cubicles or open spaces where they are frequently interrupted.

- ☐ The team should have a common area for meeting, either as an entire group or in smaller groups. This space is needed for weekly team meetings, team inspections, and design sessions.

While workspace problems are difficult to resolve, they are important and should not be ignored. Even when you cannot get an ideal arrangement, provide the members with private workspace when they need it. One approach is to have a dedicated quiet room. An alternative is to establish quiet times when phones would be forwarded or turned off and no meetings scheduled. For further discussion of the importance of team workspace, see Chapter 15.

If you cannot get agreement on the needed facilities, conduct experiments to see how various working arrangements affect the team's weekly task time. Even a brief test will likely show that you could significantly increase weekly task time at little expense. With such data, you will have a better chance of convincing management to improve the team's working environment.

14.7   Data Confidentiality

Team and team member data can be misused, particularly by managers who have not been TSP trained. In one case, Craig was PSP trained and assigned to a TSP team in another department. When Craig's manager saw that this TSP team was only averaging 14 task hours a week, he called Craig in for a review. He opened the meeting by saying, "I always knew you were not very productive and now I know why." While this manager was uninformed and unreasonable, the team leader should have talked to him in advance. Craig was very upset and threatened to quit. The team leader then had a difficult time convincing him to stay.

Don't ever provide data on any individual team member to anyone. If that team member is assigned to your team from another department and that person's manager asks for the data, explain why the data are private. Also advise your team members not to provide personal data to anyone other than the team members or the team coach. Freely discuss team data within the team and individual data with the individual and the team coach, but do not provide team data to anyone who does not understand it and know how to use it. Before you provide team data to anyone, make sure that this person has been TSP trained, understands what the data mean, and plans to use the data properly. If not, first take the time to explain the data and satisfy yourself that it will be properly used before providing it.

14.8 Balancing Priorities

Your principal job is running this project and using this team to do the work. However, once you have accepted this assignment, management's attitude will change. You now have a resource that they can use in an emergency. You will get many requests for help and, unless you speak up, your manager will assume that you are still able to meet the team's commitments.

Treat every management request in exactly the same way as a requirements change. If your actions imply that the request does not cost anything, you will get more requests. Assess the impact of every change and make that impact known before agreeing to do the work. As team leader, this is your job and your management expects you to do it. If you do not speak up, they will assume that their requests have no impact.

Since you are now on the management team, however, be cooperative and do your best to help whenever that will not jeopardize the project. But, regardless of how responsive you are, if you do not meet your project commitments, you will have failed.

14.9 Summary

This chapter describes your responsibility to protect the team from external pressures. It opens with a discussion of the management job and the pressures and crises managers must handle on a daily basis.

The typical problems team leaders face concern requests for help, additional project tasks, staffing problems, training, workspace, and data confidentiality. In handling these issues, remember that you are now a manager and must be cooperative and supportive while also assuring that your team can continue to do its assigned job and meet its business commitments.

References

Davis, Noopur, and Julia Mullaney. Team Software Process (TSP) in Practice. *SEI Technical Report CMU/SEI-2003-TR-014*. September 2003.

Humphrey, Watts S. *Winning with Software: An Executive Strategy.* Boston: Addison-Wesley. 2002.

McAndrews, Donald R. The Team Software Process (TSP): An Overview and Preliminary Results of Using Disciplined Practices. *SEI Technical Report CMU/SEI-2000-TR-015, ESC-TR-2000-105*. 2000.

PART V

Maintaining the Team

Peggy was an experienced program manager, but she was having problems with a project and was not sure how to handle some issues. This was a large multi-team TSP project with three subteams. Team A was in the application division in San Jose and team B was in the infrastructure division in San Diego. Team C, the requirements team, had members from both divisions. The leader for team C was in San Diego.

Since the members of team C had different backgrounds, locations, and management, Peggy had originally worried that they would have problems working together. However, that had not turned out to be the problem. The problem was that teams A and B were fighting with each other and were now seriously behind schedule.

Peggy discussed this problem with the leadership team. Bill, the leader of team B, suggested that they hold a team relaunch to see if that would help the teams refocus on the project goals and resolve some of the animosity that had developed. They decided to have all of the team members meet in San Diego for the relaunch.

They started the relaunch with an open management meeting at which Peggy and the leaders of teams A, B, and C described the situation and what they wanted the developers to accomplish during the relaunch. Meetings 2 (roles and goals) and 3 (development strategy) were handled as usual, but when they got to meeting 4 (overall plan), the A and B teams found that they could not make their overall plans. The problem was that the product had two principal parts—the

191

Analyzer and the Generator—and the work for these products was split between teams A and B.

The lead coach then suggested that they form an Analyzer planning team and a Generator planning team with the members taken from teams A and B. They did this and these teams completed launch meetings 4, 5, and 6 with no trouble. For meetings 7, 8, and 9, the coach then told the developers to resume working in their old teams A, B, and C. Both the Analyzer and Generator teams refused. They said that they had worked together so well in making the plan that they did not want to return to the old team A and team B structure. The project then continued after the relaunch with three teams: Team C, the Generator team, and the Analyzer team. Each team had members in both the San Jose and San Diego laboratories, and each team had a team leader in one location and an alternate team leader in the other location.

What is most interesting about this example is that the teams worked more effectively and the team members were happier and better able to settle their issues when they were distributed between the two locations than had been the case when the teams were each in one location. The lesson of this example is that a common goal and plan are more effective than a common location for building and maintaining team spirit and cooperation. Common goals and plans are so powerful that they can overcome the communication difficulties of distributed teams.

Part V concludes the book with four chapters on developing the team, handling difficult team members, benchmarking, and being a team leader.

Chapter 15 discusses how to help your team and all of its members do truly superior work, both as individuals and as a cohesive working unit. This chapter is about teams in general and the steps you can take to address the most common questions teams have about the TSP process and how best to use it.

Chapter 16 deals with the team members' needs, interests, and capabilities. Since a team's performance is determined by the skills and capabilities of its members, you must develop and improve the capabilities of your people. You may also have some team members who, for whatever reason, are unable to work cooperatively with you or with the other team members. To build and maintain a productive team, you must either change the behavior of these people or get them off the team. This chapter discuss this and related issues.

Chapter 17 is about improving team performance. After your team has learned to properly use the TSP and after it is working effectively as a unit, your next concern will be improving the team's performance. This chapter treats the team as an asset and your role in building and improving that asset's capability to do future work.

Chapter 18 closes the book with comments on the team leader's job and ways to make this job truly enjoyable. Being a team leader can be a great experience. Leading a team of motivated and skilled professionals while they build a complex and useful product is one of the most satisfying experiences of a developer's life. This chapter discusses some of the more personal aspects of the team leader's job and suggests ways to make it most rewarding for you and for all of your team members.

15

Developing the Team

Even after you and your team coach have prepared the team and formed it into a cohesive unit in the team launch, you have more work to do. You must still grow and develop your team. You would never expect a football or soccer team to play at its best the first time it went onto the field. Development teams must also build and hone their skills. Even when all of the members are highly skilled, they must learn to work together as a team. To work smoothly and efficiently, each member must view team success as more important than individual achievement. Because the team's performance will largely determine the success of the project, one of your top priority jobs as team leader is developing this team into a cohesive working group and motivating all of the members to do superior work.

While there is no magic formula for developing cohesive teams, this chapter provides some guidelines that will help. To develop a team, you must work at two levels: with the team as a unit and with each member as an individual. To develop the team, you must understand its problems and help the team address these problems. This chapter concerns working with and developing teams. The next chapter addresses the issues of the individual team members. The principal topics in this chapter are the following.

☐ Assessing the team
☐ Team membership

- ☐ Team goals
- ☐ Team ownership
- ☐ Team planning
- ☐ The team's commitment to quality

15.1   Assessing the Team

To determine whether a team has become a cohesive working unit, it is helpful to ask yourself some questions. The topics to consider are the five basic properties of self-directed teams (see Chapter 3).

1. Does the team have a common sense of membership?
2. Are all of the members committed to a common goal?
3. Does the team own its processes and plans?
4. Do all of the members have the skill to make a plan and the discipline to follow it?
5. Is the team dedicated to doing an excellent job?

If you can answer yes to all of these questions, the odds are that your team will develop into a cohesive and effective group. If the answer to any question is no, the information you gained in answering that question will point you to the causes of any teamworking problems.

15.2   Team Membership

On cohesive teams, every member feels like a member and is accepted as a member by all of the other members. While many things contribute to a feeling of membership, membership is determined by the attitudes and feelings of all of the members. The TSP launch starts the teambuilding process by providing the essential elements of team membership. It is now your job to continue this teambuilding process and to ensure that once the group has become a coherent team, the mutual feeling of membership is not lost. While the principal requirements for team membership are discussed in Chapter 3, the way to determine membership attitudes is to observe the team members' behavior. The topics to consider in doing this are team communication, team meetings, issue resolution, and the team's workspace.

Team Communication

Once a group has become a coherent team, its members will communicate in shorthand, they will share private jokes, and they will develop pet names for their most frequent issues and tasks. Close-knit teams develop a special language that helps them to communicate quickly and efficiently. This private jargon is often so specialized that outsiders will have no idea what the team members are saying. When team members communicate openly and completely, they develop an intimate understanding of what the other members think, believe, and feel. While there is no magic strategy for ensuring open and full team communication, one of the principal requirements is close and continuous interaction among the members.

Frequent Team Meetings

The weekly team meeting is an important part of maintaining team communication. While this meeting can take an hour or two a week, it is an essential part of maintaining a cohesive group. It is in the weekly meeting that the members get the feedback needed to understand their progress and to appreciate the significance of their personal contributions. Think of this feedback in sporting terms: knowing the score—precisely where the team stands—is essential to maintaining the team's energy and motivation.

An example of what can happen when a team does not hold weekly meetings is illustrated by a situation on a large development project. Shortly after the initial team launch, the team leader decided that the weekly meetings took too much time and did not add to what he already knew. He stopped these meetings and asked the lead developer to meet separately with each team member every week. The lead developer then reported back to the team leader on the members' status and any problems needing attention.

Sally was assigned to this project and had participated in the team launch. While the launch made her feel like a team member, she soon found that she no longer knew where the project stood. The team was supposed to be completing design and starting on implementation, but all Sally knew was what the lead developer told her in their weekly one-on-one meetings. Since the lead developer rarely had time to update her on project status, Sally soon lost all sense of team membership and was just doing what she was told to do. While Sally kept plugging away, she was essentially working alone and the work was neither exciting nor fun.

When development groups plod through projects, they don't have the energy or enthusiasm to produce creative or exciting results. Their task hours never get very high and the work takes much longer than it should. When properly run, team meetings need not take very long, but they provide a sense of membership and the feedback that teams need to stay involved and to maintain their feelings of excitement, commitment, and membership.

Openly Resolving Issues

Your behavior will have a major impact on the team's ability to become and stay a cohesive group. When some team member comes to you with an issue, how do you handle it? Do you ask if any other team members are involved and include these other members when you resolve the issue? You can discuss issues privately with anyone, but if you take a position or make a decision without involving all of those who are concerned, your team will quickly break into factions. Everyone will seek to settle their issues by meeting privately with you. This will destroy the team.

Make the team members work together to solve their problems and compliment them when they do so. Refuse to handle team issues by yourself, and give the team the time and opportunity to work out its own solutions. If they have trouble resolving an issue, meet with all of the involved members and guide them in defining the criteria for a successful outcome and a strategy for getting there. Then let them do the work of resolving their own issues. Finally, once they have resolved their issues, support their decisions. This will encourage the behavior you want and build the team's cohesion, morale, and sense of membership.

A Common Workspace

Even if you have been able to obtain the kind of workspace described in Chapter 14, organizations constantly rearrange their facilities, so you may have to fight to retain it. Workspace is important because when team members share a common working space, they are in frequent contact and can regularly interact with and support each other. A shared workspace allows them to meet often, to discuss ideas, and to review and comment on each other's work. With a common workspace, every team member can easily see what every other member is doing and can quickly recognize when someone needs help. A common trait of cohesive teams is that members chip in to help without even being asked.

A shared workspace is indispensable for self-directed teams. Once the members learn to communicate freely and to trust and rely on each other, it might seem feasible to physically disperse the team. However, this is risky. Teams are rarely static; new members come while old members leave. As the membership mix changes, the remote members will soon feel like outsiders and not be part of the close-knit central group. Wherever possible, keep the entire team together and maintain a common workspace where the members can meet informally in pairs, in small groups, or as an entire team. An exclusive private team workspace both sets the team apart from other groups and provides the close and intimate conditions required to sustain the team members' feelings of membership.

When the team must be distributed, pull the members together for common meetings and relaunches whenever possible. Also establish a virtual workspace where the team meets regularly for weekly meetings, reviews, and design or planning sessions. With the Internet, video conferences, and telephone conferences, it is now often possible to maintain at least a satisfactory virtual common team workspace.

15.3 Team Goals

As discussed in Chapter 3, the members of effective teams are all committed to a common set of goals. To maintain your team's motivation and energy, ensure that the members remain committed to their goals. While you and the team agreed on the goals during the project launch, these were project goals that stretched over several months or even years. To work energetically, however, the members need daily and weekly objectives. Part of your job is helping the team establish immediate and visible goals and ensuring that all of the members know these goals and understand where they stand against them.

To see whether the team has a goal-related problem, examine the way the team uses its goals. Do all the members know which team goals their current tasks satisfy? Do they know how their tasks contribute to those goals? Do they have a sense of urgency about completing these tasks on time? If not, you have a problem with the team's goals or with goal feedback.

Measurable Goals

For goals to motivate action, they must be quantified and the measures must be specific enough to tell the members where they stand against each goal. This feedback must be timely, and the more immediate the better. This requires that the team's goals be measured frequently and that the members regularly see the results of the measures.

One way to keep goal progress timely and visible is to post charts with team results and to update these charts every day. Discuss this issue with the team and try various approaches to see what measures the team finds most useful and motivating. Discuss these measures in the weekly meetings, set progress goals for each week, and review status against each goal.

15.4 Team Ownership

The transition from management-directed to team-directed work requires a fundamental change in attitude. Instead of being told what to do, TSP teams produce their own plans, allocate their own work, and monitor their own workload. As noted in the previous chapters, your team will have started building this ownership during the launch. This was when the team decided on its own strategy, defined its own processes, and produced its own plans. After the launch, the team members must continue to own their own processes and plans.

The first symptom of an ownership problem is complaints about the tools, the processes, or the plans that the team is using. One example is a team leader whose team had been using the TSP for several months. She complained that the weekly meeting script and form were a serious problem. It turned out that her team had found that the times given in the sample weekly meeting form did not work for her team. Such complaints indicate that the team, some team members, or the team leader do not understand how a self-directed team should work. You own your own process, and if some tool, form, or procedure doesn't fit your needs, you are responsible for fixing it.

No predefined schedule, process, plan, procedure, or form can possibly fit all the needs and preferences of any team. When teams have a feeling of ownership, they recognize this fact. Whenever they find that some process item is inconvenient or inappropriate, they fix it. They don't need permission from anybody, and they certainly don't complain about it. After all, they own the process; if it doesn't fit their needs, they change it. Team complaints are the first sign of an ownership problem. Software people are so used to being victims of poorly designed and inappropriate processes, plans, and tools that their first reaction to a problem is to feel helpless and complain. If your team members complain, challenge them to fix the problem. If they need help, provide it, but don't let their helplessness persist or you will not have a self-directed team.

15.5   Team Planning

An important part of developing the team is motivating the members to consistently maintain their plans after each team launch or relaunch. A **plan** is a snapshot of how your team thought the job should be done at one point in time. As discussed in Chapter 8, the members will learn more about the job as they do the work and their views of how to do that work will change. The longer they work without changing their plans, the more their views will change, and the less helpful their initial plan will become.

The plan provides the reference for everything TSP teams do. If the plan does not accurately represent the way the team members work, it will not guide their actions, the members will not be able to accurately record their time, and they cannot measure status or estimate job completion. If the members do not regularly update their plans to reflect their current work, they will no longer operate as a self-directed team.

To detect this plan-maintenance problem, check how the team members are recording their time. In their weekly summaries, do their completed tasks truly represent what they have been doing and do their plans accurately describe what they will do for the next few weeks? If not, help them update their plans so they represent their current views of the job. If the updates are modest, the members can each make their adjustments by themselves, but if the changes are more fundamental, hold a team replanning session or even conduct a complete team relaunch.

15.6 The Team Quality Commitment

The team's commitment to quality forms the basis for the team's development strategy. In software work, quality is fundamental. If just one team member is not producing quality work, the quality of the team's work will almost certainly suffer. Then testing will take longer than it should and the resulting product will be defective. The most critical ingredient for the team's quality performance is the quality commitment of every team member. Your quality strategy should be to motivate the team to manage the quality of each member's work.

When teams are fully dedicated to doing quality work, they consistently gather defect data and they analyze their performance to identify quality exposures. Initially, some team members will not spend enough time in reviews or inspections, or they may not record their compile defects. However, if you are convinced that quality is critical and that the number of compile defects is the earliest and most objective measure of the quality of the work, you should be able to convince the team. Keep stressing these points in team reviews and weekly meetings, and your people will gradually start to accept them. Then they will be more disciplined in their work.

Work with the team to convince them of the importance of quality and the necessity of following the process. It may take some time for the team to really believe the connection between the quality of their products and the discipline of their processes, but you can help them to make the connection. Start by reinforcing the importance of quality at every opportunity. If the entire team is unwilling to do disciplined work, that is a team problem, but if only one or two members are having quality problems, you must deal with them individually. Chapter 16 discusses how to do this.

15.7 Summary

This chapter describes how to sustain a TSP team as a self-directed unit. It reviews the five basic properties of self-directed teams and suggests ways for you to determine whether your team possesses these properties. If a property is missing, promptly take steps to correct the deficiency. The five questions to ask to determine if a team has these properties are the following.

1. Does the team have a common sense of membership?
2. Are all of the members committed to a common goal?
3. Does the team own its processes and plans?
4. Do all of the members have the skill to make a plan and the discipline to follow it?
5. Is the team dedicated to doing an excellent job?

You are responsible for the quality of the team's work. When team members work well together, support each other, and strive to meet their goals, team leadership is a pleasure. The members will be energized and enthusiastic, progress will be rapid, and the job will be fun. However, when the team members do not work well together, disagree about the team's goals, and are unable to work out their problems as a group, there are likely to be teamworking problems. You must then address these problems. This chapter provides guidance on how to identify teamworking problems and how to fix them. The next chapter discusses how to handle individual team member issues.

16

Developing Team Members

This chapter reviews the principal issues you will face when working with, guiding, and developing the members of your team. An effective way to maximize the performance of any team is to ensure that all of its members are assigned to tasks that suit their personal interests and capabilities. When negotiating these assignments with the team, however, recognize that most people are capable of doing far more challenging work than they are currently doing. A key part of your leadership responsibilities is keeping your people challenged with assignments that utilize their capabilities and hone their skills.

Teams are enormously varied and each can have a wide variety of capabilities, interests, and problems. This chapter discusses some of the issues that are common to many teams, and it provides general guidelines on how to address them. The topics covered in this chapter are as follows.

- □ Interests, competence, and motivation
- □ Challenging work
- □ Task and relationship maturity
- □ Measuring and evaluating people
- □ Handling difficult team members
- □ Handling poor performers

Leadership and coaching issues are covered in Chapter 18.

16.1   Interests, Competence, and Motivation

Interests, competence, and motivation are related, particularly for technical people.

> Motivated employees set their own goals and are their own toughest task-masters. At the highest level of motivation, people seek challenges and strive to overcome obstacles, not because they want any external reward or benefit, but because they find satisfaction in their own achievements. (Humphrey 1997, 64)

Technical people are motivated by new and exciting work. They like the challenge of creating advanced products and of seeing their complex creations actually work. While most developers soon realize that few jobs are interesting and challenging all of the time, they will lose interest in any repetitive or dull assignment if it continues for too long.

Interest and Competence

There is an interesting conflict between a developer's interests in some job and his or her competence to do that job. By repetitively doing a similar job, we build our skills and become progressively better able to do it. However, as a developer becomes more skilled at doing some type of work, that work becomes less and less challenging and therefore less interesting. However, the boredom of repetitively doing some practiced task is counterbalanced to some degree by the joy and satisfaction of doing a superb job.

Burnout

When the feeling of boredom with repeating similar work is not relieved, it can ultimately result in what is called **burnout**. Studies have shown that burnout is caused by an employee's feeling stuck in a repetitive and dead-end job (Brooks 1982). "It is not caused by age, overwork, or exhaustion but is more a defense against the loss of self-esteem caused by an apparent lack of personal worth" (Humphrey 1997).

Burnout is a problem for software developers, particularly when their organizations follow a traditional test-based quality strategy. The thrill of finding and fixing defects in a large and complex system can be rewarding for a time, but after repetitively doing it for months on end, it loses its charm. This is why the Bureau of Labor Statistics estimated that in the ten-year period from 1996 through 2005, over half a million professional software developers in the U.S. left the software field (Clark 2000). While most of them were too young to retire, they burned out and sought employment that provided a more comfortable home life and reasonably interesting work, even at a lower salary. This loss of professional capability is both a social and an economic tragedy.

16.2 Challenging Work

While there is no question that debugging a complex software system can be intellectually challenging, it often involves late nights and loss of home life. After a while, debugging becomes almost hypnotic as you are led hour after hour through a seemingly endless set of fixes. While many developers find that brief periods of debugging are relaxing and even enjoyable, there is a limit to how long anyone can keep it up without becoming jaded.

As team leader, your job is to keep the work interesting and challenging. While a certain amount of testing and debugging is inevitable, by properly using the PSP and TSP practices, your team can keep the test and debug time to 10 percent or less of the project schedule. Because the requirements, design, and implementation work tend to be much more intellectually stimulating, a sound and high-quality process can actually help you to minimize team turnover. Preliminary data show that the turnover of software professionals on TSP teams consistently approaches zero (Humphrey 2002, 97).

Professional Discipline

To properly use the PSP and TSP, and to consistently produce products that are of high quality at test entry, are major challenges. As noted in Chapter 10, process discipline is difficult, and it requires a level of team commitment and management support that is hard to sustain. However, since poor-quality work by any single team member can cause the team to waste months in testing and debugging the system, consistently professional performance is very important.

Fairness

There is another side to the quality issue. When everybody is producing defective code, the developers all feel equally responsible for the problems and are resigned to finding and fixing the defects. However, when most of the team is being very careful and only one or two of the members are doing defective work, the situation is quite different. Now they will know that their project is late and that they are working long hours because only a few people didn't follow the process.

They will resent the fact that a couple of teammates got away with sloppy work and they will feel that you were unfair by only insisting that some of them do a quality job.

Unfairness and unequal performance will destroy a team's spirit faster than anything else. However, the biggest problem with poor quality work is that its consequences do not show up until very late in a project. While everybody worked happily together for months, when you got into test, everything seemed to fall apart. By then it will be too late to fix the basic problem and you could easily have a dysfunctional and resentful team. This is when burnout will begin to be a problem and turnover will increase.

16.3   Task and Relationship Maturity

As team leader, you must evaluate your people. This isn't something that you can delegate to someone else. As a manager, evaluation and counseling are part of your obligations to your people. They know that you will evaluate them because they expect their performance to be recognized. They will also know because, when you do your job properly, you tell them how you will evaluate them and what you think of their performance. Evaluating people is not difficult, particularly when you know as much about their performance as you will with the TSP. But you must think carefully about how to use what you know, particularly the TSP measures.

Your principal objective in evaluating people is to help them improve. Since everyone is different, the most effective approach for one person could be totally wrong for another. The framework shown in Figure 16.1 can help you to select an evaluation and counseling strategy (Humphrey 1997, 71).

Task maturity deals with the developers' technical skills. Are they experienced, do they know how to perform their assignments, and do they have the ability to take on even more challenging work? Generally, relatively new and inexperienced team members will have low task maturity while the more experienced employees will have higher maturity. This can vary, of course, particularly when the job involves some new tool, language, or technology. When developers have low task maturity, it is usually relatively obvious where they need to improve. Your counseling and evaluation sessions can then be quite straightforward. Often, however, you will also need to build the developers' self-confidence and encourage them to take on more challenging assignments. This will accelerate their learning. This is a question of relationship maturity.

Relationship maturity concerns the developer's feelings and attitudes. Here, low maturity team members will generally be more concerned with how they are evaluated than with their job performance. Even very experienced people can have low relationship maturity and many very junior people can be quite

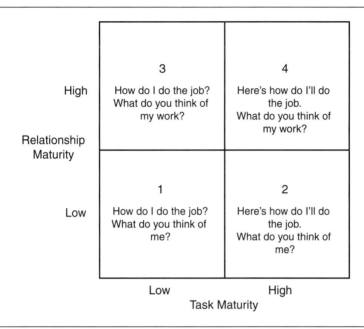

Figure 16.1 Task and Relationship Maturity

mature. While there are many possible situations, low relationship maturity can be caused by personality problems, job insecurity, or just plain confusion. If, for example, developers do not clearly understand what you expect of them, they are likely to worry. These worries can often be resolved very quickly, but only if you are aware of them and clarify the developers' job assignments. You must also honestly discuss their job performance with them.

The best approach in these cases is to be completely open with the developers and to tell them what you want them to do and how you intend to evaluate them. Frankly discuss their jobs and their performance. Explain what you are looking for, where you would like improvement, and why. The objective is to remove any confusion in the developers' minds about what they are expected to do. The team-member role assignments and detailed personal planning in the TSP launch process can help you to do this.

A Maturity Example

Ted was a new developer who had just been assigned to the team. He had been told to develop the system test plan, but he had no idea how to proceed. When he asked for guidance, Sally, the team leader, realized that Ted had both a task and a relationship maturity problem. He did not understand the system, the organization, or how to do the job he had been given. What is more, he did not have the self-confidence to start exploring this assignment on his own.

Rather than giving Ted detailed instructions on how to do his job, Sally challenged him to work it out for himself. She briefly described the organization and some of the people who might be able to help him. Then she told him to find out the rest for himself. Ted did a competent job, and he learned a great deal about the system testing process and the system his team was developing. He also learned a great deal about the organization, its various development and support groups, and the jobs of many of the key people. The most important thing that he gained was the self-confidence to solve such problems for himself.

16.4   Measuring and Evaluating People

The basic rule to remember is: don't use data—any data—to evaluate people. Don't even hint that the value of any measure will affect how you evaluate your peoples' performance. Even if you do not measure your people or use measures to evaluate them, if they suspect that you do, you will likely have problems.

Misuse of Data

As mentioned in Chapter 14, personal data are sensitive and, depending on how you use the data, you could get very different results from what you expect. The topic of people measurement and the problems of misusing data are described in a book by Robert Austin, entitled *Measuring and Managing Performance in Organizations* (Austin 1996). This is a wide-ranging subject and Austin's book is worth reading. I cover some of the highlights here.

The essential issue in misusing data concerns motivation. What makes developers want to do a good job? Are they motivated by the team's goals? Do they want to support their teammates? Are they just trying to get a raise or a promotion? While just about everybody would like a raise, that is not usually their principal concern. When, as is often the case, your people are driven by project goals or team spirit, you will have nothing to worry about. Measurement will not be a problem as long as the measurements do not relate to their personal performance. However, if the developers work hard principally because they want you to recommend them for a raise or a promotion, you will likely have problems.

While salary increases and bonuses are supposed to encourage good work, the real issue is not how you evaluate people, but how they *think* you evaluate them. If they think your evaluation will be based on some numerical measures, and that you have specific targets for these measures, they will do their utmost to meet those targets, almost regardless of how their actions impact any other objective. On the other hand, if the developers believe that your evaluation will be based on how they perform as team members or on the degree to which they contribute to the project's success, they will not be too concerned about the value of some numerical measure.

Measurement Limitations

No simple measures can possibly capture all aspects of what you want your people to do. If they feel that your evaluation will be influenced in any way by the numerical value of some measure, they will maximize that measure, and the unmeasured aspects of their work will be largely ignored. If the work is simple, and if all you care about is widgets per hour, then by all means measure your people on widgets per hour. But if you care about the quality of those widgets, or whether the widget feature mix meets the market need, or any other unmeasured characteristic, then watch out. Unless that characteristic is measured and included in the evaluation in exactly the way you want, you will not get the results you desire.

A marvelous example of the measurement problem is the Trans-Siberian Railway that was built in Russia many years ago. After the communist takeover, railroad operating personnel were measured on the number of tank cars crossing the continent. When the communist bosses discovered that many trains had empty cars, they changed the measure to require that the cars be loaded. Then, workers filled the railroad cars with anything available, including water. Of course, this was not helpful in the winter when the cars froze, and it did not address the pressing need to ship fuel and food, but water was easier to ship and it didn't spoil or cost money.

Even very simple jobs cannot be measured with enough precision and in enough detail to completely define the performance you want. This is why, when I was at IBM, the company's plan for sales commissions was described in a large volume with many dozens of pages. Because of the need to consider cancellations, product mix, new account growth, support levels, and a host of other issues, a seemingly simple sales commission plan became extremely complicated. All this plan did was describe how sales performance was measured and how salespeople were paid based on these performance measures. The plan was so complex and so much money was involved that some salespeople even hired lawyers to help them negotiate particularly large commissions.

Being a Coach

While all teams need coaching support, there are also times when it would be helpful for you to act like a coach. For example, your people will have an unconscious concern that, in spite of everything you say, you will still consider their data in evaluating them, particularly if the values are poor. Therefore, when some developer has a poor result, act more like a coach than a manager (see Chapter 18). Urge the developer to learn from what happened and then to forget it. The proper attitude is to strive to do better the next time. Point out that every job is different, and that development performance varies enormously from one job to the next. Not only are there variations in the work, but performance varies from day to day and even from hour to hour. The objective is to learn from what we do and to try not to repeat the same mistakes.

The principal challenge of the software process is to use our teams' creative talents to do superior work. The Team Software Process is designed to help teams of fallible people produce flawless products. Expect to get an occasional poor performance, but when you get it, remember that the developer is probably more upset than you are. Act like an understanding and supportive coach, and concentrate on helping that developer do better the next time.

16.5   Handling Difficult Team Members

Some people are easy to manage and some are difficult. One of the most challenging things managers have to do is to handle difficult people. Here, a difficult person is someone who requires special attention. He or she may ignore the guidance you give, argue with the team's proposed strategy, have a unique way to do things, or just be hard to communicate with. Since these can also be the characteristics of very intelligent and creative people, you must be careful how you deal with these "difficult people."

Difficult people will be your greatest challenge. The reason is that these are generally very bright people and many of them will know precisely how to get under your skin. In fact, that is precisely what some of them will try to do. Your job, however, is to get the best possible work from *all* of your people. You may have an occasional developer who is incapable of doing any of the jobs you need done and that topic is covered in the next section of this chapter. This section illustrates the two basic ways to handle difficult, but potentially productive, people.

Jake Refused to Use the Process

Jake had a great deal of development experience and had already written many successful programs, so he did not feel he needed to use the PSP and TSP. The team leader asked him to make a plan that used the organization's process. Jake did what he was told but then he did not even try to follow that plan. He spent very little time in design and did superficial design and code reviews. He refused to have the team inspect any of his programs, and he started integration and system test more or less on schedule. However, testing found more defects in his programs than in the rest of the team's components combined. Testing took much longer than planned, and after the system was shipped to the customer, several defects were reported in Jake's components.

When the team leader reviewed these results with him, Jake argued that he had developed the largest and most difficult parts of the system and that the other developers were just lucky not to have defects. When the team leader reviewed Jake's performance with the laboratory director, however, the director's first reaction was to fire Jake. Jake had cost the company several months of testing time, produced poor-quality products, and delayed product delivery. The laboratory director did not want Jake to work on any other projects.

The team leader argued that they should not fire Jake for two reasons. First, firing Jake would frighten the other developers. Even though she had not used Jake's personal data to evaluate him, the team would suspect that she had. They would then be nervous about accurately reporting their own data in the future. Second, Jake was a competent developer and she needed him. They had a large backlog of maintenance work and she would like to have Jake fix customer-reported defects. The director agreed, but only on the condition that Jake not work on any new development unless he understood that management was serious about quality and agreed to follow the company process.

When the team leader explained the situation to Jake, he was not happy. He liked development work and viewed himself as a superb designer. However, he took the maintenance assignment and worked at it for nearly a year. Finally, he went to the team leader and told her he would follow the organization's process if he could get back into development. She gave Jake a place on the next project and he did a superb job. He delivered his part of the product ahead of schedule and it had no customer-reported defects.

The moral of Jake's story is that even very capable people can have hang-ups and be hard to work with. In fact, some of the very best people are also the most difficult. They may disagree with the process, be convinced that they know more about the job than you do, or refuse to do something just because you told them to do it. While the team leader could have easily fired Jake and told the team the reason, she knew that Jake was very bright and she didn't want to lose his talents. She also felt that, even though she had not used Jake's data to evaluate him, the team would think that she had.

Think of your job as not just getting products built but of also building your people's skills. If some people do not perform up to their potential, figure out how to help them improve. While this may be hard to do, it is invariably rewarding and, for the team leader, it is a top priority job.

Janet Would Not Join the Team

The second example concerns Janet. She had been a long-time employee and resented having a new manager who was young enough to be her son. For years Janet had come to work late, but she left at the regular quitting time. She didn't want to change her personal schedule, so she refused to attend the weekly team meetings. She had also refused to take a team role. She argued that she had worked late on the previous project and deserved a rest. She had also developed software for many years and didn't need to be told how to do it.

Fred, the team leader, felt that this behavior would destroy the team as a cohesive unit. Janet was putting in far fewer hours than any of the other members and she was not behaving as a cooperative member of the team. When discussing this issue, Fred's manager suggested that he tell Janet that if she didn't work regular hours and participate as a full member of this team, she would have to get another job. They would give her 30 days' severance pay plus any accrued vacation. When Fred explained this to Janet, she was shocked. She had worked for the company for many years, was nearing retirement, and had never had a manager talk to her like this. The next day, however, she was at the team meeting on time and agreed to take the test manager role.

While it is never pleasant to take a hard line with any employee, there are times when you have no alternative. Janet presented just such a case. However, experience shows that difficult employees will often turn around when management takes a firm position. Many of these people can become valued and productive employees. Some people have never had firm guidance, even as children, and they may still be looking for it. An important part of your job as a manager is to provide this guidance.

General Principles

From these examples, you can see a couple of ways to handle difficult people. Since this is such a large subject and there are an almost infinite variety of cases, it is important to understand the four general principles for handling difficult people. First, everyone is different, and many seemingly difficult people are merely confused or not yet comfortable working with you. Take the time to listen to and understand these people, and try to establish a degree of personal rapport. Usually, the initial difficulties will disappear and these people will become productive team members.

Second, if you continue having problems using a particular employee on the team, discuss the problem with your own manager and agree in advance on precisely how to handle it. Third, even if it takes time, continue trying to motivate the employee to do good work. Finally, when nothing else works, don't hesitate to take a hard line; it will frequently work. In all cases, remember that your job is to help every one of your people. Whatever you plan to do with a difficult employee, first make sure that your boss agrees with your plan of action. Since misunderstandings are common in these situations, write down your plan and then review it with your manager. Then make any suggested changes and confirm your manager's agreement before taking action.

16.6   Handling Poor Performers

Occasionally, you will have an employee who is incapable of doing the job. There are lots of reasons for poor performance, but only a few of them warrant dismissing an employee. The general situations are

☐ Skill mismatch

☐ Overpowering ambition

☐ A disabling personality

Skill Mismatch

Some people just do not have engineering skills. Product development is challenging work and it requires many skills and abilities. If one of your people does not perform as expected, it could be due to inadequate training or an improper assignment. Some superb designers are terrible implementers, and some marvelous troubleshooters couldn't design to save themselves. Even when developers are capable of doing some jobs, if they are not interested in the work, you cannot expect good results. If they need special training to handle some job that you both agree would be a good fit, arrange for that training, but try to match the developers' talents and interests to their assignments. If some developers still can't do good work, maybe they are not cut out to be developers.

Overpowering Ambition

With very capable people, overpowering ambition is a particularly common problem. Some people get stars in their eyes and focus on the next promotion instead of concentrating on what they are doing right now. Symptoms of this problem include angling for visibility, wanting to be included in every meeting, or seeking opportunities to give management presentations. These employees probably have ambition problems. While they may handle these special tasks very well, they are paid to do their current jobs. If they do that work with distinction, they will almost certainly get a raise or be promoted.

Usually, all these people need is a good counseling session. They need to understand that if they do not do a good job on their present assignments, they will not get promoted or even get a raise. Get them to devote their energies to the current jobs and let you take care of their promotions.

A Disabling Personality

There are as many kinds of personalities as there are kinds of people. However, with reasonable care you can help almost all employees to be productive. Sometimes these employees' personality problems will be so severe that they cannot be productive, or they will disrupt the team and limit everyone's performance. Such problems often show up as drug or drinking problems, excessive absenteeism, chronic lateness, anger, or depression. Since many people with these problems are adept at taking advantage of the laws on discrimination, safety, disability, and unemployment, unwary managers can get into serious trouble before they know that they have a problem. Also, remember that such people are occasionally even dangerous. If you even suspect that you might have an employee with such problems, talk to your manager and get professional advice.

Personality problems are a common reason for poor employee performance, and they are also the most difficult people-related problems to handle. When very bright people have personality problems, they can be particularly troublesome. They can make very convincing arguments about why their performance is really superior or how they have suffered from mismanagement. They will often argue that they have been unfairly treated, have an unusually difficult assignment, or deserve a promotion and a pay increase.

When you have determined that you have such employees, treat them with care. While they could potentially be very good employees, you may have to treat them harshly to shake their odd convictions or hang-ups. When and if you do take a hard line, however, be prepared for a fight. One difficult developer can easily take more of your time than all of the other team members combined. He or she is likely to pull every trick in the book, plus some you have never heard of.

When you encounter such a person, the first step is to listen and take notes, both because he or she could be right, and also because if you don't listen, you are vulnerable to retaliation. Next, before you say anything to the employee (other than to ask questions), get advice from your manager and from the personnel department. Finally, once you have decided how to handle the situation, make sure that you are in complete agreement with your manager and have documented this agreement. Then, review this document with your manager and with the personnel department. Finally, deal with the employee exactly as you all have agreed.

In dealing with the employee, don't hurry. If something comes up that you had not thought of, stop and look into it. Remember that if you mistakenly try to push a resolution through too quickly, the case could drag on for years. Many years ago I was asked to fix such a mishandled case. However, since too many management mistakes had been made, I could not resolve it. Six years later, I was called to testify in the resulting lawsuit. So, take a few days or weeks to do your homework and to ensure that you have a completely supportable case. Then take action.

While very few people have truly disabling personality problems, when you have such employees, treat them with great care. If you don't, they are likely to destroy your team and they could destroy your career as well.

16.7 Summary

This chapter focuses on the team leader's responsibilities for coaching, guiding, and evaluating individual team members. To do their best work, developers need to be committed to the job, but they also need to find the work interesting. This chapter discusses the close relationship among interests, competence, and motivation, particularly for technical people. It also discusses burnout and how boring or highly repetitive work can destroy a developer's motivation and even cause him or her to resign.

One way to look at people's performance is in terms of task and relationship maturity. This framework provides a useful basis for understanding a developer's capabilities and for selecting a coaching, evaluation, and support strategy.

As team leader, you must evaluate your people. Evaluating people is not difficult, particularly when you know as much about their performance as you will with the TSP. However, personal data are sensitive. The best approach is to avoid using data for people evaluations and to be completely open with your team members about how you intend to evaluate them.

Some people are easy to manage and some are difficult. Since the difficult people are often very intelligent and creative, you must be careful how you deal with them. Think of your job as not just getting products built, but also building your people's skills. If some people do not perform up to their potential, figure out how to help them improve. While this may be hard to do, it is invariably rewarding and, for the team leader, it is a top priority job.

The four general principles for handling difficult people are, first, take the time to listen and understand; second, discuss the problem with your manager; third, try to motivate the employee; and finally, when nothing else works, don't hesitate to take a hard line. Before doing anything, however, first write down your plan of action and make sure that your boss agrees with it.

References

Austin, Robert D. *Measuring and Managing Performance in Organizations*. New York: Dorset House Publishing. 1996.

Brooks, Patricia. Burnout. *Think*. Vol. 48, no. 1, January/February 1982. Armonk, NY: IBM Corporation, p. 26.

Clark, David. Are too many programmers too narrowly trained? *IEEE Computer*. June 2000, pp. 12–15.

Humphrey, Watts S. *Managing Technical People*. Reading MA: Addison-Wesley. 1997.

———. *Winning with Software: An Executive Strategy*. Boston: Addison-Wesley. 2002.

17

Improving Team Performance

As noted in Chapter 15, teams grow and improve with experience, but they don't improve unless they are motivated to do so. When groups are serious about improvement, they define their goals, make plans, and establish dedicated improvement resources. However, to decide what to improve and how to do it, you need performance measures and feedback on improvement progress. This chapter is about ways to improve the performance of your team and some things to do to make sure that it does improve. The following topics are covered in this chapter.

- ☐ Motivating improvement
- ☐ Improvement goals
- ☐ Improvement strategy and process
- ☐ Improvement plans and resources
- ☐ Improvement measures and feedback
- ☐ The elements of benchmarking
- ☐ Benchmark measures
- ☐ Dynamic benchmarking
- ☐ Benchmarking yourself

17.1 Motivating Improvement

You cannot improve a team unless it is motivated to improve. When a team is just plodding along and doing whatever it must do to stay on the payroll, it will not get better by itself. In fact, it may not even sustain its current performance. When people are content just to do their jobs and to collect their paychecks, they often become bored and uninterested in the work. If this situation continues for long, team performance not only will not improve, it will likely deteriorate.

Even when teams are doing a good job, continuing to do similar work in much the same way for many years can become boring and, over time, lead to the burnout problem discussed in Chapter 16. Under these conditions, the team leader or a higher-level manager must figuratively light a fuse under the team to wake it up and to regenerate the members' energy. You must motivate them to do even better work than they have done before. An aggressive set of improvement goals with strong management justification and support can provide the stimulus teams need to stay excited and enthusiastic and to make the work both interesting and enjoyable.

Few software teams are truly lethargic, but many of the teams I have known were perfectly content to continue working just as they had in the past. While they were energetic and working hard, it was clear that they would continue to face precisely the same problems year in and year out. For example, one software manager once told me that his company had 10 years of data on defects found in final testing and maintenance. These data showed that this company's software teams had, for over 10 years, produced programs that consistently had 20, plus or minus 1, defects/KLOC on entry to integration and system testing. Since the average cost to find and fix each defect was 1½ engineering days, this company was spending an enormous amount of money on defects. Fortunately, this manager convinced his management to introduce the TSP and, with their very first TSP project, they reduced this 20-defects/KLOC level to less than 1. This was a quality improvement of over 20 times, and it saved the company over $5 million in the next two years.

Motivating development teams to improve is not difficult. In fact, you can do it in exactly the same way that you motivate TSP teams to do their projects. First, establish goals and convince the team that the goals are important, then work with the team to define roles, make a plan, assess risks, and assign resources. Since these are the steps used to launch TSP teams, you should consider using the TSP launch process to initiate the improvement effort. Even for an effort that is too small to justify a full launch, it is usually helpful to follow the approach used in the TSP launch and to have the improvement team establish its own goals, roles, and plan for the work. The following discussion assumes that you will use something like the TSP launch process to initiate the improvement work and that you will include these improvement activities in the team's planning during its project launch. However, if you launch the improvement work at the same time you launch the development work, the improvement focus will likely get lost in the rush to complete the project launch. If this happens, consider holding a separate and later mini-launch for the improvement effort.

17.2   Improvement Goals

The first time you launch a TSP team, you will have many potential measures of team performance but little or no historical data for setting objectives. However, since first-time TSP teams generally get substantially improved performance, they do not need special sets of improvement goals. The principal improvement objective for such a team is to make an aggressive plan and then to follow that plan in doing the work. Once you have completed several TSP team projects, you will begin to see a performance pattern and can define meaningful improvement goals.

Rather than just start the launch with some general improvement ideas, however, talk to your management and any business or technical staffs to get their ideas for improvement objectives. Whenever possible, also get estimates of the benefits these improvements would provide for the organization. During the launch, review the team's prior performance and compare it with the suggested goals. Then work with the team to decide on the goals the members are willing to commit to and define the role responsibilities for each goal. Then incorporate these improvement goals and responsibilities into the team's plan. At the end of the launch, publicly commit to these improvement goals in the final management meeting. Finally, after the launch, track both the improvement and the project tasks and have each team member review the status of his or her improvement work in the weekly team meeting.

17.3   Improvement Strategy and Process

Suppose, with the prior project, that your team had taken 12 weeks to complete integration and system test. Suppose also that this was four weeks longer than had been planned. While 12 weeks was presumably a substantial reduction from prior test times, it delayed the product's release and cost the company money. You and the team have set a goal of six weeks for integration and system testing for this product, and you are now producing the improvement plan to help you accomplish this. To decide how to proceed, the quality manager has gathered data on the prior product's system testing. These data are shown in Table 17.1.

Table 17.1 Prior Project Testing Data

Test Cycles		Defects	Days
	Cycle 1	63	24.4
	Cycle 2	47	18.4
	Cycle 3	18	10.5
	Cycle 4	3	5.9
	Totals	131	59.2
Defective Modules		**Number**	**Total Defects**
	0 Defects	430	0
	1 Defect	43	43
	2 Defects	31	62
	3+ Defects	6	26
	Totals	510	131
Defect Categories			**Total Defects**
	Requirements misunderstandings		14
	System timing, performance, etc.		20
	Coding and detailed design		97
	Totals		131

In examining the module data, the quality manager concluded that the requirements and system-level defects were important, but that the first improvement priority should be to manage the detailed design and coding problems. All of the modules with multiple test defects had poor quality profiles. These modules accounted for 86 of the coding and detailed design defects, and the team concluded that if they could eliminate most of these defects, they could cut testing time to at most 2 cycles. This would reduce testing time to about six weeks.

In examining the multiple-defect modules, the quality manager found that either the review rates were excessive, the design time was inadequate, or no inspections had been conducted. This meant that every multiple-defect module could have been identified before test entry. The team decided to follow a three-fold strategy to find and fix the most defective modules before test entry.

1. Every team member would strive to meet the team's quality goals for every module he or she produced.

2. The quality manager would review the data for every module before the code inspections, before unit test, and before release to integration and system test.

3. If the quality manager found problems with any module in any of these reviews, she would bring those problems to the team meeting together with a recommendation for what to do about it.

The team would then decide whether the module should be

☐ Rereviewed

☐ Reinspected

☐ Retested

☐ Redeveloped

With this overall quality strategy, the team proceeded to make its improvement plan.

While there are many ways to approach process improvement, it is generally wise to identify the one or at most two significant problem areas and tackle them first. By focusing on a relatively narrow improvement scope, you are more likely to accomplish the objective. Then you can start on the next improvement cycle.

17.4   Improvement Plans and Resources

In making the improvement plan, the developers reviewed their personal plans to ensure that they had allowed adequate time for design, design reviews, code reviews, and inspections. They also allocated time for the quality reviews with the quality manager. The quality manager found that the quality reviews would probably take her about four task hours per week. Since this would not leave her enough time for all of her development work, the team decided to reassign one of her modules to another team member. With these changes, the team's plan was balanced and all of the members felt that they could do their development and improvement tasks in time to meet the team's commitments.

Planning for process improvement is no different than planning for any other kind of activity. The key point to remember, however, is to put the improvement tasks into the team plan and to ensure that they are not forgotten. If, as in this case, the improvements concern product quality, they will have a major schedule impact so they should get priority attention. If the improvements were not successful, the product's quality would suffer and the schedule would be delayed.

17.5   Improvement Measures and Feedback

To track its progress against the improvement plan, the team decided to use run charts on review rates, compile defects, and unit test defects. The quality manager agreed to produce these charts and to review them with the team every week. The test manager also agreed to gather test data from the test group every week during testing and to plot the cumulative test defects compared to the cumulative defects for the prior project. He would also review these data with the team in each weekly meeting.

Tracking and feedback are critically important. If you don't regularly track progress, the team members will not know where they stand or whether they are making progress against the improvement goal. Pretty soon, they will forget about the improvement goal and just concentrate on doing their jobs in whatever way they had always done them. Under these conditions, improvement is highly unlikely.

17.6   The Elements of Benchmarking

A **benchmark** is a standard or reference against which similar things can be measured to determine their quality (Random House 1983). Benchmarks are particularly useful for TSP teams because they provide a rich and comprehensive source of performance data. Benchmarks can also show teams how much room there is for improvement.

To use benchmarking, you must have three things. First, there must be general agreement on the need to do quality work. Whether this need is to meet a particular standard, to perform better than some competitor, or to improve your own performance, everyone knows what they are supposed to do and that it is important to do so. Second, you must have a standard against which to evaluate performance. This could be an arbitrary corporate, industry, or government requirement; a competitor's level of achievement; or your own prior performance. In any case, you must have a known and defined standard that is recognized and well understood. Third, you must have measures that tell you whether or not you have met the standard or benchmark. This measure or set of measures must be precise and timely and it must be sufficiently comprehensive to show performance against the standard.

Once you meet these three conditions, the next steps are to identify the benchmark, establish measures, and define the benchmarking process. Then you are ready to use benchmarking to manage and motivate your team. In doing this, the criteria to consider are as follows.

☐ The benchmark is relevant.

☐ The benchmark is measurable.

☐ The benchmark is available.

☐ The benchmark is timely.

☐ The benchmark is challenging.

☐ The set of benchmarks is representative.

The Benchmark Is Relevant

To be useful, the benchmark must relate to the type of work you do. Assuming that you are benchmarking against another project, the benchmark team should be doing a similar kind of work. If possible, you should be developing similar products for similar customers on comparable schedules and with roughly the same size teams. You probably will not be able to use an organization that does precisely the same kind of work since that would almost certainly be a competitor. However, try to minimize the differences, since too many variations would make useful comparisons difficult.

The Benchmark Is Measurable

Generally, measurable performance is only possible if the benchmark team is also using the TSP. If not, there will be little comparable data, and what data there are would be at too high a level to motivate the team. While some high maturity organizations will have data, if their teams are not using the TSP, the data may not be comparable. However, you could probably use their quality measures for system-test, acceptance-test, and customer-reported defects as benchmarks. Although benchmarking with teams that are not using the TSP might be helpful to those other teams, it would probably not be of much help in motivating your team.

The Benchmark Is Available

In selecting a team with which to benchmark, pick one that is nearby and willing to discuss their data with you and your team. Ideally, you would like a TSP team that you could visit to discuss issues and to brainstorm about common problems and ideas.

The Benchmark Is Timely

The best choice for a benchmark team is one that has completed a prior TSP project and is launching a new project at about the same time as you are. This would provide performance data on the earlier job and timely updates on current performance.

The Benchmark Is Challenging

To be challenging, the benchmark team's performance should be better than yours but not so good as to seem unreachable. Goals are only motivating if the team feels they are achievable.

The Set of Benchmarks Is Representative

As noted in Chapter 16, measurements can be misused. Therefore, in measuring something as complex as a development project, it is important to use a complete enough set of benchmarks to truly represent the project and how it is performing.

17.7   Benchmark Measures

Benchmarking measures are useful in two ways: to demonstrate to management and to the customer how well your team is doing and to motivate the team to do even better work. The key measures to use with management are the following.

- ☐ **Estimating accuracy.** Here, show weekly plots of planned versus actual task hours for completed tasks for your team and for the benchmark team. When the team starts producing code, you can also show plan to actual size comparisons like those shown in Figure 17.1 (Humphrey 2002, 173). In this example, after 16 weeks, the team has developed 7,561 LOC for modules that were only estimated to have 6,295 LOC. When the actual size of these modules is used in the estimate, the total project size estimate becomes 25,996 LOC instead of 24,730.

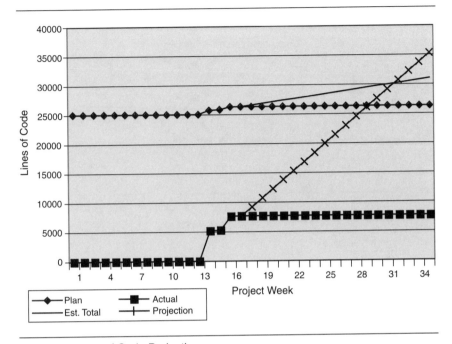

Figure 17.1 Line of Code Projections

- □ **Weekly task time.** A comparison of weekly task hours per full-time team member would show how your developers are improving against the benchmark team. Figure 17.2 shows that the other team started before you did, but that your team is catching up and will likely pass the benchmark team in about three weeks.
- □ **Productivity.** Show the LOC per hour for the entire job for a completed benchmark project compared to your team's plan. You could also give a productivity projection based on the actual versus planned task hours for completed tasks and the latest size projection. Since productivity measures are easy to misuse, use several and be careful not to motivate shoddy work. When available, consider using task hours per LOC, LOC per developer week, or function points per month, for example.
- □ **Defects.** Show the planned versus actual defect removal profiles for your team and for the benchmark team. Also show yield goals and yield estimates for both phase and process yields. Where available, also show data on system-test, acceptance-test, or customer-reported defects.
- □ **Percent Defect Free (PDF).** Where the data are available, the PDF measure can be used to compare most types of program products.

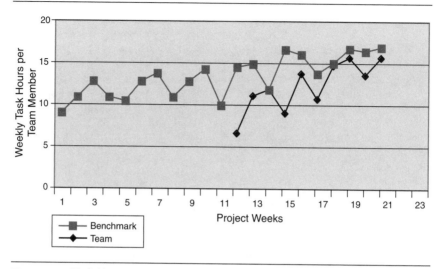

Figure 17.2 Task Hours Benchmark

The best measures for motivating a team are

☐ Weekly task hours as shown in Figure 17.2
☐ Review and inspection rates
☐ Defect densities by phase
☐ Percent defect free (PDF)

With any measure, and particularly the task-hour measure, directives to improve will demotivate the team rather than encourage improvement. These measures show the team members how their personal performance affects team performance and what they need to do to help the team meet its goals. To be most effective at motivating the team, involve all of the team members in defining the benchmarks and then have a team review with your TSP coach.

17.8   Dynamic Benchmarking

Benchmarks are motivating because they represent real performance for real teams. People are competitive and are readily motivated by a race, as long as the benchmark is relevant and challenging. People also perform better with live competitors than when racing against the clock. Even world class runners have pacers to provide a tangible and compelling benchmark. The difference is dynamic feedback. In a competitive race, the dynamic benchmark shows the runners exactly where they stand. However, when goals are just numbers, they often seem arbitrary or theoretical and are not especially compelling. By comparing with a real team, you can make the benchmarks more like a race. Then the team members can see how they are doing and strive a little harder to win.

Assuming that you have selected a benchmark team, you can generate benchmark charts like those in Figures 17.3 and 17.4. The defect profiles in Figure 17.3 show the defects per KLOC found to date for both teams. Here, for example, the team line shows that 65 percent of the product has completed detailed design (DLD) review, 28 percent has been code reviewed and compiled, and only 16 percent has been inspected. Your team is doing better than the benchmark team, since it has found more defects in the design and code reviews and fewer in compile, code inspection, and unit test. However, since only 16 percent of your code has completed unit test, your defect rates could easily get worse. It is therefore important that the team carefully monitor the rates for every review.

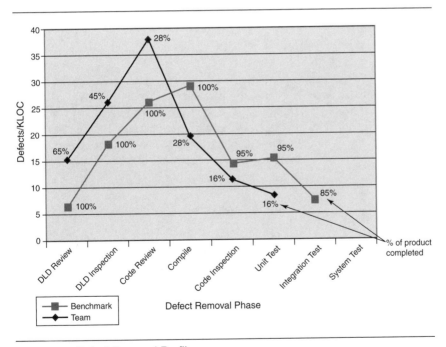

Figure 17.3 Defect Removal Profile

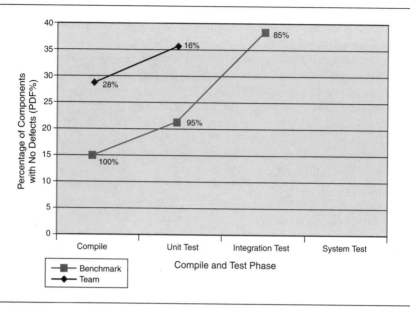

Figure 17.4 Percent Defect Free

Figure 17.4 shows the percent defect free (PDF) curve for your team and the benchmark team. This plot shows the percentage of the product's components that had no defects in a compiling or testing phase. The benchmark team has entered integration testing with all components through compiling and 95 percent through unit test. Your team has compiled 28 percent and unit tested 16 percent of its components and is doing substantially better than the benchmark team.

17.9   Benchmarking Yourself

Since you may not find a suitable benchmark in your organization or elsewhere, you will often have to benchmark against yourself. If the team has completed a prior project or project cycle, the data from that earlier work can provide a comparative benchmark for the next and subsequent phases. Here, the objective is to motivate the team members to do even better work than they did the last time. Whenever such data are available, it is always a good idea to use them as a benchmark.

Another approach is to use the variations in the team's weekly performance. Do not compare individuals, as this can lead to internal team competition and destroy the team's cooperative spirit. The idea is for the team to track its best overall performance in any area and to continually strive to equal or exceed that performance. For example, if the team's best average task-hour rate was 17.3 task hours per developer week, that would be the goal for subsequent work. Each team member should then strive to personally meet or better that team goal for every week. When every team member does this, the team's performance will improve quite rapidly.

Being a Benchmark

One of the joys of superior work is the pride of being a model for other teams. As teams build a performance track record, we will see best-in-class performance for every important measurement. Imagine the pride and satisfaction for being on a team that was best-in-class on an important benchmark measure.

When to Benchmark

While benchmarking can be done throughout a project, it is particularly important during the launch, relaunch, and postmortem. During the launch, use benchmarks to help set the team's goals, and then review the team's performance against these benchmark goals every week as well as in each cycle postmortem. Also, if you didn't meet the goals, discuss why not and what you should do differently in the future. During the relaunch, reset the team's goals based on the postmortem results and try to set new goals that are challenging but achievable. However, try to set goals that are a stretch but seem realistic to the team. While you want the team members to strive, you also want them to win.

17.10 Summary

This chapter describes how to improve a team's performance and some of the key issues to consider in motivating team improvement. In setting an improvement strategy, the first requirements are establishing improvement goals and motivating all of the team members to achieve these goals. Motivating teams to improve is much like motivating teams to do a project. This suggests that you follow a process much like the TSP launch in establishing the improvement plan.

In managing and tracking the improvement work, timely measures and regular performance feedback are important. The TSP provides many useful improvement measures. Management and customers will be most interested in estimating accuracy, weekly task time, productivity, and defect profiles. Motivating measures for the team are weekly task hours, review and inspection rates, defect densities, and percent defect free.

Benchmarking can be very helpful for TSP teams. The three requirements for benchmarking are, first, general agreement on the need to do quality work, second, an available standard, and third, measures that can verify that the team is meeting the standard. Assuming that the team is ready to participate in a benchmark program, with the team's help, identify potential benchmark teams. These teams must do relevant work, have available measures, and provide timely data. Their performance should also provide challenging goals for your team.

Dynamic benchmarking compares weekly team performance with the benchmark team. With the proper measures, this can lead to substantial performance improvements. Teams can also benchmark themselves. The ways to do this are to compare with prior performance on other projects or to use performance fluctuations to set more immediate goals.

References

Humphrey, Watts S. *Winning with Software: An Executive Strategy.* Boston: Addison-Wesley. 2002.

Random House Dictionary of the English Language. New York: Random House. 1983.

18

Being a Team Leader

Chapter 2 described *what* leadership is. This chapter addresses *how* to provide leadership and what you must do to be an effective team leader. It provides perspective on the issues that affect your performance as a leader and it suggests steps you can take to do an effective leadership job. Each section of this chapter deals with different facets of leadership. These sections are as follows.

- □ What is leadership?
- □ Being a leader or a manager
- □ The leadership role
- □ Coaching while leading
- □ The challenges ahead

18.1   What Is Leadership?

Leadership is described in Chapter 2 as the act of leading. It means going before, preceding, guiding the way. It requires that you be in front of the team, know where it must go, and guide the way. As leader, you cannot force your people to follow; you must motivate them. Napoleon once said, "One does not *make* a French army cross the Alps; one *leads* it across" (Brown 1981).

Convincing the Team to Follow You

The best definition of a **leader** is one who has followers. Without followers, after all, you cannot lead. To get followers, you need to do only one thing: motivate your people to follow. While this sounds simple, there is more to it than meets the eye. First, you must know where you want to go. Second, you need to show your people why this goal is worth striving for. And finally, you must actually start going and induce your people to follow.

Knowing Where You Want to Go

In the software business, defining the goal is rarely a problem. Management has decided on the job that they want done and they have asked you to lead a team in doing it. So, your goal is to get this job done. While you need to define more precisely what management wants you to do, the overall goal is clear. This is what meeting 1 of the TSP launch process is about: for management to explain to the team what they want you to do. The TSP launch process will help you with the first step of becoming a leader—at least it will if management clearly describes what they want you to do.

Convincing the Team That the Goal Is Worth Striving For

Another place where the TSP launch will help is in convincing the team that the goal is important. When management explains what they want the team to do, they should also explain why. Then, if they do not give a convincing story, perhaps you can help them make it convincing. The objective is to convey to the team why this job is important to the organization, to you, and to them. That, of course, is why the launch process starts the way it does: to help you explain the goal to the team and to help you motivate your people to put their hearts and souls into this job.

Launch meeting 2 is designed to reinforce the goals and to make them meaningful to all of the team members. Your objective is to convince the team that the goal is important and worth striving for. To do this, you must appreciate the members' interests so you can help align their personal goals with those of the team and management. By convincing each member that the team goal is consistent with his or her personal goals, you can help the group coalesce around a common team goal.

Getting the Team to Follow

The TSP launch process can help you with defining the goal and convincing the team members that it is worthwhile. The final step of getting them to follow is up to you. This step is largely a matter of trust and of mutual support. Building trust starts in the team launch. If, as you make the team plan, you demonstrate that you rely on the members to make the best and most aggressive plan they think they can meet, you are showing that you trust them. Then, in launch meeting 9, when you defend the plan to management and when you refuse to change the plan without the team's agreement, you have proven that you are trustworthy. After the launch, the team is ready to trust you. While you still don't have their complete trust, you are almost there.

Your First Leadership Challenge

Leadership and trust are not popularity contests. One of the most difficult issues is balancing the need for team agreement with the occasional need to get the members to do things they would not naturally or normally do. While you want to be accepted as a full member of the team, there are times when you must take charge and act like a boss. This is a difficult balancing act, and it involves standards and discipline. You have an objective to meet and you know that, to be successful, the team must do the job in the right way. The example of Ben, the marine lieutenant in Vietnam (Chapter 2), emphasizes the importance of trust. It also shows how important discipline is in getting people to do things they really don't want to do, just because they are following their leader.

With the TSP, your most difficult leadership challenge will be discipline— the discipline to do the job in the way that you know it should be done. While this is not as difficult as getting a team to charge into machine-gun fire, people naturally resist discipline. It is hard and it is rarely fun, but it pays off in the long run. To establish and maintain discipline, however, you must truly believe that discipline is required and that it will help the team to do the job in the most effective and efficient way.

Disciplined work involves planning and following the plan, tracking and managing personal time, and remembering that quality is the top priority. It requires that you demand superior work and that you know what superior work looks like. You must also strive for superior work yourself. While discipline sounds simple, it is exceedingly difficult. That is where leadership and trust come in.

Building Trust

After the team launch, you must continue to build on the initial trust you have established. The basic needs are to be honest, to be yourself, and to consistently focus on helping the team to do its work in the best possible way. The TSP process can help you to do this as long as you consistently do what you say and don't pretend that you are something you are not.

Keith was a new manager who sat in his office by the hour, figuring out what his people should do and how they should do it. Then, one by one, he would call them in and tell them what to do. His people viewed Keith as a tyrant. He never listened to them or asked them what they thought. He just gave orders.

It turned out that Keith was scared to death of his people. He felt that, as a manager, he was supposed to be the all-knowing mastermind for all of the work in his department. Since he knew he wasn't all-knowing, he was afraid to expose his fallibility. His gruff and impersonal management style was a façade to protect himself from his people.

This is a problem of trust. Keith was a brilliant developer but also a fallible human being. He could not understand that all people make mistakes, even managers, and he did not trust his people to respect him if they discovered that he could be wrong. He could not understand that the only way humankind has survived through the ages is by working together, learning from each other, and supporting the group. But working together takes reliance, learning requires humility, and reliance takes trust.

Maintaining Team Communication

Trust is a rather nebulous property that may seem hard to establish. However, it is not that difficult if you know how to start. The best place to start, in fact, is with team communication. When developers evaluate their managers, their most frequent complaint is about communication (Raudsepp 1981). When I worked at IBM, we conducted periodic employee satisfaction surveys. The single greatest complaint that the employees made about managers was that they did not adequately communicate. This was true in every opinion survey. Development professionals are intelligent and creative people; they have ideas and opinions, and they want to participate and to have an influence over their work. Communication is critical, not only as a way to tell developers what to do, but also as a way to show respect for them and to enlist their minds and energies in meeting the project's goals.

18.2   Being a Leader or a Manager

We have already discussed what a leader is, but what is a manager? Here we have another circular definition: a **manager** is someone who manages. However, now we must look at what it means to manage. **Managing** means controlling, directing, giving orders, and expecting obedience. This is strong stuff. It sounds like managers leave little room for their people to use judgment or to take the initiative. Managing sounds like something we might not mind doing, but we don't want it done to us.

In general parlance, a manager is viewed as someone who controls an organization or a facility. Thus, a manager typically determines how people are evaluated, whether they get a salary increase, and how much. So, being a manager is not necessarily bad, as long as the manager concentrates on managing the mechanics of employment and does not try to manage the details of the work.

However, maintaining this balance between managing the employment details and guiding the work is difficult. It is particularly difficult because your people know that you are their manager and that you have control over how they are evaluated and paid. Therefore, they will behave differently toward you than if you were just another member of the team. A discussion of two leadership topics will clarify these issues: leading teams that you manage and leading teams that you do not manage.

Leading Teams That You Manage

The principal problem with leading people that you manage concerns motivation. In essence, the question concerns whether they are doing the job because they want to do it or because they want to please you. As discussed in Chapter 2, **transactional** leadership is when people are working for some reward, while with **transformational** leadership they are doing the work because they believe it is important and they are excited about the opportunity to participate and to contribute.

While transactional leadership is the norm for most work, it has one fundamental drawback. The true objective of the team member is to please the manager, not to do a superior job. While pleasing you may not seem like such a bad idea, such a motivation often leads to bad decisions. This is not because you would necessarily support a bad decision, but because your team members do not know what you would support. They end up doing what they *think* you want. Such second-guessing often leads to confusion and mistakes.

When you lead teams that you manage, you will rarely have problems getting the people to do what you want. However, you will often have problems getting them to take the initiative and to do what they think is right. The principal issue you will then face is the need to do superior technical work. Urge the team members to think for themselves, to take initiative, and to be creative. You picked these developers because they are capable of doing the job. You could not do it by yourself, and you need more than just their arms and legs; you need their minds and hearts.

The TSP process is designed to address this problem. By focusing on goals, plans, and performance, you can help the team members to concentrate on doing the job rather than thinking about your evaluations of them. This is the subject of task and relationship maturity which is discussed in Chapter 16. As you walk the team through the TSP launch process, and as you guide the members in planning and tracking their own work, you are helping to develop their task and relationship maturity. This, in turn, helps you become a transformational leader.

Leading Teams That You Do Not Manage

When some or all of the team members do not report to you, you no longer have the leverage of transactional leadership. This should not be a serious problem, however, since you can still provide transformational leadership. Unfortunately, there is another complication. These team members report to someone else, and it is these other managers who control their evaluations and decide whether or not they will get salary increases. Now, instead of a management problem, you have a political problem. Here, we define **politics** as the art of obtaining power, while power is the ability to cause action (Humphrey 1997, 233).

When you need the allegiance of people who do not work for you, you first need their managers' support. Since these managers have the power to force the team members to do what they want, you need these managers to tell those team members the importance of fully participating on your team and that if they do fully participate, they will get a positive evaluation. While this is transactional leadership, it is a transaction between the team member and his or her manager. That transaction is important, however, since you do not want your team members to have conflicting loyalties.

Once you know that the team members do not have conflicting loyalties, you can focus on transformational leadership. Now, your objective is to excite them about this job and to motivate them to do superior work.

Being a Transformational Leader

To be a transformational leader, you must get the team excited about doing this job. While there are many ways to do this, the TSP helps you by satisfying the five basic conditions for self-directed teams. As described in Chapter 3, these are as follows.

1. A sense of membership and belonging
2. Commitment to a common team goal
3. Ownership of the process and plan
4. The skill to make a plan and the discipline to follow it
5. A dedication to excellence

As described in Chapter 7, the TSP launch process was designed to establish these conditions. However, after all of this preparation, how do you know that the team will be excited about the job? Here, you are fortunate to have a development team. These developers have spent years preparing to design and develop systems. They will be excited about the job because it is what they have dreamed about doing. By the end of the launch, the developers will have made a start at becoming a close-knit energetic and cohesive team. Your challenge is to maintain and to build on this energy and enthusiasm. The next sections of this chapter discuss your role as a leader in establishing and maintaining these five conditions for self-directed teams.

18.3 The Leadership Role

The TSP team leader's roles and responsibilities are summarized in Table 18.1 on the next page. The following subsections describe how, by properly performing these responsibilities, you will satisfy the five basic conditions for self-directed teams. You will then be well on the way to being a transformational leader.

A Sense of Membership and Belonging

The feeling of membership and belonging has two parts: being included in all of the important team activities and having an accepted role on the team. The role topics are discussed in Appendix A, and the sense of membership and belonging is also covered in Chapter 15.

With few exceptions, your leadership, management, and coaching responsibilities will involve communicating with the team members both individually and as a group. The challenge is to handle these communications so as to know and understand each team member while treating the entire group as a cohesive team. As discussed in Chapter 15, you must have a common workspace, hold frequent team meetings, openly resolve issues, and objectively use facts and data.

While these responsibilities sound relatively straightforward, the way you handle them is not as clear. For example, when one team member does work of

Table 18.1 TSP Team Leader Roles and Responsibilities

Objective	When all team members consistently meet their role responsibilities, follow the defined process, and work to agreed goals and specifications, the team will be most efficient and effective.
Goals	The team leader's goals are to • Ensure that the project is successful • Build a motivated and effective team • Fully utilize the talents and abilities of all team members • Keep management informed
Role Characteristics	The characteristics most helpful to the team leader are • You enjoy being a leader and naturally assume a leadership role. • You are able to identify the key issues and objectively make decisions. • You do not mind occasionally taking unpopular actions and are willing to press people to accomplish difficult tasks. • You respect your team members, are willing to listen to their views, want to help them perform to the best of their abilities, and will support them to higher management.
Team Member Responsibilities	All team members, including the team leader, are responsible for meeting their responsibilities as team members. • Meeting their team member commitments • Following a disciplined personal process • Planning, managing, and reporting on their personal work • Cooperating with the team and all team members to maintain an effective and productive working environment
Leadership	The team leader leads the team. • Maintains a clear and continuous focus on the team's goals • Ensures that all team members are working productively and effectively • Maintains a sense of urgency and pushes to accelerate tasks where practical • Consistently presses for daily results, recognizing that schedules slip a day at a time • Motivates and supports the team • Challenges the team's and team members' decisions and asks what alternatives they have considered • Maintains awareness of other related work and ensures that the team takes advantage of applicable prior results • Represents and supports management to the team • Represents and supports the team to management
People Management	The team leader handles all team personnel issues. • Manages project staffing, recruiting, and training • Is sensitive to team interaction issues and takes steps to resolve such problems when the team cannot resolve the issues itself • Considers team members' interests and abilities in making job assignments • Ensures that the tasks and work pressures are consistent with each developer's skills and abilities • Protects the team from diversions and time-consuming distractions

Table 18.1 (continued)

Team Coaching	The team leader maintains a disciplined and effective working environment. • Facilitates team communication • Keeps the team informed and leads the weekly project status meetings • Ensures that the team and the team members produce their own plans • Reviews individual and team plans to ensure that they are aggressive but realistic • Ensures that team members follow disciplined personal practices • Ensures that team members adhere to the agreed team standards and processes
Quality Management	The team leader maintains a consistent focus on quality. • Ensures that quality metrics are regularly gathered and analyzed • Regularly motivates the team to meet its quality goals • Leads the team reviews of every valid integration, system test, and user-reported defect (form DEFECT and script TESTD).
Project Management	The team leader manages the project. • Handles funding issues • Resolves issues with management and other teams or departments • Where possible, delegates all defined project tasks to team members • Handles all ill-defined issues and problems, at least until they can be defined and assigned to the team or a team member for attention • Maintains awareness of schedule status and chances of acceleration or delay • Regularly reports project status to management and the customer • Leads risk evaluation and tracking • Leads issue tracking and resolution • Ensures that all requirements and design assumptions and uncertainties are promptly and thoroughly verified • Participates in the configuration control board • Ensures that all requirements and design changes are promptly assessed for impact • Where a change significantly impacts the project cost or schedule, ensures that the plan is adjusted and approved before the change is implemented
Principal Team Leader Activities	The team leader motivates the team to perform their tasks and resolve issues. Every week, the team leader holds a team meeting to • Track that all committed tasks have been completed • Check that all team members have submitted the required data • Check that the TASK and SCHED templates are up to date for the team and each team member • Check that all INS, SUMP, and SUMQ forms have been completed on work accomplished to date • Check on the status of development tasks • Check on change, ITL, and risk activity • Press late team members to promptly provide the required data Weekly, the team leader • Reports team status and progress to management and the customer • Maintains the project notebook At each phase postmortem and at project conclusion, the team leader leads the team in producing or updating the project final report (specification SUMMARY).

such poor quality that it jeopardizes the entire team's performance, how do you avoid separating out the guilty team member while still treating the team as a unit?

This is a question of attitude. Since our earliest childhood, we have played the "blame" game. Whenever anything was spilled, broken, or missing, the first question was, "Who did it?" The view was that the guilty party is to blame for this disaster and must be convinced not to ever do such a thing again. While this may be an effective way to train children, it is not an effective way to deal with the developers of complex systems.

An instructive example is the way mistakes are handled on nuclear submarines. Any problem involving the propulsion system causes an immediate captain's mast—all the involved crew members assemble to understand what went wrong and how to prevent a repetition in the future. Whoever was responsible is expected to speak up, describe what he did, and explain why. While problem prevention might involve remedial actions for individuals, everybody concentrates on avoiding future accidents that could jeopardize the submarine. The captain then reports the incident and its resolution to the admiral.

In handling such situations with your team, treat purely individual problems privately, but for anything that involves the team, handle it with the team. For example, if one team member's component had serious quality problems in an inspection, involve the team in deciding what to do. Since the responsible developer will almost certainly feel defensive, at least at first, discuss the problem privately in advance and explain what you intend to do and why. Also point out that anyone can make mistakes. The important point is to learn from these mistakes and to minimize their impact on the team.

Commitment to a Common Team Goal

Because they are so important, goals are discussed in many places in this book: in Chapter 4 on motivation, Chapter 7 on the TSP launch, Chapter 9 on maintaining product focus, Chapter 12 on management support, Chapter 15 on developing the team, and we'll discuss them again here. Goals are an important element of team motivation and they require your continuing attention. The principal leadership need is to maintain a constant and visible focus on the team's goals.

To maintain this focus, break the goals into intermediate milestones so you can regularly track progress against them. Also, ensure that every team member always knows the next milestone and understands how his or her work impacts the team's ability to meet it. One way to do this is to schedule periodic management reviews, and then hold weekly team updates to check milestone status and to identify bottlenecks and problems. Another helpful step is to identify all of the tasks involved in meeting a milestone and list them on a chart with assignments and dates. Then have the team members check off their tasks when they complete them. If this status chart is publicly posted, everybody will always know milestone status and what they must do to meet the next milestone goal.

Ownership of the Process and Plan

When you own something, you feel responsible for taking care of it, improving it, and seeing that it is properly used. That is the way you want your team to feel about this project. There is a big difference between owning something yourself and group ownership. When management specifies the process and plan, most of the members will feel that the team leader really owns them. It's like the distinction between owning and renting a car. With a rental, you will still drive carefully, but you would never consider washing it or taking it in for service.

While you want your team members to properly use the process and to follow the plan, you want them to do more than merely drive carefully; you want them to act like owners: identify problems, suggest improvements, and take responsibility for making these improvements. In fact, you would really like them to do this without your having to tell them and without their needing to ask anyone's permission before they do it. This is a feeling of ownership.

So what is ownership? **Ownership** is defined as responsibility for, control over, and the right of possession of something. Ownership, however, means more than this. It also implies uniqueness: you own this and nobody else does. As the owner, you are the sole proprietor and have the final say regarding this property.

While a sense of ownership would produce the kind of behavior you need for a self-directed team, there is a conflict between the cohesiveness and cooperative spirit of a team and the unilateral and exclusive nature of ownership. This dichotomy is resolved in the TSP by establishing team roles and having the team agree on who will "own" each role and take unique responsibility for handling its defined functions. The purpose of the TSP roles is threefold.

1. To define the key team activities that must be handled properly to produce a successful project
2. To specify the person to handle each of these activities
3. To give each team member a sense of ownership and responsibility for a part of the team's work

The role managers are identified in TSP launch meeting 2, but team members typically will not immediately understand or appreciate the importance of their roles. This will take time and it will also take reinforcement. To provide this reinforcement, consider the role responsibilities in every team activity and make sure that all of the role managers know what you and the team are counting on them to do. If some role manager does not know what to do, think about that role and any relevant issues or problems that you have or anticipate. Then get the role manager to address these areas in advance and to make sure that any problems are resolved before they impact team performance. For some ideas on how to do this, see Appendix A.

After the TSP launch, you and the team will believe in your process and plan. As you accomplish the work, however, you will learn more about the job and see how to change the plan to better reflect what you now know. While the gradual divergence between the plan and the work is normal, you must correct it before the plan becomes unrealistic. If it does, the team will not be following the plan you, your team, and your management agreed to. What is worse, you will not be able to report progress or warn them of problems. When management finds that they can no longer rely on you to follow the committed plan, they will start to direct your work. You will then no longer have a self-directed team.

Since it takes time to adjust the team's plan, you do not want to do it too often. However, if you wait too long, you will soon be unable to track project status, rebalance team workload, assess the impact of changes, or predict when the job will be done. When the team's plan has these problems, get it fixed right away. While there are many ways to attack this problem, some typical examples are as follows.

☐ **Changed goals.** If the project's goals have changed, do a complete relaunch. This problem could be caused by an accelerated delivery date, by adding functions, or by a change in the team's resources.

☐ **Staffing changes.** For minor changes, you can generally hold a brief team planning meeting to reestimate and rebalance the workload.

☐ **Discovery.** If you find that the product is substantially larger than estimated or that some planned commercial off-the-shelf functions will have to be developed instead of being reused, hold an overall replanning meeting as soon as possible. If the schedule impact is substantial, inform management and then hold a complete team relaunch with meetings 1 and 9.

The general guidelines for handling such situations are as follows.

1. For major changes affecting the team's goals and resources, hold a new launch or a relaunch as soon as possible. If the changes impact the schedule so significantly that they jeopardize the project, include launch meetings 1 and 9.

2. For changes that do not have a major impact on the team's goals or activities, hold an overall replanning meeting and then inform management of any likely schedule adjustments as soon as possible. Also, review your prior relaunch plan with the team and with management to see if it should be changed.

3. For changes that affect the team's current work, hold a rebalancing and replanning session as soon as possible.

4. For changes that only affect one or two team members, have them adjust their plans and, if the changes impact anyone else, have them review these plan changes with the team.

The Skill to Make a Plan and the Discipline to Follow It

To make accurate, precise, and complete plans, all team members must be PSP trained before the first team launch. However, the discipline to actually follow a detailed plan can only be developed over time. If you have not been updating the plan to accurately reflect the work, the team will not be able to follow it. However, if you have kept the plan up to date, you can ensure that your people follow it by doing two things.

1. Make sure you follow the plan yourself. Use the plan in reviews and team meetings, regularly check project status against the plan, and use the plan to define work priorities and prepare for management reviews.

2. When you meet with team members, check that their plans are current and that they are following them. If they are not, find out why not and get any problems fixed. Then insist that the team members follow their plans.

If you do these things regularly and consistently, the team will almost certainly follow its plan.

A Dedication to Excellence

The ultimate performance standard is excellence. Excellent work is demanding and demanding jobs are rarely easy. Tell your team that if the job were easy, you wouldn't need such good people. Don't let them give up at the first sign of trouble. Don't accept excuses. Be creative. Treat problems as challenges. The right way is always the best way. When someone is in a hurry and wants to cut corners, remind that person that while there may not be time to do the job the right way, there is certainly not enough time to do it the wrong way. Use judgment and common sense, and when the developers have defined the best way to do a job, insist that they do it that way.

The discipline of excellence is extremely difficult to maintain. This is why professional athletes have trainers and coaches and performing artists have directors and conductors. Doing difficult work in a superior way is not natural, and it can't be learned from a book or by casual observation. With almost any demanding task, human performance improves gradually. But it is never improved by "just trying harder." It takes training and informed practice, it requires data and feedback, and it takes time. Sustained improvement takes defined methods, precise measures, and professional guidance.

With a job as challenging as product development, the only way to consistently improve is with the informed guidance of a trained coach. This coach must have the knowledge to understand what the people are doing and how. This means that if your developers are to improve, they must use a defined process, and they must measure and track their work. Only then will you and the team coach have the data to support them.

Discipline also involves trust. On one hand, you must trust that the developers want to do good work, while on the other, you know that they are only human. If you were guiding an Olympic athlete, you would not doubt that athlete's dedication; dedication is a given. No athlete gets to the Olympics without dedication and personal commitment. In the software business, we often deal with world champions but we don't know it. These are extraordinarily capable people. It took them great effort and lots of time and money to get where they are. They are almost certainly committed to doing superior work, but they are also human. Therefore, they need guidance and support. Think of your role as providing the extra push that your people need to do truly excellent work.

A Sense of Urgency

In addition to the five basic properties of self-directed teams, you also need to impart the energy and enthusiasm required for superior work. As noted in Chapter 1, "The speed of the boss is the speed of the team" (Iacocca 1984, 186). If you are easygoing and not in much of a hurry, your team will relax and coast. If this is an important project, act as if it is important. Don't accept delays and excuses. "Schedules slip a day at a time" (Brooks 1995, 154). Energy and enthusiasm are contagious. Keep charging up the hill. Trust your people and they will follow.

The critical issue is your behavior. Do you really believe in the team's goals yourself, and are you working aggressively to meet them? Are you supporting and using the team, and are you challenging the developers to do their best? Product development is not easy, but you have capable people. Your job is to motivate them to do the best work they are capable of doing. It must be a top priority.

One team had been working for several months on designing a new hardware-software product, and when they took their plan to finance for initial pricing, they were told that at the prices they needed to make a profit, there was no market. The developers then went to Judy, their manager, and told her that she would have to cancel the project. Judy didn't accept their story. She told them that their job was to develop this product, and if finance didn't buy their first plan, they must figure out why and develop a better plan. After several months of hard work, the team did develop a plan that met the financial criteria, and the team produced a successful product.

Problems are normal in development work. That's what development is: solving problems. If the job had been done before, we would not be needed. So, when the developers are up against a stone wall and ready to quit, challenge them to surmount that wall, to get around it, or to find a better way. Don't get discouraged too quickly and, above all, don't let the team quit.

18.4   Coaching While Leading

In leading a TSP team, the principal challenge will be motivating your people to do a superior job. Since many of your interactions with the team members will concern how they are dong their jobs and how they could do them better, you will often find yourself acting more like a coach than a manager. This raises the question of how you coach people while leading them. The obvious answer would be to do both jobs at the same time. However, there are two reasons that this is not possible. First, you will not have the time to do everything that both a team leader and a coach must do. Second, as team leader, the team members will treat you as team leader and not as coach.

Team members see the team leader as a manager and the coach as an advisor and confidant. Even if you wanted to, you could not completely adopt the coaching style, at least not at first. However, if you begin to think and act like a coach, show concern for your peoples' interests, and ask about their personal goals, your people will begin to think of you as a coach. So how do you do all of this and still have time to lead the project? Answering this question involves your leadership tasks, your coaching tasks, and the overall coaching attitude.

Leadership Tasks

Although many factors contribute to a developer's behavior, the demands that you, the team leader, place on your people and the way that you guide and reward them will have more effect on their behavior than anyone else in the organization. As a leader, you must meet the team's commitments, build the team's capabilities, and keep management informed. You must also set the team's pace, establish and maintain high standards, and support and protect the team. To do all of this, you must delegate much of what has traditionally been a management responsibility.

The role managers can help you prepare for the weekly team and management meetings, review team members' data, and handle the team's control and support tasks. If the organization has support groups, they can also help. A quality assurance group could alert you to quality control problems or planning oversights, and a process group could analyze the team's data and provide process improvement guidance. To be a coach and a leader, you must have time to spend with your people. That means taking advantage of any individual or group that can help you to run the project.

Coaching Tasks

The principal coaching job is building talent. The coach cannot think about the team members in general terms; he or she must think of them as individuals. This requires spending time with each developer every week. For a reasonably sized team, this can take a substantial amount of time.

On my first project, I had eight developers designing a complex cryptographic communication system. Since I was new to the organization and had never worked on such a system, I had a lot to learn. I started by asking questions. I would chat with each developer every day to ask what he (in those days we didn't have women developers) was doing and why. I could immediately see when anyone had a technical issue, was held up by someone else's work, or had a personal problem. After a couple of weeks, I knew the developers' strengths, weaknesses, and interests. I now understood how to do my own job and I could also see where each team member needed help or support.

When you spend time with each developer every day, you will know who is having problems and will understand who is misassigned or could handle a greater challenge. As long as your team is not too large, these daily discussions need not take very long. However, they will give you the intimate knowledge needed to be an effective coach.

To help your people improve, build on each developer's skills. Focus on what that developer can now do and recognize that improvement will be gradual. Look for incremental improvements and applaud every achievement. Concentrate on motivation; it is the most powerful improvement tool you have.

Don't just focus your efforts on the newer developers or those who need help. Meet also with the experts and with the developers who work in disciplines you do not know. Ask these developers what they are doing and why. When they have problems, ask about alternatives and where they are looking for guidance. You can learn a lot from your best people, and you can also stimulate and motivate them by asking questions. They will learn more from answering your questions than you will learn from asking them. As long as you ask questions and are willing to learn, you will have no trouble coaching even the best developers.

The Coaching Attitude

The acid test of your coaching attitude is the way you handle promotions. Suppose your lead designer tells you that he or she would like to be a team leader. Then, when you hear of a team leader opening in another department, and assuming that you think he or she is a good candidate, do you recommend your lead designer? If not, you are acting like a team leader and not like a coach. While you may not want to lose this developer, if you do pursue the promotion, word will soon get around that you promote your best people. Then you will have no trouble getting more good people.

The key to being an effective coach is treating your people as more important than the job. While this may seem unrealistic, it is actually the only way you can earn your developers' allegiance. These are smart people, and they will quickly sense your interests and priorities. If your top priority is the job, they will know that they cannot trust you to look out for their interests. However, if you are truly concerned with their development, they will be less likely to worry about their careers and better able to concentrate their energies on the job. That is what produces superior work.

18.5 The Challenges Ahead

The trends in modern technology require that the leadership and coaching roles converge. The reason for this is connected with the trends in the work, and how these trends impact the nature of engineering work. Changes in engineering, in turn, impact the nature of the engineering workforce and the leadership role. Finally, these changes call for a people-centered leadership style, or more specifically, leaders who act much more like coaches.

Integrated Engineering

When the computer revolution started shortly after World War II, system development involved many technical and business disciplines. Projects needed circuit designers for the logic, hardware designers for packaging, architects to create the instruction set, and logic designers to produce the detailed system logic. Programmers then developed systems programs, maintenance people produced diagnostics, and manufacturing defined the tooling, assembly, and test procedures. Installation, application, and marketing people were also involved, as were human factors, materials, styling, advertising, and financial groups. System design involved many activities, and although these activities were all related, they could be treated as largely separate groups with limited interfaces and interdependencies.

Today, as improvement in individual disciplines approaches limits, developers must look across disciplines to find further opportunities. Think of system management as a multidimensional problem where each new technology adds a new dimension. Issues that seemed insoluble in one or two dimensions often seem trivial in three or four. For example, early integrated circuits had two-dimensional layouts. Improving performance by cutting lead length was often impossible. When technology allowed multilayered chips, however, many of these two-dimensional problems became trivial in three.

Similarly, eliminating a month from a design schedule is often out of the question. However, by considering design and manufacturing as one integrated activity, several months can often be saved through early tooling, phased design releases, and design for manufacturing. Similar savings are possible through interleaving almost any set of disciplines. When organizations don't see the potential for savings, it generally means that they are not thinking in multiple dimensions.

With growing competition and the wide availability of skilled development talent, there are increasing pressures for improved performance, lower costs, and shorter schedules. It is hard to find any aspect of development that can be treated as an island. Modern engineering is becoming integrated in almost every respect.

When we seek cost, schedule, performance, or quality improvements, integration is often the answer. We can expect more pressure for integration in the future.

Integrated Leadership

If you are like most team leaders, you have spent most of your career in a single discipline. While previously you viewed the world from one dimension, you must now see things in a broader context. You must look at the full product life cycle. For example, could the requirements and design work be interleaved? How about the systems, hardware, software, test, release, manufacturing, or service groups? Could any sets of involved disciplines be better related to improve overall performance?

To integrate multiple specialties, you must eliminate interfaces among the groups. However, without interfaces, communication through managers is slow and the bandwidth too narrow. There isn't time to pass information through intermediaries, and there is simply too much information to pass. Since you can no longer rely on the managers to relay instructions among the developers, the professionals must interact directly, and they must be empowered to solve problems without management intervention. The challenges of leading integrated project teams are several, and they require a workforce-centered view of leadership. These challenges include

- ☐ Leading in a multidimensional environment
- ☐ Developing multidimensional developers
- ☐ Delegation and involvement
- ☐ Building the workforce

Leading in a Multi-Dimensional Environment

When leading a team in a multidimensional environment, you are likely to manage several different disciplines, and you will almost certainly work closely with many more. Whether these disciplines are on the same team, on related teams, or in separate groups, you must orchestrate all of the work.

When you have team members from other disciplines, they are likely to be matrix-managed by you and their specialty managers. In a matrix structure, the developers are typically managed by a technical manager who understands the details of the discipline and can ensure that the professionals are properly trained and evaluated. These developers are then assigned to project teams on which the team leaders guide and manage the development work. As you use more complex and more integrated technologies, such matrix structures will become more common, and you will need to rely on the specialty managers for guidance in many of the disciplines.

Developing Multi-Dimensional Developers

In leading an integrated project, try to integrate the team as thoroughly as you plan to integrate the technologies. To get the loyalty and dedication of all of the developers, focus on goals and on involving the entire team in planning the work and running the team. Have everyone make personal plans, join in the team meetings, and participate in the strategy sessions. Unless the developers behave like an integrated and interdependent team, they are not likely to create an integrated and interdependent product.

Delegation and Involvement

When you lead work that involves more than your own specialty, you must start to act like an executive. Now you are managing work that you do not fully understand. Some people feel uncomfortable in this situation and try to become masters of these new fields. As technology accelerates and cross-discipline integration increases, however, this approach is impractical. What is more important, it misses the point. Developers should handle their own specialties. You need to focus on the quality and discipline of the work, the project goals, and the interfaces among the project's many specialties and technologies. The interfaces are important because no one else can manage them. Unless team leaders and program managers take care of the interfaces among the technologies, no one else can.

Building the Workforce

The modern development workforce must be more flexible, heterogeneous, and interdependent than ever before. Capable developers are in great demand, and this demand will likely continue for the foreseeable future. To manage your workforce assets, you must get capable people, build and properly apply their skills, and somehow manage to retain them. The more skilled your people, however, the more attractive they are to competitors, and the harder it will be to keep them. Turnover is a major problem in most development organizations and it must be one of your key concerns. Studies show that developers leave organizations not because they wanted to go but because they had been mistreated and started to look elsewhere (Shellenbarger 2000; McLean 1966).

Experience shows that when employers offer their developers competitive salaries and benefits, treat them with respect, and provide them substantial control over the way they do their jobs, they will be loyal. How you treat your people largely determines their loyalty, and employee loyalty largely determines turnover. As the team leader, you personify the organization to your people, and your treatment of them will be seen by them as the organization's treatment. This is why coaching and leading must merge. Leadership focuses on project goals while coaching focuses on people. To do your job effectively, you must be an effective leader but you must also think and act like a coach.

18.6 Summary

This chapter discusses the team leader's role and the key elements of effective leadership. Leadership is defined as the act of leading. Leading means going before, preceding, guiding the way. Leaders do not demand or force their people to follow; they make them want to follow. Leadership also involves discipline and the team leader's ability to get people to follow, even when this means that team members must do things they would not normally want to do. The team leader must embody the behavior that he or she wants the team members to emulate. The TSP launch process can help to develop such leaders.

When you lead a team that you manage, you will rarely have problems getting the people to do what you want. However, you will often have problems getting your people to take the initiative and to do what they think is right. This takes transformational leadership. The TSP launch process builds the conditions for transformational leadership, and it will even be effective for teams where the members do not all work for you. By the end of the launch, the developers will have made a start on becoming an energetic and cohesive team. Your challenge is maintaining and building on this energy and enthusiasm.

To be a transformational leader, you must establish five conditions: a sense of membership and belonging, commitment to a common team goal, ownership of the process and plan, the skill to make a plan coupled with the discipline to follow it, and a dedication to excellence. The TSP launch process provides a start on establishing these conditions, but you must continue that process. This chapter provides guidance and suggestions on how to do this.

Your responsibilities to the team are to set the pace, establish and maintain high standards, maintain process discipline, and support the team. Energy and enthusiasm are contagious, and discipline is extremely difficult to maintain. To be effective, you must believe in your team and drive the members to do excellent work. The best leaders get more from their teams than their people thought was possible. The key is to trust and believe in the team and to keep motivating the members to strive until they win.

You must also learn to act more like a coach. Consistently doing disciplined intellectual work is difficult and it can't be done by unmotivated people. By acting like a coach and by working with each member as an individual, you can provide the kind of coaching guidance and support required for superior work.

This chapter concludes with a discussion of the changing nature of professional work and the demands this places on team leaders. Today, there are increasing pressures for improved performance, lower costs, and shorter schedules. Integration is often the answer to these pressures, and we can expect more pressure for integration in the future. But integrated engineering requires integrated leadership and an increasingly diverse workforce.

The integrated leadership strategy concentrates on the quality and discipline of the work, the project goals, and the interfaces among the specialists and technologies. Finally, it focuses on building the workforce. To do this, you must get capable people, build their skills, and give them control over their own work. You personify the organization to the team, and your behavior will directly impact their loyalty to the organization and to the team. To get the best work from the team, you must be an effective leader while thinking and acting more like a coach.

References

Brooks, Frederick P., Jr. *The Mythical Man-Month.* Reading, MA: Addison-Wesley. 1995.

Brown, Arnold, and Edith Weiner. *Supermanaging.* New York: Harper & Row. 1981, p. 182.

Humphrey, Watts S. *Managing Technical People.* Reading, MA: Addison-Wesley. 1997.

Iacocca, Lee, and William Nova. *Iacocca: An Autobiography.* New York: Bantam Books. 1984.

McLean, E. R., S. J. Smits, and J. R. Tanner. The importance of salary on job and career attitudes of information systems professionals. *Information & Management.* Vol. 30, No. 6, 1966. Elsevier Publishing, pp. 291–299.

Raudsepp, Eugene. Teamwork: Silent Partner in the Design Group. *IEEE Engineering Management Review.* Vol. 9, no. 4, 1981, p. 94.

Shellenbarger, Sue. To win the loyalty of your employees, try a softer touch. *The Wall Street Journal.* January 26, 2000, p. B1.

A

Team Roles

This appendix describes the TSP team-member roles, and it provides the background you need to take advantage of these roles in guiding and leading your team. It describes why roles are needed and the standard TSP roles. It also suggests ways to help the role managers handle their role responsibilities.

A.1 What Roles Are

A role is defined as "the rights, obligations, and expected behavior patterns associated with a particular social status" (Random 1983). All the elements of this definition are important. By holding a team role, the developers have certain rights and they are active participants in managing the project. They do not just do what they are told—they develop their own plans, manage and track quality, and lead the design work. The TSP roles cover all aspects of team management, from customer interface issues to testing, and from process management to quality control. Thus, TSP team members own their processes and plans, decide how they will work, and control how their project is run.

The role managers are responsible for carrying out their roles, and they are expected to act accordingly. They are active and thinking team members. When they see a problem, they get it fixed. When they anticipate problems, they address them, either personally or by alerting the team member with the appropriate role responsibility. This is the most important aspect of the TSP roles: team members feel responsible for the success of the team and they take that responsibility seriously.

Finally, the ownership of a TSP role confers status. When team members have role responsibilities, they know that those responsibilities are theirs and that no one will object or interfere when they handle them. This gives them the authority to speak out on role-related issues. Nobody will ask why they are concerned; it is their responsibility. They are expected to be involved, even if it means taking the issue to senior management or to the customer. While they must keep their team and team leader informed, they are expected to be proactive.

A.2   Why Roles Are Needed

While we don't question the reasons for athletic teams to have playing positions, it is not as obvious why development team members need roles. Roles provide a defined and accepted working framework. With roles, members can specialize and focus on specific objectives. Roles help to divide the work, and they allow team members to concentrate on specific aspects of that work. With roles, each member can handle a specific subset of the overall job and no one else needs to worry about doing it. To be fully effective, however, each team member must not only know his or her personal role but also must be generally familiar with all of the other roles.

It would be hard to imagine a baseball, basketball, hockey, rugby, or cricket team where the positions had not been defined and the players assigned to positions before the play began. Similarly, with the TSP, the standard roles divide the principal team responsibilities among all of the members. They identify the team member who covers each key area, and they ensure that the normal issues of running a team are handled expeditiously and effectively. Roles fill human needs, they accelerate teambuilding, and they help to handle necessary team tasks.

To Fill a Human Need

Humans are social animals. We need the association of others, both in our work and in our personal lives. People need membership in groups; this satisfies the basic human need to belong and to be accepted. By agreeing that a group member can have a defined role, the group signifies its acceptance of that member and demonstrates its confidence that he or she will handle the assigned role responsibilities. Finally, and most important, when the team members handle team roles, they are part of team management and feel powerful and important.

To Accelerate Teambuilding

The TSP roles accelerate teambuilding. They do this by allocating responsibilities and by giving the team members specific tasks. This helps to overcome the negative and defeatist character of the traditional storming phase, when the members struggle to establish their personal positions in the team's informal hierarchy. As noted before, the first sign that a team is starting to coalesce as a productive unit is when the members start resolving issues rather than merely complaining about them. The TSP roles help to focus the team on addressing its problems and establishing the plans and actions needed to accomplish the assigned mission.

To Handle Necessary Team Tasks

For teams to operate smoothly and efficiently, the members must handle a wide range of tasks. If your team members did not have assigned roles, these role tasks either would not get handled, or you, as the team leader, would have to handle them. This would have three unfortunate consequences. First, because there are many tasks involved, you would not have the time to handle them all. Therefore, many of these tasks would not get done or would not be done as well and as expeditiously as they should be. Second, if you were fully occupied trying to handle the various role responsibilities, you would not have time for the true leadership tasks of motivating the team, monitoring the process, resolving issues, and managing the team's external relationships. Third, since the members would consider you responsible for all the roles, they might not feel comfortable telling you about role-related problems. As a result, many such issues could be left to fester.

When the team members do not have assigned roles, many important team-management tasks are not addressed, at least not until they became crises. Plans become out of date, project status is not tracked, and the team's standards and procedures are not defined or followed. If you are distracted by all of the team's operational details, you will not have the time to be an effective leader. Then team performance will almost certainly suffer.

A.3   Assigning Role Responsibilities

During the TSP launch, the team members select their own roles. However, since the standard TSP roles provide only a general definition of what each role manager is supposed to do, most team members need further guidance. The most effective way to provide this guidance is for you to discuss the roles with the team members and to make sure that they each know what you expect from them. As team leader, you should follow a basic principle in assigning tasks to the role managers: if you can define a role or a task, delegate it. Thus, your first reaction to a problem or an issue should be to define it as a task for the team or some team member to handle. If you can't do that, it is your job. Your job as team leader is to guide and support the team in performing its defined tasks. To have the time to be an effective leader, you must not do any job that you could assign to a team member.

In delegating tasks to team members, don't flatter yourself by thinking that you are the only person who can handle them. There was a time when you were new and didn't know how to handle many of the tasks you were assigned. Give your new people a chance to learn—they can do a lot more than you or they think they can. So delegate, and if you are worried that the task might not be done properly, periodically check to see if the developers need help. But let them do it—that is the only way they will learn.

When teams are newly formed and the members have not used the TSP before, they will not know how to handle the role assignments. Then they will wait until you tell them what to do. Work with each role manager to define the responsibilities of that role and the specific tasks to be done. Think about the team's risks and issues and consider the problems that lie ahead. The role manager's job is to anticipate problems and to ensure that they are addressed before they impact team performance. You must hold them to that responsibility.

If you can't think of anything for a role manager to do, don't invent useless tasks. However, keep thinking of possible jobs that must be done. To get the most benefit from the team roles, challenge the team members with useful and important role tasks.

A.4   The TSP Team-Member Roles

The TSP process defines eight standard team-member roles. These are

- ☐ Customer interface manager
- ☐ Design manager

☐ Implementation manager

☐ Test manager

☐ Planning manager

☐ Process manager

☐ Quality manager

☐ Support manager

These roles cover much of the management work that must be done by the team. The objective of the roles, however, is not to do everything implied by each role, but rather to provide a team focus and leadership for that activity. By providing consistent attention to the roles, the role managers can ensure that all of the relevant issues and concerns are identified and handled in a timely way.

A.5   Other Team-Member Roles

In addition to the roles defined by the TSP, many others are possible. Examples of additional roles are the following.

☐ COTS (commercial off-the-shelf) manager (design, implementation, or test manager)

☐ Installation manager (customer interface, support, or test manager)

☐ Hardware interface manager (design, implementation, or test manager)

☐ Performance manager (design, implementation, or test manager)

☐ Privacy manager (customer interface, design, implementation, or quality manager)

☐ Safety manager (design, implementation, test, or quality manager)

☐ Security manager (customer interface, design, implementation, or quality manager)

☐ Subcontract manager (planning, design, implementation, or test manager)

During the launch process, the team should think about the special issues of the project and identify any additional roles that might require special attention. When any of these additional roles are assigned, make sure that the selected role managers define their role responsibilities and review these responsibilities with the entire team for agreement. Often, when some additional responsibility is identified, it could logically be added to an existing role. Suggestions for doing this are shown by the roles in parentheses in the preceding list. However, in making the choice about adding responsibilities to an existing role, be sure to consider what else that role manager has to do.

A.6   Selecting Team Roles

Team members must be involved in selecting their own roles and they must agree with the selections. While you may influence the role-selection process and you certainly can lobby for particular developers to fill certain roles, it is important that you do this subtly and that you not assign the roles to the team members. Generally, the developers will know the roles for which they are best suited and you and the TSP coach need not do more than facilitate the role selection process.

You will depend on the planning, process, quality, and support managers for process fidelity and on the customer interface, design, implementation, support, and test managers for product management. The implementation and test managers must also ensure that the team is properly prepared for the implementation and test phases. Therefore, all of the team roles must be handled efficiently and effectively or the team will almost certainly have problems. That is why you must ensure that all of the team members are assigned roles that you believe they can handle effectively.

Role selection is relatively straightforward when there are eight or more team members. Then one member can take each role and the leftover members can act as alternate role managers. You could also add one or two additional roles if that seemed appropriate. For smaller teams, however, role selection will be easier if you follow these general guidelines.

☐ The planning manager role generally takes the most work and should be assigned as the only role for one team member.

☐ The quality manager role can also take a substantial amount of work, but only if the role manager understands what is needed and is willing to take the time to do the job properly. During detailed design, implementation, and test, this should be a single role assignment for a team member.

☐ Depending on the status of the project, it might be possible to assign some or all of the customer interface, design, implementation, and test manager responsibilities to a single team member. However, in the early requirements phase, you will almost certainly need a separate customer interface manager, and in the final test phases you will probably need a separate test manager.

☐ The support and process manager roles can often be combined and handled by a single team member.

The key to selecting the roles for small teams is to be clear on what you want the role managers to do. The later section on role manager responsibilities suggests some of the topics you could ask the role managers to address.

A.7   Coaching the Role Managers

Some of the TSP roles have relatively obvious responsibilities while others are not so clear. Make sure that the developers know that their job is to think broadly about their role responsibilities and to act as if they were running the project in all aspects that relate to that role. If you hold the team members responsible for their role tasks and consistently ask them to handle all role-related issues, pretty soon they will begin to behave like role owners.

One of your principal jobs as team leader is to help the team members understand their responsibilities as role managers. In a nutshell, the role job involves acting as the team's conscience in the particular area involved. Without consistent coaching and periodic review, however, the role managers will often let their role responsibilities slide. Ask about their role responsibilities whenever you talk to a team member and review the role activities in the weekly team meetings. Think about the issues that the role managers should be handling and ask about them. Also, encourage all of the team members to raise issues that the role managers should address.

One way to think about the roles is as an extension of the team leader's job. Thus, think about what you want done and then ask the role managers to handle it for you. Once you have decided what you want each role manager to do, discuss these tasks with each team member and make sure that he or she understands what you want. Then check periodically to make sure that these tasks are being done.

When a team member takes a role assignment, he or she makes a commitment to you and to the team to handle the issues covered by that role. This means that they will have to allocate some of their time to handling the role responsibilities. However, the amount of time need not be excessive, particularly if the organization has process, support, quality, and testing groups. The role managers should make a practice of asking the software engineering process group (SEPG), quality assurance, test, and any other support groups to handle many of the role tasks for them. While this can reduce the role managers' workloads, the role managers should still monitor these role-related tasks to ensure that they are being properly handled.

A.8   Role Manager Responsibilities

The following sections provide examples of the kinds of responsibilities the role managers can handle for you and the team.

Customer Interface Manager Responsibilities

The customer interface manager is responsible for the team's relationships with its customers. Since every group to which the team provides work products could be considered a customer, it is important to be precise in defining the particular customers you want the customer interface manager to handle. The most common definition is the end user for the products the team is developing together with any groups that represent or speak for that user community. This could, for example, include systems groups, requirements groups, the marketing people, contract negotiators, or actual end users. The TSP role manager specification for the customer interface manager is given in Table A.1.

Table A.1 TSP Customer Interface Manager Roles and Responsibilities

Objective	When all team members consistently meet their role responsibilities, follow the defined process, and work to agreed goals and specifications, the team will be most efficient and effective.
Goals	The customer interface manager's goals are to • understand the customer's wants and needs • lead the team in providing a product that delights the customer
Role Characteristics	The characteristics most helpful to the customer interface manager are: 1. You like working with people. 2. You understand people's needs and can empathize with their concerns. 3. You can describe technical problems in nontechnical terms. 4. You are interested in defining and building a superior product.
Team Member Responsibilities	All team members are responsible for meeting their responsibilities as team members (see Team Member Roles and Responsibilities). • meeting their team member commitments • following a disciplined personal process • planning, managing, and reporting on their personal work • cooperating with the team and all team members to maintain an effective and productive working environment

Table A.1 (continued)

Customer Focus	As customer interface manager, you will lead the team's interactions with the customer. • maintain a focus on the customer's needs throughout the project • ensure that the customer agrees with the product requirements • where needed, define prototypes to help the customer understand proposed product features • guide the team in establishing customer training and documentation plans • work with the customer to establish acceptance test criteria and plans • document the agreed acceptance test criteria and plans and ensure that the customer reviews and agrees with them
Define Requirements	As customer interface manager, one of your principal responsibilities is to lead the development and evolution of the product requirements. • identify and define requirements issues and manage their resolution • document and confirm requirements issue resolution • lead the team in producing, refining, and verifying the product requirements • lead the team in specifying, testing, analyzing, and resolving product usability issues • ensure that all the requirements assumptions are identified, documented, and verified • ensure that installation issues are addressed by the team in a timely way
Manage Requirements Changes	The customer interface manager also • manages the requirements change process • leads the team in estimating and documenting the impact of every requirements change • ensures that the configuration control board is provided with complete and timely data for requirements change decisions
Establish and Manage Requirements Standards	As customer interface manager, you also establish team standards and procedures for documenting and reviewing the product requirements.
Reporting	The customer interface manager tracks and reports weekly to the team on the status of the requirements standards and requirements development.

One way to clarify the customer interface manager's responsibilities is to consider some of the questions you might want to ask. The following are some possible examples.

☐ Are we being responsive to customer requests?

☐ Are we handling customer requests properly?

☐ Is every requested change being evaluated, planned, and approved before being implemented?

☐ Is the interface between the developers, the requirements, and the systems people working properly? If not, what should be done to improve this interface?

☐ Is development being delayed by the requirements work?

☐ Is the quality of the requirements sufficient to guide the development work?

☐ Are the right people reviewing and approving the requirements?

☐ Do all team members understand the environment in which the system will be used?

☐ Are there any other customer-related issues that the team should be aware of?

Design Manager Responsibilities

The design manager is responsible for the quality of the team's design work. He or she should track the design work and ensure that all appropriate design standards are being met and that the designs are properly recorded. The design manager may be able to get help from other team members, but it is generally not practical for this role to get assistance from outside the team. The TSP design manager role specification is given in Table A.2.

Table A.2 TSP Design Manager Roles and Responsibilities

Objective	When all team members consistently meet their role responsibilities, follow the defined process, and work to agreed goals and specifications, the team will be most efficient and effective.
Goals	The design manager's goals are to • lead the team in producing a superior design • fully utilize all the team's skills and ideas in producing this design • ensure that the design and its documentation are of high quality

Table A.2 (continued)

Role Characteristics	The characteristics most helpful to the design manager are 1. You like to design and build things. 2. You are generally familiar with design methods. 3. You are most interested in producing a superior design, even if it is not the one you originally thought of. 4. You can objectively compare other people's designs with your own.
Team Member Responsibilities	All team members are responsible for meeting their responsibilities as team members (see Team Member Roles and Responsibilities). • meeting their team member commitments • following a disciplined personal process • planning, managing, and reporting on their personal work • cooperating with the team and all team members to maintain an effective and productive working environment
Lead the Design	As design manager, you • maintain a focus on design issues throughout the project • identify and resolve all design issues • document and confirm design issue resolution • provide the team focus for anticipating and addressing product performance and size issues • lead the team in producing, refining, and verifying the product design • using analyses, prototypes, or experiments as appropriate, ensure that all the design issues and assumptions are identified, documented, and resolved
Manage Design Changes	As design manager you • manage the design change process • for product elements under configuration control, lead the team in estimating and documenting the design impact of every change • for product elements under configuration control, ensure that the configuration control board is provided with complete and timely data to make design change decisions
Establish and Manage Design Standards	As design manager, you also establish the standards and procedures the team will use to produce the design materials.
Reporting	The design manager reports weekly to the team on the status of design standards and product design work.

Some sample questions you might ask the design manager are the following.

☐ Are all of the team's design methods and notations capable of producing a quality design?

☐ Do all team members understand how to use these design methods?

☐ If some team members are not fluent with the design methods, what remedial action do you recommend?

☐ Is the team's design work of high quality?

☐ Has a sound system architecture been produced and documented?

☐ Is the architecture properly controlled and maintained?

☐ Does the architecture consider future product evolution?

☐ Does the design conform to the architecture?

☐ Is the design properly documented and maintained?

☐ Are the interfaces and other design dependencies properly identified and managed?

☐ Are there any other design issues that the team should be aware of?

Implementation Manager Responsibilities

The implementation manager is responsible for the overall quality of the team's implementation work. For example, he or she should be concerned with the adequacy of the design being produced during the design phase. The implementation manager is also responsible for any required implementation standards as well as the degree to which these standards are followed.

For example, the implementation manager should ensure that the coding and commenting standards are proper and that they are being followed. You should also clarify whether the implementation or test manager is verifying the adequacy of the unit test plans and the completeness of unit testing. The TSP implementation manager role specification is given in Table A.3.

Table A.3 TSP Implementation Manager Roles and Responsibilities

Objective	When all team members consistently meet their role responsibilities, follow the defined process, and work to agreed goals and specifications, the team will be most efficient and effective.
Goals	The implementation manager's goals are to • lead the team in producing a superior implementation • ensure the implementation fully conforms to the design • produce an implemented product that is of high quality

Table A.3 (continued)

Role Characteristics	The characteristics most helpful to the implementation manager are: 1. You like to build things. 2. You understand the implementation tools and environment. 3. You are most interested in producing a high-quality product.
Team Member Responsibilities	All team members are responsible for meeting their responsibilities as team members (see Team Member Roles and Responsibilities). • meeting their team member commitments • following a disciplined personal process • planning, managing, and reporting on their personal work • cooperating with the team and all team members to maintain an effective and productive working environment
Lead the Implementation	The implementation manager • maintains a focus on implementation issues throughout the project • identifies and resolves all implementation issues • documents and confirms implementation issue resolution • leads the team in planning for and handling product packaging, distribution, and installation problems • leads the team in producing, refining, and verifying the product implementation • leads the team in measuring and identifying any performance and size issues • using prototypes or experiments as appropriate, ensures that all the implementation issues and assumptions are identified, documented, and resolved
Manage Implementation Changes	As implementation manager, you • manage the implementation change process • for product elements under configuration control, lead the team in estimating and documenting the implementation impact of every change • for product elements under configuration control, ensure that the configuration control board is provided with complete and timely data to make implementation change decisions
Establish and Manage the Implementation Standards	The implementation manager establishes the standards and procedures the team will use to produce the product implementation and its documentation. • ensures that the team has standards for coding, LOC counting, language, and documentation
Reporting	The implementation manager reports to the team weekly on the status of implementation standards and product implementation. • These reports include the plan and actual LOC coded, reviewed, compiled, inspected and repaired, unit tested, and released to integration.

Some sample questions you might ask the implementation manager are the following.

☐ Are all of the team members fluent in the languages being used?

☐ If any team members are not fluent in these languages, what remedial actions do you recommend?

☐ Have the proper implementation standards been developed and adopted?

☐ Are the implementation standards being used consistently?

☐ Are the team members taking advantage of shared and/or reused code where they could? If not, what improvement actions do you recommend?

☐ Are there any other implementation issues that the team should be aware of?

Test Manager Responsibilities

The test manager is responsible for the quality of all the testing and test-related work for the project. This includes testing standards, test plans, test procedures, and the degree to which the testing work is done in accordance with the team's and organization's plans and standards. The TSP test manager role specification is given in Table A.4.

Some sample questions you might ask the test manager are the following.

☐ Are test plans being produced when the process requires them?

☐ Are these test plans complete and thorough?

☐ Do the developers understand how to produce suitable test plans? If not, what remedial actions do you recommend?

☐ Are the system test plans being reviewed when the requirements are reviewed, the integration plans when with the design is reviewed, and the unit test plans when the implementation is reviewed?

☐ Are sufficient test facilities planned for integration and system testing?

☐ Are the needed test tools available?

☐ Do the developers know how to use the test tools? If not, what remedial actions do you recommend?

☐ Are there any other test issues that the team should be aware of?

Table A.4 TSP Test Manager Roles and Responsibilities

Objective	When all team members consistently meet their role responsibilities, follow the defined process, and work to agreed goals and specifications, the team will be most efficient and effective.
Goals	The test manager's goals are to • lead the team in developing comprehensive test plans • ensure that the system is thoroughly tested and properly performs all important functions
Role Characteristics	The characteristics most helpful to the test manager are 1. You like to understand and take things apart. 2. You are intrigued by puzzles. 3. You like the competitive challenge of testing products to find their defects.
Team Member Responsibilities	All team members are responsible for meeting their responsibilities as team members (see Team Member Roles and Responsibilities). • meeting their team member commitments • following a disciplined personal process • planning, managing, and reporting on their personal work • cooperating with the team and all team members to maintain an effective and productive working environment
Test Planning	The test manager supports the customer interface manager in getting acceptance test criteria defined and agreed to by the customer during the requirements phase. The test manager also leads the team in • maintaining a focus on testing throughout the entire development process • defining and planning the system tests during the design phase • defining and planning the integration tests during the implementation phase
Test Support	The test manager supports the team members with • planning and executing all test activities • establishing unit test standards • reporting and reviewing all integration and system test defects (see script TESTD and form DEFECT)
Test Analysis	The test manager • analyzes data from every test phase to identify defect-prone product elements • maintains a defect density map of all product components and the overall system for every test phase • works with the quality manager to find areas that need reinspection or retest
Reporting	The test manager tracks and reports weekly to the team on the status of the team's test planning, development, and execution work.

Planning Manager Responsibilities

The planning manager is responsible for maintaining the team's plans, reporting on plan status, and supporting the team with any plan-related issues. The TSP planning manager role specification is shown in Table A.5.

Table A.5 TSP Planning Manager Roles and Responsibilities

Objective	When all team members consistently meet their role responsibilities, follow the defined process, and work to agreed goals and specifications, the team will be most efficient and effective.
Goals	The planning manager's goals are to • help the team run a well-planned and tracked project • help the team members with their personal planning and progress tracking • regularly track and report the team's status against plan
Role Characteristics	The characteristics most helpful to planning managers are the following. 1. You have a logical mind and feel most comfortable when following a plan while doing your work. 2. While you may not always be able to produce a plan, you tend to plan your work when given the opportunity. 3. You are interested in process data and are willing to press people to track and measure their work.
Team Member Responsibilities	All team members are responsible for meeting their responsibilities as team members (see Team Member Roles and Responsibilities). • meeting their team member commitments • following a disciplined personal process • planning, managing, and reporting on their personal work • cooperating with the team and all team members to maintain an effective and productive working environment
Lead the Team's Planning	The planning manager • ensures that the team is always working to a defined and documented plan • assists the developers in generating their personal and team estimates and plans • ensures that plans are revised at every team launch and relaunch or whenever the project schedule or resources change substantially • helps the team maintain a balanced plan at all times

Table A.5 (continued)

Track Team Progress	The planning manager • tracks team progress against the plan and reports to the team weekly on project status • supports the team leader in tracking project issues and risks • maintains an updated copy of SUMP for the system and each of its parts • keeps the team TASK and SCHEDULE templates updated and ensures that each developer updates a personal TASK and SCHEDULE template
Reporting	In addition, the planning manager • ensures that team members report data on their progress in time for the weekly team meeting • produces a composite report of team status against plan and distributes it at or before the weekly team meeting • based on the rate of schedule and resource progress, keeps the team and management informed of likely phase and project completion dates • supports the Team Leader in producing weekly management and customer status reports • maintains the data to produce the schedule, resource, size, and productivity sections of the project report during the phase and project postmortems (see SUMMARY specification and PM script)

Some example questions you might ask the planning manager are the following.

☐ Is each developer's plan sufficiently detailed?

☐ Do these plans accurately represent the work that the developers are currently doing?

☐ If any of the developers' plans do not represent their current work, what actions do you recommend?

☐ Is the team's workload reasonably well balanced? If not, what actions do you recommend?

☐ Is the workload with any cooperating groups reasonably well balanced? If not, what actions do you recommend?

☐ Are dependencies within the team and with other related groups known and tracked?

☐ Are there any other planning issues that the team should be aware of?

Process Manager Responsibilities

The process manager is responsible for ensuring that the team's processes and procedures are properly defined, that they are used as defined, and that team members who have problems or suggestions submit process improvement proposals (PIPs) on their suggestions. The process manager is also responsible for handling the PIPs. The TSP process manager role specification is given in Table A.6. Some sample questions to ask the process manager are the following.

- ☐ Does the team have defined processes for its principal activities? If not, what processes do you recommend be defined, and by whom?
- ☐ Do these processes reasonably represent the way that the work is currently being done? If not, are PIPs being submitted to correct the processes?
- ☐ Are the developers following the processes that they have?
- ☐ Is management providing the support needed to get the defined processes followed? If not, what remedial actions do you recommend?
- ☐ Do you have a defined process for handling the team's PIPs? If not, what steps are planned to define such a process?
- ☐ Are the developers submitting PIPs for the process problems they encounter? If not, what actions do you recommend?
- ☐ Is the team's project notebook complete and up to date?
- ☐ Are there any other process issues the team should be aware of?

Table A.6 TSP Process Manager Roles and Responsibilities

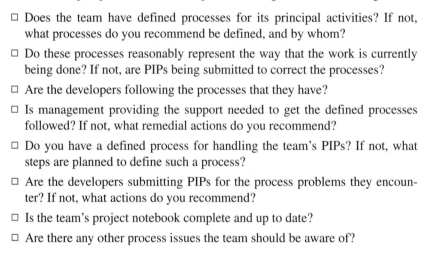

Objective	When all team members consistently meet their role responsibilities, follow the defined process, and work to agreed goals and specifications, the team will be most efficient and effective.
Goals	The process manager's goals are to • ensure that the team has defined processes available for all key activities • assist team members in defining and using processes • ensure that team process data are promptly reported and analyzed • assist the team in identifying and resolving process problems
Role Characteristics	The characteristics most helpful to the process manager are 1. You are interested in processes and process measurements. 2. You know how to define, use, measure, and analyze processes.

Table A.6 (continued)

Team Member Responsibilities	All team members are responsible for meeting their responsibilities as team members (see Team Member Roles and Responsibilities). • meeting their team member commitments • following a disciplined personal process • planning, managing, and reporting on their personal work • cooperating with the team and all team members to maintain an effective and productive working environment
Process Support	The process manager • ensures that defined processes are available for the major development, management, and team activities • leads the team in developing the processes the team needs • ensures that team members are familiar with each defined process and, where necessary, are trained in its use • ensures that the team always follows a defined and documented process
Process Tracking	The process manager is responsible for ensuring that • all team members report their process data in a timely way • where members are late providing their process data, promptly gets their data or calls on the team leader for help • the project notebook is complete and up to date
Process Analysis	The process manager • analyzes the team's process data • identifies where the team or any team member has problems following the defined process • assists that team member's improvement efforts
Process Problems	Where there are process problems, the process manager • alerts the team • suggests actions to resolve the problems • provides needed assistance in resolving the problems
PIP Handling	The process manager manages the elicitation, gathering, recording, tracking, and handling of the team's PIPs.
Reporting	The process manager • reports weekly to the team on the status of all team process development and analysis work • alerts the team and team leader when process problems need their attention • maintains the data to produce the process section of the project report during the phase and project postmortems (see SUMMARY specification and PM script)

Quality Manager Responsibilities

The quality manager is responsible for ensuring that the team members are recording their data, examining these data, and helping the developers properly follow the process. While the team leader can help in analyzing the team's data and in motivating developers to follow the process, the review of individual developer's data should generally be left to the quality manager or to the team coach. The quality manager should review all of the team's quality data on a weekly basis and alert the team and team leader to any work that is not of high quality. The quality manager role specification is given in Table A.7.

Table A.7 TSP Quality Manager Roles and Responsibilities

Objective	When all team members consistently meet their role responsibilities, follow the defined process, and work to agreed goals and specifications, the team will be most efficient and effective.
Goals	The quality manager's goals are to • lead the team in producing and following a quality plan • provide timely analysis and warning of quality problems • perform effectively as the team's inspection moderator
Role Characteristics	The characteristics most helpful to quality managers are the following: 1. You are concerned about software quality. 2. You know how to measure, analyze, and improve software quality. 3. You have some experience with or awareness of inspection methods. 4. You are willing and able to constructively review and comment on other people's work without antagonizing them.
Team Member Responsibilities	All team members are responsible for meeting their responsibilities as team members (see Team Member Roles and Responsibilities). • meeting their team member commitments • following a disciplined personal process • planning, managing, and reporting on their personal work • cooperating with the team and all team members to maintain an effective and productive working environment
Quality Support	The quality manager • maintains a focus on product and process quality throughout the project • leads the team in developing and following the quality plan
Inspection Support	The quality manager • ensures that a qualified moderator is available to lead team inspections or acts as inspection moderator

Table A.7 (continued)

Quality Tracking	The quality manager • regularly tracks product and process quality measures • where members are late providing their quality data, promptly gets their data or calls on the team leader for help
Quality Analysis	The quality manager regularly • updates a SUMQ form for the system and one for each of its parts • analyzes team quality data • ensures that these analyses are available for team reference • alerts the team whenever the defined process is not being followed • recommends how to correct the problems • alerts the team and management whenever quality problems require special attention The quality manager determines when and where there are quality problems and recommends corrective actions, such as • selective reinspection • component rework • in severe cases, scrap and redevelop
Reporting	The quality manager • reports weekly to the team on quality measures and product quality status • maintains the data to produce the defect, yield, ratio, rate, and component sections of the project report during the phase and project postmortems (see SUMMARY specification and PM script)

Some sample questions to ask the quality manager are the following.

☐ Are the developers recording their data properly?

☐ Do they record the data as they do the work?

☐ Are the data complete and of sufficient quality to permit analysis? If not, what remedial actions do you recommend?

☐ Are the developers using their data to assess the quality of their work?

☐ Do the developers' data indicate that the work is of high quality? If not, what remedial actions do you recommend?

☐ Are the developers holding team inspections of the requirements, design, and implementation products and are these inspections being done properly?

☐ Are the developers conducting personal design and code reviews and are these reviews being done properly?

☐ Is component and/or module quality being reviewed before integration and system test?

☐ Does the quality of all the components and modules meet the team's quality guidelines before integration and system test? If not, what is being done to fix the quality problems?

☐ Do you need further support from management or the team leader in assuring quality work?

☐ Are there any other quality issues that the team should be aware of?

Support Manager Responsibilities

The support manager's job is to ensure that every team member has the proper tools and support and knows how to use these tools correctly. The support manager also makes advance plans for the development environment and establishes and administers the team's configuration management system. The TSP support manager role specification is given in Table A.8.

Table A.8 TSP Support Manager Roles and Responsibilities

Objective	When all team members consistently meet their role responsibilities, follow the defined process, and work to agreed goals and specifications, the team will be most efficient and effective.
Goals	The support manager's goals are to • help the team use proper tools and methods • handle the team's configuration management and change control functions • act as the team's reuse advocate
Role Characteristics	The characteristics most helpful to support managers are the following: 1. You are interested in and like to use software support tools. 2. You are a competent computer user and feel you could assist the team with their support needs. 3. You have some experience with support tools and systems. 4. You are generally familiar with the tools that will likely be used with the current project.
Team Member Responsibilities	All team members are responsible for meeting their responsibilities as team members (see Team Member Roles and Responsibilities). • meeting their team member commitments • following a disciplined personal process • planning, managing, and reporting on their personal work • cooperating with the team and all team members to maintain an effective and productive working environment

Table A.8 (continued)

Tool Support	The principal role of the support manager is to • ensure that the team has an appropriate development support system • track the performance and effectiveness of the support system • maintain awareness of support system developments both in this and other groups • recommend to management and the team whenever support system changes or enhancements are needed to improve team performance • lead the team in developing or obtaining special support tools or facilities • ensure that the team members are familiar with support tools and, where necessary, trained in their use
Configuration Management	The support manager obtains and manages the team's configuration management system. • maintains a protected master copy of all controlled items • only makes approved changes to this controlled version • maintains master copies of all controlled items and versions
Change Control	The support manager leads the configuration control board. • reviews all changes to controlled products • evaluates each change for impact and benefit • recommends to the team which changes to make
Reuse	The support manager acts as the team's reuse advocate. • maintains a listing of potentially reusable parts • alerts the team to reuse opportunities
Reporting	The support manager also tracks and reports weekly to the team on • the status of all support procurement and development work • reuse status and opportunities

Some sample questions you might ask the support manager are the following.

☐ Does the team have suitable tools to support its work? If not, what additional tools do you recommend?

☐ Are all team members fluent with the available development tools?

☐ If any team members are not fluent with these tools, what remedial actions do you recommend?

☐ Does the team have adequate tool support for the configuration management process? If not, what actions do you recommend?

☐ Is the change control board working effectively?

☐ Are all changes to baselined products being managed through the configuration control system?

☐ Have all products that should be baselined been baselined?

☐ Are there any other support issues that the team should be aware of?

A.9 Summary

This chapter discusses why TSP roles are needed, the role-selection process, and suggestions for coaching and guiding the TSP role managers. The TSP roles cover all aspects of team management from customer interface issues to testing and from process management to quality control. TSP team members own their processes and plans, decide how they will work, and control how their project is run. Roles help to accelerate teambuilding and to handle necessary team tasks.

The TSP process defines the eight standard roles of customer interface manager, design manager, implementation manager, test manager, planning manager, process manager, quality manager, and support manager. The objective of each role is to provide the team focus for that activity. In addition to the standard TSP roles, other roles are possible. Examples are installation manager, hardware interface manager, performance manager, privacy manager, safety manager, security manager, and subcontract manager. The team members must be involved in selecting their own roles, and they must agree with the role selections. Generally, the team members will know the roles for which they are best suited, and the team leader and coach need not do more than facilitate the role selection process.

In defining team-member roles, the TSP follows the basic principle that if you can define a role or task, then you should delegate it. Your job is to handle all of the project unknowns. One way to think about roles is as an extension of your job. Think about what you want done and then ask the role managers to handle it. Once you have decided what each role manager should do, discuss it with the role managers to make sure they understand their responsibilities. Then check periodically to see that these tasks are being done.

Some of the TSP roles have relatively obvious responsibilities while others are not so clear. You or the coach should make sure that the developers know that their job is to think broadly about their role responsibilities and to act as if they were running the project in all respects relating to that role. One of your principal jobs is to help the team members understand their responsibilities as role managers. In a nutshell, the role job involves acting as your conscience in the particular area involved.

Reference

Random House Dictionary of the English Language. New York: Random House. 1983.

B

Networking

Most of this book is about you and your team. With the exception of Part IV, where we discuss your relationships with management, the topics concern ways to lead, guide, coach, and support your team. However, you and your team work within an organization, and this organization has many groups and individuals who can help you to do your job. Knowing how to use these groups could make your job much easier.

This appendix discusses many of the networking and interrelationship issues you will face in leading a team. It describes some of the groups and individuals with whom you should work, and it reviews some of the key things to consider as you establish relationships with these other groups. The following topics are covered in this appendix.

- ☐ Organizational networks
- ☐ Executive style
- ☐ Working with the coach
- ☐ Working with the software engineering process group (SEPG)
- ☐ Quality assurance
- ☐ Configuration management
- ☐ Independent testing

☐ Staff and support groups

☐ Multi-team networks

B.1   Organizational Networks

While organizations typically have organization charts that show the official reporting structure, these charts are usually simplistic and can often be misleading. Organizations are run by people, and these people use various communication and decision-making networks to make decisions and to accomplish what they want done. Understanding and knowing how to use these networks can greatly simplify your job. The following are examples of common communication and decision-making networks.

☐ The **financial network** concerns the organization's financial controls. It includes the people who authorize spending as well as those who influence the people who authorize spending. This latter group provides information and advice to the decision executives before they make financial decisions. This network is the fundamental control network of the organization, and you should understand it and know how to use it when you need funding or staffing changes.

☐ The **advisory network** consists of the staff members who influence decision makers and whose agreement and support you will need before taking an issue to senior management. To get a decision quickly, you must know which executive will make the decision and have the support of that executive's advisory staff.

☐ The **informal information network** is also important. For example, shortly after I was appointed to a corporate staff position at IBM, I got involved in a debate with a senior vice president about funding the marketing division's systems engineers. The VP wanted to cut the systems engineering staff by 15 percent while the division argued that it should be increased by 12 percent. When the VP asked for my views, I supported the division. However, instead of accepting my recommendation, he asked a lot of questions. Every time I met with the VP, he had new facts that contradicted what I was telling him. While I made every effort to get all of the key information, the VP always seemed to have some fact that I was not aware of. One of my people found out that an old timer named George, the marketing division records manager, lived next door to the VP and talked with him all the time. Before my next meeting with the VP, I went to see George to review my proposal. He gave me some information that I was not aware of, and after suggesting a number of changes he agreed with my recommendation. When I next met with the VP, I explained that George had been very helpful in clearing up several points but that he agreed that the division needed more systems engineers. The VP just smiled, but he approved the 12 percent increase for the systems engineering staff.

In leading your team, you will often need management support. You may need added staff, more funds, support in customer negotiations, or help with almost anything. To be most effective, you need to know who the key decision makers are and to understand the networks these executives and managers use in making decisions.

B.2   Executive Style

As executives move higher in the management ranks, they get information from an increasing array of sources. While some executives rely entirely on their line managers for information, the most capable executives get information from many different sources. For example, in the IBM example described in the previous section, I knew that the IBM senior VP was talking to the division general manager, the corporate marketing staff, and corporate finance, so I had reviewed my recommendations with all of these people in advance. While I thought that everyone but corporate finance agreed with me, the VP had a secret information source that I was not aware of. He was not trying to trip me up or to be clever; he just wanted to make sure that I knew what I was talking about before he agreed. He trusted George to give him objective facts and wanted to make a sound decision.

While your management may not follow this networking style, there is a good chance that they will. Then they will be getting information about your project directly up the chain of command from you but also from several other sources. The most common sources for such information are the following:

- □ Finance
- □ Personnel
- □ Quality assurance
- □ The SEPG
- □ The test department
- □ Marketing

Your management will also usually get information from the systems group, the requirements people, and the other projects as well as from their friends and former associates throughout the organization. If you are dealing with a very senior executive, he or she will almost certainly also get input from your organization's customers.

As you run your project, be sensitive to these information networks and recognize that many of the groups you work with are not just doing a support job—they are also learning about your project and providing information to management on how they think you are doing. While your principal focus should always be on getting the job done in the best possible way, you will frequently need management support. To get this support when you need it, build a network of people that you can rely on to give you information, to help you when you need assistance, and to support you with management.

B.3 Working with the Coach

As discussed previously in this book, the TSP coach can help you in launching your team and in running the project. If the coach is the person who trained your team in the PSP, then he or she will already know your developers and will almost certainly have developed a trusting relationship with many of them. The coach should then be able to look at their data and comment on their work without causing undue concern.

Right after the team launch, meet with the coach and agree on the level of support that he or she can provide to you and to your team. Ideally, the coach will be able to meet with all or some of your team members every week to help them with process, data collection, and analysis problems; to assess the adequacy of their data; and to review the quality of their work. To take full advantage of the coach, meet with him or her every week to discuss the team's work and to see who on your team needs guidance or support.

Since the coach may be supporting several teams and may not be able to meet with each of your developers every week, discuss the highest priority areas needing attention. Then, when these initial problems are handled, pick another set of priority concerns. Once the team is following the process reasonably well, you can examine quality issues with the coach and decide where to make improvements. Finally, when the team is doing a competent job of managing product quality, you can begin thinking about benchmarking. If you treat the coach as a partner and work jointly to improve team performance, you will be most effective in doing your development job and you will earn the coach's support.

B.4 Working with the SEPG

Many organizations have SEPG groups that are charged with helping the organization define, adapt, and improve its processes. These groups sometimes view the

TSP as a threat and are concerned about their job security. Unless they have been PSP trained, they may think that the TSP competes with the Capability Maturity Model Integration (CMMI) (Chrissis 2003). The best way to deal with this issue is right after the team launch. You should first discuss the team's process needs with the process manager and agree on where you would like the SEPG's help. Then meet with the SEPG manager and agree on how to work together. Discuss where and how you need the SEPG's support, and describe how working with your team could help the SEPG in its work.

If some or all of the SEPG members have been PSP trained, they can help you define and improve your processes. However, if they have not been PSP trained, they can still help you in defining design and coding standards, establishing a change management and configuration control system, or defining and supporting the PIP handling process.

Since the SEPG staff is likely to be busy and reluctant to commit very much support for your team, keep asking for their help. This may not get you the needed SEPG support, but it will certainly demonstrate that you respect the SEPG's capabilities and need their help. As the SEPG members learn more about the PSP and TSP, they will begin to understand how these methods can help them. For example, one SEPG group that was working towards CMM level 3 produced a 450-page process description. After PSP training, the SEPG members could see how to cut this description to 50 pages. If they had known how to use the PSP methods at the outset, they could have saved a great deal of work. Several references show how using the TSP can accelerate CMM and CMMI process improvement (*CrossTalk* 2002, 2005).

B.5   Quality Assurance

Quality assurance (QA) groups are often concerned about the TSP team's quality manager role. They believe that they should assign a QA representative to your team and that this representative should be your quality manager. This would be a serious mistake. The QA job should be to audit the work of the development groups and to provide management with impartial assessments of your team's work. If QA had a full-time member on your team, they would either not be impartial or they would not be able to work closely with you and your team. Finally, unless you were developing a very large system, there would not be enough quality work to occupy a full-time team member. However, if the QA representative was PSP trained, was willing and able to moderate the team inspections, would be a full-time team member, and would use the TSP personally, then that person would probably be a useful team member and quality manager.

Explain that your team's quality manager will serve as your interface to the QA group and that you will count on the QA group for quality advice and assistance.

Before getting too embroiled in debates about the QA mission, however, first determine if you are dealing with a true QA group. Many organizations have independent testing groups that they call quality assurance. True QA groups are concerned with analyzing product and process quality. They rarely do any testing.

If you have a true quality assurance group, the best approach is for you and the quality manager to agree on a strategy and then to meet with the QA manager and staff to review that strategy. The QA people can generally help by regularly reviewing team data and alerting the quality manager to potential problems. If any of the QA people have been PSP trained, they could be a big help. If not, then you, the quality manager, or the coach could show them the kinds of analyses that would be most helpful.

Initially, these examinations should be of all the developers' plans and the degree to which they meet the team's quality criteria. As the work progresses, the examinations could consider actual performance compared to the plans, the quality profiles, and the process quality index (PQI). With a little guidance, QA people can be very helpful. In providing this help, they could also get a great deal of useful data to use in their regular QA job.

While it may not be immediately clear how helpful such QA support could be, there is an enormous amount of potentially useful TSP data. Since you and your team will be busy with development work, you cannot spend much time reviewing all of these data. By working with the QA people, you can get valuable assistance with the team data and be aware of any QA concerns with your project. You could also gain a strong and very helpful supporter for your team's work.

B.6   Configuration Management

If your organization has a software configuration management (SCM) organization, you will almost certainly want use it. The project SCM guidelines will then have been established and you and your team will merely have to use them.

If your organization is just forming an SCM group, you could offer your project as a test bed. First decide with your support manager what kind of configuration management support you need, and then talk to the SCM manager about how your group could help in establishing an initial SCM capability. However, do not commit to anything other than developing and sharing an initial team SCM process. Establishing such an initial process could accelerate the organization's SCM capability and provide valuable support to your group.

If no SCM group has been or is being formed, establish your own team's SCM procedures and then describe them to management. Offer to make these procedures available to any new SCM group if and when one is formed. To accelerate your SCM process definition work, start with a relatively simple initial process.

An example of such a process is given in Appendix B in my book *Introduction to the Team Software Process* (Humphrey 2000).

B.7   Independent Testing

Regardless of whether they are called quality assurance or testing, independent testing groups can be enormously helpful. If your organization has such a group, there are probably established procedures for how to do testing and your team will have to conform. Assuming that there is a testing group, the test manager will probably be concerned about your team's test manager job and argue that the test group should provide the team's test manager.

As was the case with QA, it would be a mistake to have someone from the test group act as the test manager. The exception would be if that test representative would be PSP or personal process trained and be essentially full time on the team. Personal process training is for those team members who are not program developers and it omits the software design and software quality topics. As a result, this training only takes a few days. With personal process training, the test representative would be able to make a detailed plan, take responsibility for team tasks, and use the TSP process along with everyone else. If the test representative will not be a full team member, accept him or her as the official test contact point but do not include him or her in TSP launch meetings 2 through 8. During the job, only include that person in those team meetings where testing is the principal issue.

The test department can be very helpful in preparing and/or reviewing test plans, gathering and providing test data, developing test cases and scripts, and running tests. This can be an enormous amount of work, and you need agreement on the precise allocation of this work between your team and the test organization. Make the test manager responsible for reaching agreement with the test department on the work allocation, for documenting that agreement, and for ensuring that everyone involved agrees with that document.

B.8   Staff and Support Groups

In most organizations, many different groups can have an impact on your team. Examples are finance, personnel, facilities, and any corporate or division staffs. Since you will almost certainly face various kinds of financial and personnel issues, early contact with the financial and human resources staffs is important. When starting as a new team leader, it would usually be a good idea to stop by and introduce yourself to the financial people and then meet separately with the personnel people.

With both groups, explain what your team is doing and tell them that while you don't know of any problems right now, you expect to need their help from time to time during the project. Also, ask if they have any suggestions for things you should watch out for and to let you know if they hear of anything that you should know about or do. Since development people generally ignore these staffs until they have problems, these groups will likely be surprised at your visit. However, you will have laid the groundwork for a useful and productive relationship. Many team problems start with either financial or personnel issues, and often these staffs get advance warning and can help you resolve the problems before they reach crisis proportions.

Depending on the size and structure of your organization, there may also be various other technical, quality, or administrative staffs that senior management uses to monitor organizational performance and to help them direct operations. To the extent that such groups are concerned with your team's work, establish an open and constructive relationship with them. Their support will be important to you whenever you need senior management support or guidance.

B.9   Multi-Team Networks

If your team is part of a large project, you will likely be using the TSP multi-team process. That process defines a family of networks that facilitate communication and decision making across the team. These networks are managed by a set of teams, responsibility definitions, and team meetings. The leadership team guides and leads the overall project, and the role-manager teams support the leadership team in identifying issues, handling cross-team assignments, and maintaining coordination among all of the subteams.

The Leadership Team

In a large multi-team project, the leadership team is composed of the overall program or project manager and the leaders of each of the individual teams. This leadership team is the principal mechanism for managing the multiple team. It is through the leadership team that program management learns about your team's status and how you are progressing against your plan. The leadership team also provides feedback on overall program status and advice on how to handle many of your team's problems and issues.

As a member of the leadership team, you must balance your loyalty to your subteam against your allegiance to the leadership team. While you must forcefully represent your team in the leadership debates, you must also be willing to resolve issues in the best interests of the overall project. When the leadership team makes a decision that is counter to your team's interests, you will need to explain that decision to your subteam. To do this, you must understand the logic for the decision, be able to explain that logic, and be able to demonstrate that you were an effective advocate for your team.

The Role-Manager Teams

The role-manager teams provide a key resource for managing multiple teams. These teams are composed of the role managers from each subteam. For example, all of the design managers would form the design role-manager team, the planning managers the planning role-manager team, and so forth. The role managers provide the glue that holds the multi-team together. They can provide the leadership team with the information and the insight needed to understand complex technical issues and to anticipate serious problems.

Since these role-manager teams usually have questions about what they are supposed to do, the leadership team must decide what they want the role-manager teams to do and explain these responsibilities to each of these teams. Generally, the leadership team will assign one of the team leaders to mentor each role-manager team. Assuming that you end up with one or more of these mentoring assignments, you will not only be leading your own development team but guiding and coaching one or more of the role-manager teams. To minimize the time that this mentoring takes, have the role-manager teams select their own team leaders and then periodically observe and advise these teams as they do their work. Also sit in on occasional role-manager weekly meetings and make yourself available to these teams whenever they ask for help.

For role-manager teams to be effective, most of the role managers should already understand their role responsibilities and be able to think about their broader scope as members of a role-manager team. As long as most of the members of the multi-team project have previously worked on TSP teams, this should not be a problem. Occasionally, however, organizations first use the TSP on a large multi-team project. Under these conditions, it is generally best to defer introducing the role-manager teams until the first or second relaunch.

Before forming the role-manager teams, the leadership team should consider chartering working groups to address specific problems. One example of such a group would be to assign the design managers from all of the teams to produce a common cross-project design standard. This working-group approach could be used, for example, to help the leadership team manage subteam interdependencies (planning managers), coding standards (implementation managers), configuration management needs (support managers), and the inspection process (process managers). The role-manager teams are a potentially powerful mechanism for integrating multiple groups, particularly when they are distributed. Use them whenever you can.

B.10 Summary

Organizations contain many communication and decision-making networks that can be useful in leading a team project and in getting support. This appendix discusses the typical networks in organizations and how, by building and using such networks, you can make your job easier.

In large organizations, many groups can help and support you in leading a project. The most important individuals and groups to work with are the TSP coach, the SEPG, quality assurance, the configuration management group, and the testing organization. In addition, various administrative and technical staffs can be helpful by providing guidance and support.

This appendix discusses many of these staff groups and provides suggestions on how to work with them as well as on how to obtain their support.

References

Chrissis, Mary Beth, Mike Konrad, and Sandy Shrum. *CMMI: Guidelines for Process Integration and Product Improvement.* Boston, MA: Addison-Wesley. 2003.

The September 2002 and March 2005 issues of *CrossTalk* feature several articles on the TSP, including some that discuss the TSP's relationship to the CMM and CMMI process improvement frameworks.

Humphrey, Watts S. *Introduction to the Team Software Process.* Boston, MA: Addison-Wesley. 2000.

INDEX

The SEI Series in Software Engineering

CMMI Distilled
SECOND EDITION
A Practical Introduction to Integrated Process Improvement
Dennis M. Ahern
Aaron Clouse
Richard Turner

ISBN 0-321-18613-3

CMMI SCAMPI Distilled
Appraisals for Process Improvement
Dennis M. Ahern • Jim Armstrong
Aaron Clouse • Jack R. Ferguson
Will Hayes • Kenneth E. Nidiffer

ISBN 0-321-22876-6

Managing Information Security Risks
The OCTAVE Approach
Christopher Alberts
Audrey Dorofee

ISBN 0-321-11886-3

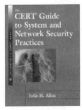

CERT Guide to System and Network Security Practices
Julia H. Allen

ISBN 0-201-73723-X

Software Architecture in Practice
Second Edition
Len Bass
Paul Clements
Rick Kazman

ISBN 0-321-15495-9

CMMI Assessments
Motivating Positive Change
Marilyn Bush
Donna Dunaway
Foreword by Watts S. Humphrey

ISBN 0-321-17935-8

The Capability Maturity Model
Guidelines for Improving the Software Process
Carnegie Mellon University
Software Engineering Institute

ISBN 0-201-54664-7

CMMI
Guidelines for Process Integration and Product Improvement
Mary Beth Chrissis
Mike Konrad
Sandy Shrum

ISBN 0-321-15496-7

Documenting Software Architectures
Views and Beyond
Paul Clements • Felix Bachmann • Len Bass
David Garlan • James Ivers • Reed Little
Robert Nord • Judith Stafford

ISBN 0-201-70372-6

Evaluating Software Architectures
Methods and Case Studies
Paul Clements
Rick Kazman
Mark Klein

ISBN 0-201-70482-X

Software Product Lines
Practices and Patterns
Paul Clements
Linda Northrop

ISBN 0-201-70332-7

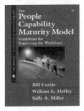

The People Capability Maturity Model
Guidelines for Improving the Workforce
Bill Curtis
William E. Hefley
Sally A. Miller

ISBN 0-201-60445-0

Measuring the Software Process
Statistical Process Control for Software Process Improvement
William A. Florac
Anita D. Carleton
Foreword by Watts S. Humphrey

ISBN 0-201-60444-2

Software Design Methods for Concurrent and Real-Time Systems
Hassan Gomaa

ISBN 0-201-52577-1

MANAGING RISK
METHODS FOR SOFTWARE SYSTEMS DEVELOPMENT
ELAINE M. HALL

ISBN 0-201-25592-8

MANAGING TECHNICAL PEOPLE
INNOVATION, TEAMWORK, AND THE SOFTWARE PROCESS
WATTS S. HUMPHREY

ISBN 0-201-54597-7

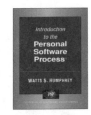

Introduction to the Personal Software Process
WATTS S. HUMPHREY

ISBN 0-201-54809-7

PSP
A Self-Improvement Process for Software Engineers
Watts S. Humphrey

ISBN 0-321-30549-3

Managing the Software Process
Watts S. Humphrey

ISBN 0-201-18095-2

The Complete PSP Book
A DISCIPLINE FOR SOFTWARE ENGINEERING
WATTS S. HUMPHREY

ISBN 0-201-54610-8

Introduction to the Team Software Process
TSP
Watts S. Humphrey

ISBN 0-201-47719-X

TSP
Leading a Development Team
Watts S. Humphrey

ISBN 0-321-34962-8

Winning with Software
How to Transform Your Software Group into a Competitive Asset
An Executive Strategy
Watts S. Humphrey

ISBN 0-201-77639-1

CMM in Practice
Processes for Executing Software Projects at Infosys
Pankaj Jalote

ISBN 0-201-61626-2

Managing Software Acquisition
Open Systems and COTS Products
B. Craig Meyers
Patricia Oberndorf

ISBN 0-201-70454-4

Architecture-Centric Software Project Management
A Practical Guide
Daniel J. Paulish
Foreword by Len Bass

ISBN 0-201-73409-5

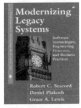

Modernizing Legacy Systems
Software Technologies, Engineering Processes, and Business Practices
Robert C. Seacord
Daniel Plakosh
Grace A. Lewis

ISBN 0-321-11884-7

Secure Coding in C and C++
Robert C. Seacord

ISBN 0-321-33572-4

Estimating Software-Intensive Systems
Projects, Products, and Processes
Richard D. Stutzke

ISBN 0-201-70312-2

SOFTWARE PROCESS IMPROVEMENT
Practical Guidelines for Business Success
Sami Zahran

ISBN 0-201-17782-X

Please see our web site at www.awprofessional.com for more information on these titles.

Register Your Book

at www.awprofessional.com/register

You may be eligible to receive:

- Advance notice of forthcoming editions of the book
- Related book recommendations
- Chapter excerpts and supplements of forthcoming titl
- Information about special contests and promotions throughout the year
- Notices and reminders about author appearances, tradeshows, and online chats with special guests

Contact us

If you are interested in writing a book or reviewing manuscripts prior to publication, please write to us at:

Editorial Department
Addison-Wesley Professional
75 Arlington Street, Suite 300
Boston, MA 02116 USA
Email: AWPro@aw.com

Visit us on the Web: http://www.awprofessional.com